Aniyunwiya / Real Human

Aniyunwiya / Real Human Beings
An Anthology of Contemporary Cherokee Prose

**Edited by
Joseph Bruchac**

GREENFIELD REVIEW PRESS
Greenfield Center, New York

Publication of this book has been made possible, in part, through a Literary Publishing Grant from the Literature Program of the New York State Council on the Arts.

Introduction copyright © 1995 by Joseph Bruchac

Library of Congress #94-78574

ISBN 0-912678-92-5

FIRST EDITION
Printed in the United States of America

Cover Illustration "Booger Dance" by Murv Jacob

Distributed by The Talman Company, Inc.
131 Spring Street
New York, N.Y. 10012
(212) 431-7175 Fax: (212) 431-7215

ACKNOWLEDGEMENTS

Rilla Askew's "The Gift" first appeared in "Nimrod."

Marilou Awiakta's "Red Clay" is from *Selu: Seeking the Corn Mother's Wisdom* (Fulcrum Publishing, Golden, Co.)

Betty Louise Bell's "Beat the drum slowly . . ." is from *Faces in the Moon* (University of Oklahoma Press, Norman, Ok.)

Robert Gish's "First Horses" is from *First Horses, New Stories of the American West* (University of Nevada Press, Reno, NV)

Diane Glancy's "A Sense of Continuity and Presence" is from *Trigger Dance* (The Fiction Collective, Boulder, Co.)

Rayna Green's "A Tribe Called Wannabee" was published in *Folklore*, Vol. 1, 9: 1988

Geary Hobson's "The Literature of Indian Oklahoma" appeared in *World Literature Today*, Summer 1990.

Wilma Mankiller's "Keeping Pace With the Rest of the World" appeared in *Southern Exposure*. Marilou Awiakta's interview with her appeared in *Southern Style*.

Ron Rogers' "What Became of Tribal Europe?" is from *Man Spirit*, Greenfield Review Press.

Glenn Twist's "The Dispossession" appeared in *Moccasin Telegraph*, 1994.

PREFACE

Few Native peoples have had more written about them and, in the long run, been less understood than the people most Americans call "Cherokee." Their own name for themselves, however, is Ani-yun-wiya, "real human beings," and it is as human beings, not noble savages, regally distant ancestors or pathetic figures on that Trail of Tears which shamed America, that contemporary Cherokee people continue to see themselves.

In this collection, 23 contemporary writers, all of whom claim Cherokee ancestry as a defining point in their artistic vision, speak their own words. Some, like Cherokee chief Wilma Mankiller, have told the stories of their lives, some, like Robert Conley, have mastered the genre of historical fiction. Others craft stories taking place within the world of America in the 20th century, while still others, such as newcomer Eddie Webb, retell the ancient tales which have always given their people not only delight, but also a moral framework for their lives.

The variety and complexity of their voices are, though they stem from one particular Native people – only one out of the more than 300 still surviving Native nations within the borders of the United States – emblematic of the vitality and the range of experiences which characterize contemporary American Indian lives.

– Joe Bruchac

Carroll Arnett

FROM LA DENE

(An Unpublished Novel)

SHE REACHED ABOVE the cash register to take down a large card reading $5.00 LIMIT ON CHECKS, DOLLAR SERVICE CHARGE ON ALL RETURNED ITEMS. WE HAVE A DEAL WITH THE BANK – THEY DON'T SELL BEER, WE DON'T LEND MONEY. Locating a blue crayon and a thumb tack in the catch-all cigar box under the bar, she printed on the back of the card OPEN 12:30 TODAY ONLY, STICK AROUND. When she had posted this on the front door she gave the cement floor a hit-or-miss sweeping. Let the wet mop go till tomorrow. Most of these maltheads wouldn't care if you served them in a pigpen.

At twelve thirty-five she opened the door to remove the sign and encounter there a tall, lean, heavily tanned man, his fist raised to knock. Beneath the greasy white straw cattleman's hat his hair was black and straight and hung like fine mercerized thread to almost shoulder length. His gauze shirt was sweated out and draped over the waistband of faded starched denims which in turn draped with proper casualness over the tops of a pair of highly polished black boots. La Dene stepped out of the doorway as he lowered his arm to ask:

"Y'll open now? Mam?"

His good-natured sneer awaited her answer.

"Sure, c'mon in."

Lifting his hat in a half-mocking bow, he replied:

"After you, mam."

"Go ahead in," said La Dene, moving behind him to untack the sign. "Be right with you."

She followed him through the tavern's dusty gloom, suddenly dejected, emptied of any immediate sensation; even the clonk of the man's leather heels sounded delayed and distant. A quick, stabbing desire to scream, loud as she could, fell just as quickly into its own ridiculousness. Sleep. Keeson said you gotta get enough sleep, and you still don't. The exhilaration of a changed mood draining to mere reassurance, she blotted the moisture from her palms on her skirted hips. Back of the bar as the man straddled a stool, she asked:

"Yessir?"

"Draw."

He cracked his hat loose from the ring of sweat that sealed it against his forehead, wiped the inner band with a fresh handkerchief, and sighed:

"Oooo-ee. Gonna be another pistol today."

When the frosted mug of beer foamed before him he poked the hat low on the front of his head, squinting at La Dene from under the brim as if she owed a response to his bromide in the same way she owed him silver from the dollar bill he was sliding out of a long, intricately tooled Mexican wallet which he then let plop on the bar so loudly that she jumped at the noise. He pinched his shirttails, shaking them to fan himself, adding:

"Downright chilly in here though."

La Dene ignored the bait and laid his change on the bar.

"Yeah, I suppose Bea's been fooling with the thermostat again. I'll go see in a minute."

She moved to replace the sign above the cash register and heard the man give a low laugh. Turning around, she demanded:

"What's so funny, cowboy?"

He resettled the hat on the back of his head, grinning to show a big gold tooth.

"That there sign." He admired one higher on the wall which read THE HURRIER I GO, THE BEHINDIER I GET. "That's the doggone truth, ain't it?"

As he held up the beer mug in one hand, the wallet in the other, La Dene foresaw that he was about to affirm the sign's truth by slapping the bar again, and she flinched prematurely. The instant the wallet struck, a thunderous explosion filled the barroom, rattling the glassware; every fixture and furnishing, the building itself, trembled in the rumbling echoes of what might have been a dynamite blast.

"God*damn* it!" shouted La Dene. "Oh I hate those sonsabit-ches."

"Now I didn't do that," said the man, pointing a finger at her.

"I know it, goddamn it." She clutched her head with both hands, still shouting, howling with anger. "Oh those *fuck*ass jet jockeys! Goddamned moonmen, shitass progress. Jesus!"

The man sat open-mouthed, engrossed in her evaluation.

"There's where our goddamned tax money goes," she continued, rolling her eyes to the heavens. "So those clowns can fart around breaking everybody's eardrums. Scuse my French."

"I know what you mean," said the man, who took a long swallow of his beer. "Damned crime against the human race."

La Dene drew a small tumbler half full and closed the tap abruptly. Leaning on the backbar to sip her beer, she regarded the stranger; in hopes of improving, at least cooling, the conversation she asked:

"You haven't been in before, have you?"

"I was here all day Saddy afternoon. Didn't see you here though or I'd a been in Sunday too."

"I'll betcha would."

She straightened up as in came three young men all dressed in white T-shirts and plaid walking shorts, one barefoot, two wearing tennis shoes without socks, one of whom on sighting La Dene threw his arms over his crewcut head and shrieked:

"Lover!"

"Frat rats!" she answered, recognizing these three of her steadier customers from last winter and spring. The one who had greeted her left the other two at the shuffleboard table and proceeded to the bar, digging in his pocket, glowing with good will and sunburn.

"Hey when'd you get out?"

"Two three weeks ago," said La Dene, not allowing him to clarify by adding – "of the hospital"; she asked quickly: "Three Schlitz?"

"Please."

While she reached into the cooler the boy smoothed a wadded ten on the bar's edge, folded the bill lengthwise once, twice, saying:

"We heard you were sick, just after school was out."

"Yeah, that's what the man said."

"We thought about coming down to see you."

"Lot of people thought about it." She turned for glasses to go with the three bottles she had opened. "What're you characters doing here so early? I thought school didn't start for another couple weeks."

"Rush," said the boy.

"Now look, buster." She banged the glasses on the wood and snatched the folded ten from him. "No snotty frat brat comes in here and tells me to rush."

"Hey hey hey." The boy backed off, hands crossed in front of his face. "Rush, like in fraternity rush. At the house? Getting ready for pledging?"

"Oh."

"Sheeze!" said the boy. "So touchy."

"So I'm sorry," said La Dene. "I was up all night. This the smallest you got?"

She waved the now unfolded bill.

"At the moment it is. Me, I was down all night."

"Sure you were," she said from the cash register. "Big cocksman like you's got tallow on his pole ever' morning."

Stricken with hilarity, he accepted his change, gathered bottles and glasses, and slouched happily to the shuffleboard. La Dene pointed to the quarter inch of beer remaining in the mug and asked the cowboy, who had begun to look like an Indian:

"Care for another?"

"Please mam."

She filled a fresh mug and set it beside the man's wallet.

"That's a handsome piece of leather."

"Ain't it pretty?" He turned it so she could see the design right side up. "Got that down in Chihuahua, Old Mexico."

"Didcha."

"Yeah, I was down there runnin cattle for a big Meskin rancher—*big* outfit, hunnerd thousand acres, I s'pose—he come all the way up to Fo'Worth lookin for a foreman, hired me. Drove a Cadillac pickup. Anyhow, I won . . . ."

"Whaaat?" said La Dene. "A Cadillac pickup?"

"Yeah, he took and had the ass—the rear end of a brand new Caddy cut out and had 'em put a truck bed in. All customized, looked real nice. Even kept the fishtails. Had a white boy drivin for him, chauffeur. Anyhow, as I's sayin, I won this here wallet off a drunk Meskin kid in Chihuahua City."

"Won it, huh?"

"Well," he displayed his gold tooth again; "he might not a knowed he was bettin. He'd done drunk a whole great-o big jug a that there mescal. D'you ever drink any that mescal?"

"Never did," said La Dene. "Heard of it, course."

"I got some," said the cowboy, who she was almost sure must be an Indian; "if you wanted to try some. Later on."

"There's the sign," she indicated one on the wall behind him which read NO LIQUOR, PROFANE OR OBSCENE SPEECH, THIS MEANS YOU.

"Naw," said the cowboy Indian, "I mean later, after you git off."

"We'll see," she answered.

Sloshing it about in his mouth before swallowing the beer, he swiveled on the barstool, saying as he lifted his booted feet:

"You like good leather, I can tell. Noticed ya lookin at my boots when I come in."

La Dene sought to remember, couldn't, but couldn't avoid looking now.

"Hunnerd dollar Judsons," he explained. "Won 'em off an ole boy in Elk City, there at the rodeo. Crazy fool had no better sense'n to let me try 'em on, and once I seen they was a perfeck fit I made up my mind to own 'em. I see somethin I like that's a perfeck fit, *into* the bargain, I sho git that ole stealin feeling."

"Thought you were a gambler," said La Dene.

"Oh now and agin, little poker."

"You ride in the rodeo?"

"Yeah, I done some rodeo-in'. Not this year though. Mostly I do steer wrasslin, but a damned big-o rubberneck steer last year busted my leg in two places." He marked the points of fracture by drawing the edge of his hand across the crease in his denims. "It was kinda stiff for workin cattle, or rodeo-in' either, so I went and got me a job as swamper on a drillin crew out north a Enid — that new Sinclair field? — paid better too, hunnerd dollars a week. Anyway, I'd just nearly got this stiffness worked out and one day this assho — scuse me — this ole boy let a five-ton crown drop clear from the top a the rig to about three feet from where I'm standin there on the drillin table. Missed me a course, but it bounced me right off that table onto a pile a casin', and damned if it didn't break one a the broke places agin."

"Jesus," said La Dene. "That's pretty tough luck."

"Sheee-it," he dispensed with apologies as he drained his beer mug. "Damned ole Indian boy ain't got no other kind."

"I was thinkin you looked Indian."

"Full-blood Apache," said the man, suppressing a belch while he pushed the empty mug toward her. "Almost full. My ma was half white. Betcha never heard a my grandpa."

"Not that I know of." She refilled the mug. Nobody beats an Indian when it comes to bullshit. A name came to mind and she asked, unable to control her smile:

"He wasn't Quanah Parker, was he?"

"Naaaw, sheee-it, Quanah was a damned ole Comanche half-breed, damned red nigger, agency chief, went to school and all. You heard a Geronimo, I bet."

"He was your grandpa?"

"Hell no." The Indian drank off three quarters of his new beer, licking the foam from his upper lip. "I just meant you *heard* a him, everbody does. In all the movies, big goddamned hero. But ya never hear nothin about Red Sleeves. Do ya?"

He drained the mug again, shoved it toward her again as La Dene answered:

"Red Sleeves?"

"Mangas Coloradas," he translated. "Mangas for short. Last great chief of the Jicarilla Apache, fiercest fighters in the whole of the Apache Nation."

He spoke in slow indignation as if he were reading aloud.

"I know exactly what's gonna happen," said Bea.

"No listen, I know who the very first customer's gonna be today."

"Who?"

"John One Shoe, that crazy cowboy-Indian. I'll betcha he's the first one in. All primed to lap up that free beer."

"So?" said Bea.

"So nothing," said La Dene, walking out among the tables to set down the chairs. Fuck her. Let her stew.

She couldn't help smiling at the sister-in-law, however, when a moment later the Indian man pushed the front door open. Above a fire-engine red satin shirt his gold tooth was agleam, and the hundred-dollar Judsons clacked up to the bar.

"Mornin," he said confidently to Bea's half-turned back. "Or afternoon I guess tis. You feelin better, Miz Washburn?"

"Yes thanks."

"Miz Womack?"

La Dene wasn't sure whether this was a question or a greeting; she joined Bea behind the bar and answered:

"Hi John. The name, in case you're interested, is La Dene."

"Yes mam, I shore am interested, I purely am. La Dene." The tooth shone again.

"You're here," said La Dene, "for beer. Right?"

"For the next two hours. From now"—he glanced at the clock—"till two-oh-three, yes mam, I'm here for beer fast as you kin draw it. You said two hours, nothin said 'bout how much."

"That's right." La Dene was already pulling the tap for the first one: "You gonna make a race out of it?"

"No mam. I'm not a hog, just thirsty."

At the end of the bar Bea had filled the stainless steel urn with water for the day's coffee. When the Indian had drunk the first beer in two gulps he exhaled a long sigh of relish, set the empty mug gently on the wood, and declared to the cash register since both women were busy:

"You know you're breakin the law."

The aluminum coffee basket slipped from Bea's fingers and clattered on the floor as she whispered aloud, "Damn!" La Dene looked round to ask:

"What do you mean?"

"They're still a law in this state forbiddening the sale of alcoholic beverages to Indians. Didn't you know that?"

"No," said La Dene, "and I think you're puttin me on."

"Hell I am. It's a God's truth. They don't *en*force it a course, but the law's still there on the statue books. Lawyer I know told me. It's against the fu — scuse me — against the law to sell, even *give*, a Indian person anything with alcohol in it. Whatta ya think about that?"

La Dene set another beef before the man and said, "Seems sorta silly."

"Par'n me?"

"I said it seems silly."

"Silly my ass. It's a goddamned crime, that's what it is. Silly!"

While the man sneered at the feebleness of La Dene's response she reached to snap on the transistor radio nestled among the cellophaned goodies on the backbar. She dialed the volume down until the simulated electronic bee-bee-beep should announce the noon news at 12:10. The Indian resumed:

"It just ain't right that the laws ain't right. Laws oughta *be* right, just naturally."

"Since when?" asked La Dene. "Laws're made by people who don't have to break 'em."

"Well they usta be right. In the olden days."

"That no-alcohol-for-Indians law comes from the olden days."

"I mean *real* olden days, couple hunnerd, three hunnerd years ago."

"How d'you know they were right then?"

"That's awright," said the Indian. "I know. My blood tells me so."

"Your blood."

"Yes mam, a Indian boy's got differnt blood than you palefaces."

"Maybe," said La Dene, "that's why they made the no-alcohol law."

"Sheee-it."

He finished the second half of the second beer and handed the mug to La Dene who refilled it as she asked:

"Wanna hear the news?"

"Why not. We could use some fresh misery, reckon?"

La Dene raised the volume and was told:

. . .*He urged that new anti-inflationary measures be given immediate and top priority. Turning now to the local scene, two men arrested in a nearby area motel, then later released by police last night after an anonymous tip proved to be what at first appeared a practical joke, again figure in the news. Authorities revealed this morning that the body in an oil drum at the municipal dump on Monday* has *been identified by fingerprint records as that of Heinz Schell, thirty-seven, an unemployed violinist from Linden, New Jersey. Leon Weinstein, one of the two men arrested on the false tip at the motel earlier and who claims to be a retired Jewish rabbi,* has *confessed killing Schell, whom Weinstein in a signed statement alleges was a former Hitler Youth who turned in Weinstein's mother to the Gestapo thirty years ago in Nazi Germany. Weinstein* is *being held on suspicion of murder. The other man arrested at the motel and later released, Hamilcar Otis, a local attorney, has told KNOW newsmen that he* has *been retained as Weinstein's legal counsel. Stay tuned for KNOW sports and weather, but first this message. Do you want a full-service bank, a* modern *bank? Take advantage of First Nation's* complete, modern b*anking facilities: drive-up windows, all-night suppository . . .*

La Dene clicked the off-button as her gaze met both Bea's and the Indian's in a store of astonishment.

"*What* did he say?" Bea exclaimed. "Did he say *suppository?*"

"I'd swear . . .," La Dene's answer was drowned by the Indian's choking fit of laughter.

"He did, dumbass sonofabitch. Suppository! All-night sup*pos*itory!"

All three roared at the victory.

O great god or great chief, wherever ya are, of the downtrod Indians, specially the Jicarilla Apache (he was in truth a renegade Choctaw), where *are* you? In the land of the skyblue slushpits? Where is my soul? Whatcha do with it? It was here a *minu*te ago. I need it. Feller can't git long thout his *soul*, specially a ole Indian boy. I ain't so fuckin old. Life be*gins* at forty-four. Gittin old for rodeo-in' though. Hurts more ever fuckin year. Why time was, five or ten years ago, I coulda made old Jim Byrum look like a kid on a shitland poly. If I'd a tried, I coulda.

Big fuckin rodeo star, posin for them cigarette ads, signin his name and all. So he kin write, so what? Bet his ole lady signed *for* him. Go to smokin them hunnerd-millimeter cigarettes, gittin them big ideas. Bet he's took to drinkin blended whiskey. I knew him, hell yes I knew him, to *speak* to. Dumb sonofabitch. Why he's so fuckin dumb he don't know if Christ was crucified or stabbed in the ass with a butcher knife. And tight? He's so fuckin tight he wouldn't give a dime to watch a piss ant eat a bale a hay. All them drugstore-cowboy clothes he wears. Tacky. But where in hell is my soul? O chief-god up there that usta look out for us Indian boys, they ain't but four, three, more minutes a this here free beer left and ain't but two shots left in this ole pint. God bless this here old pint and don't you dumbass paleface woman wish you knew I had it tucked down in my boot. Hunnerd-dollar Judsons. From Elk City, Oklahomer. I don't hafta go back to them godfuckin oilfields, let some sombitch kill me. Don't *haf* to. Got me a good ole woman, ole Tilly. She dumb and she don't talk English real good, but she's a good fuck. And she works, lordy lord, she does work. Gimme a baby daughter too, lil ole Calypso. Calypso One Shoe, lil ole shitpot. *She* don't want her ole daddy to git killed in the fuckin oilfields. She's gon a grow up to *love* her ole daddy, not take flars outha graveyard for him. Ain't no *sense* workin the oilfields. Just git your fuckin ass killed. Money's good awright but what good's the money when they bust ya all up, thow y'in the hospital, and say don't worry you'll git workmen's computation. Sheee-it. After the fuckin redtape and worryin, what's left? Same thing with the unemployed computation. Tell ya one thing, it's easier to work'n it is to beg, not just better, *eas*ier. Oooo-ee, that ole leg's hangin in 'ere, ain't she? Where'sat ole gal, there she is talkin to that sojer boy. Come on outa that boot, ole pint. Whiskey, do your work. Why you lil fucker, you's plumb full when I come here. Whoa there, hold off on that last shot, that's tomorra's breakfast. Or tonight's supper. Dumb fuckers. If y'all hadna give us Indians the whiskey you coulda wiped us *all* out. You give a Indian boy whiskey, he's got it *made*. Can't *noth*in hurt him then. But I ask ya agin, where's my soul? I done *lost* that sombitch. Ahhh, wait a minute, I bet I know where that sombitch's at. I bet I lost that fucker in that fuckin slushpit out north a Enid. How bout that? I's so fuckin drunk I fell flat in that ole slushpit. Got baptized all over agin, by god. Got myself washed in the blood a the fuckin lamb, by god. Come outa that ole slushpit a black sheep, by god. Les go out that ole slushpit and git that sombitchin soul back agin. Quick's I git her back we'll go tell ole Till, and she'll say, Hoo-awn you good man, heap good man. You don't bring home no bacon, nor no wampum, but you bringum soul home, by god. Then we'll give ole Tilly a little tallywhacker. Which she does just purely love. She *is* a good fuck. Yessir, we'll just step out the back door, have that ole shot a super, and go git that fucker outa that slushpit. How ya git outa this sombitch? Wait just a by-god minute, whoa up, lookee lookee in 'ere. Now this's a helluva place to have a slushpit. Betcha this sombitch's sup*posed* to be locked up. Just lookee lookee what's in this ole slushpit. There's ole Jax and Lone star and Schlitz and Pabst, Pearl, Budweiser, there's ole Carling busthead and *ever*thing, *cases* of it. You ole slushpit you. Them's empties. Ahhh, but these ain't. No sir-ee, there's full. Full a my ole long-lost fuckin *soul*. Dark as a fucker in here. Yeah you ole pop-top can, pop right outa there. We'll just scrunch us down here outa sight and *find* that ole soul, that ole fucker. Now pop-top can, I know you's warm, but don't you spew at me when I pop ya. Don't go spillin soul all over me. We take juuust a leetle soul at a time, comprende? Easy does here, there! Now. We'll find that ole soul, we'll *find* that fucker, by god.

La Dene laid a newspaper before him folded to the front-page article headlined WITNESS'S WIFE DEAD AFTER ME-LEE.

"Headline's all I can make out," said Tiger. "Didn't bring my glasses."

La Dene turned the paper and bent to read aloud:

" 'A 32-year-old mother was pronounced dead on arrival at Mercy Hospital Wednesday afternoon after an altercation with sheriff's deputies at 119 David Street, where she reportedly resisted arrest in connection with the serving of a subpoena on her husband, John One Shoe. One Shoe had been named earlier Wednesday as an eyewitness to the killing of Heinz Schell, whose body was discovered Monday in an oil drum at the city dump.

" 'Leon Weinstein, who has confessed killing Schell and is

being held for investigation, told the county attorney's office early Wednesday afternoon that One Shoe had seen him kill Schell and could confirm Weinstein's confession.

" 'When sheriff's deputies went to the One Shoe residence to summon him for a preliminary hearing scheduled for Friday, Mrs. Tilly One Shoe, wife of the alleged witness, became violently agitated, according to Deputy Marvin Stone. She reportedly threw a bucketful of ammonia water in the eyes of Deputy Jesse Winkler and attempted to run from the house, attacking Deputy Stone so savagely, he said, that he was forced to strike her with his billy club. The coroner's office reports Mrs. One Shoe died from cerebral hemorrhage following multiple skull fractures. Deputy Winkler, who suffered chemical burns in both eyes, was listed in fair condition at Mercy Hospital Wednesday night.

" 'An infant girl, apparently Mrs. One Shoe's daughter, who was found in a basket in the backyard has been placed in the county welfare home. Neighbors said they knew little of the One Shoes, who have lived at the Davis Street address about six months.

" 'The dead women's husband is still being sought.' "

La Dene leaned up as Tiger said:

"Ain't it though. Wonder if ole John knows he's wanted."

Tiger Ragsdale reflected, rubbing the gray stubble on his chin, then commented:

"Everybody's wanted by somebody for something at some time. It's part of growin up."

La Dene was often uncertain of the relevance of his observations; this one she postponed by saying:

"John's a pretty good ole boy."

"He's all right," said Tiger. "Talks too much with his mouth."

La Dene smiled for him and for the sailor who had just come in with what looked like an underage girl who, after they had sat at a table in the back of the room, wanted a limeade but settled for a Seven-Up. La Dene had almost rather have gone to the Rexall to get the limeade than to have to watch to see whether the Seven-Up was used as a mix. When she had served the couple and was returning to the bar she heard a muffled noise, a rustling, from the storeroom. Bea was at the hairdresser's; so far as La Dene knew, she, Tiger, and the couple were the only ones in the tavern. She dismissed it as some racket in the alley when she heard a bottle shatter, then another, followed by a shivering crash of breaking glass from, she was sure, the storeroom. Tiger hopped off his stool and padded after her as she went to find out what was going on. Opening the door and pressing the light switch on the wall inside, she confronted a scattered mass of broken brown glass, the better part of a case of empties, behind which John One Shoe stood holding the cardboard box out of which the bottles had fallen.

"Mornin," said John. He yawned and set the carton on the floor. "Or is it afternoon agin? Hadda lil accident."

"So I see," La Dene scolded. "How long you been in here?"

"Week, seems like." He yawned again and sat down on another beer case, testing it for firmness. "Hi Tiger."

"Hi John. Have a party, didcha?"

"Yeah I did. Got a thirst on me and thought I'd drink some beer."

"You mean," asked La Dene, "after all the free beer you had at the bar—must've been ten or twelve. . . ."

"Only 'leven," said John.

"After that much," La Dene continued, "you came in here and drink a whole nother *case*?"

"Only had twenty-two outa that case. They's twenty-four in a case, ain't they? Two left makes twenty-two. And it wans't *that* case." He focussed on the one at his feet. "I's just movin that one and slipped. I drunk cans, back there." He pointed.

"Thought you said you weren't a beer hog."

"Well hell it uz *there*, so much of it. It won't keep, beer'll go bad on ya."

"Not with you around, it won't," said La Dene. "I came in here couple times last night, how come I didn't see you?"

"I's over there behind that stack a empties. I heard ya come in. I didn't wanna make no trouble."

"Didn't you even go to the john all that time?"

"Why course." The Indian grinned his gold tooth. "I refilled some a the cans."

"Well you damned well better empty them," said La Dene.

"I awready did, last night after y'all shut down. Damned near broke my fu—my neck gittin to the john in the dark."

"John—" She paused, thinking of Tilly's always calling him

Juan. Anything to keep from saying what had to be said. Go on and get it done.

"John," she began again. "There's something you gotta know sooner or later."

"I'll *pay* for the damned beer. One a these days."

"No, forget the beer. It's about Tilly."

"What about her?"

"First though," she felt a quick relief to be able to digress, "you know Weinstein, that rabbi-preacher that comes in here, that says he killed that guy?"

"Yeah, I know him, talked to him couple times. Crazy sombitch."

"You know anything," asked La Dene, "about him killing that guy?"

"Whatta ya mean? What's that gotta do with Tilly?"

"He says you saw him kill that guy."

"He does?"

The Indian was logy from the night of beer. He closed his eyes and with each hand finger-combed his long hair at the temples.

"I'm tryna remember." He shook his head, opening his eyes to ask, "What about Tilly?"

La Dene looked at Tiger who said:

"She's dead, John."

The Indian showed his gold tooth again, not quite grinning:

"Awright now quit funnin."

"He's not funning," said La Dene.

John surveyed the scattered glass on the floor, and said:

"Naw, I kinda thought he wasn't. What happened?"

La Dene explained the particulars of yesterday afternoon's events, rehearsing the newspaper account as much as she could without denying her own grief. She finished by saying:

"And that's it. I'm awful sorry, John."

She started to touch him but didn't, feeling that she did not now have that privilege.

"Where's the baby?"

"She's okay. They put her in the welfare home, they'll take care of her."

"That ain't where she belongs;" said the Indian. "She belongs over in Talihina with her grandma. It wouldn't a happened, would it, if that Weinstein hadna said I seen him kill that guy. Would it?"

"I don't know," said La Dene. "Maybe not."

John sniffled and brushed his nose with the back of his thumb.

"Awright by god." He began to shout. "Yes by god that jew-nigger-wop sombitch done it, I seen him, he done it, and I'll see him fry for it, by god. Call up 'em cocksuckin po-lice. Call 'em, goddamn it. Call 'em shitheads."

He sat, as had the deputy with the burned eyes, elbows on knees, head in his hands, weeping in soft spasms.

Tiger came and laid his hand on the Indian's shoulder, turning to see the sailor from the barroom standing in the doorway.

"Listen jack," said the sailor, "watch your language. There's a lady out here."

All three stared at him before La Dene blared:

"Well what the fuck you think *I* am? If you don't like the language in here just get your ass out."

The sailor pursed his lips and clenched his fists.

"Ya heard the lady," said Tiger.

The sailor stepped and set himself to swing on the older man; John moved fast to get between them.

"Wait! wait, god*damn* it," yelled La Dene; all three stopped to stare at her: "We got enough goin' for us without a fistfight. I'm sorry, sailor, we'll watch it. Now go enjoy your beer. Please, go on."

He went, grudgingly. John poked in his shirttail, drew a bandanna from his pocket and blew his nose, then followed the sailor into the bar with La Dene and Tiger at his heels. Stalking past the couple at the table, the Indian headed for the front door.

"Where you going?" hollered La Dene.

"Where ya think?"

She noticed that he'd forgotten his hat, but the hundred-dollar Judsons still clonked as he walked.

Born and reared in Oklahoma and the Marine Corps, the old one. Transplanted to west central Michigan in 1970. Most recent book: *Night Perimeter: New & Selected Poems, 1958–1990* (Greenfield Review Press, 1991). Book of newer poems called *Spells* coming out from Bloody Twin Press in the summer of 1995.

I make money, spend money, clean, and repair. I write poems, shoot all manner of small arms, and smoke cigarettes, these last three no longer being socially acceptable behavior. I pray to and for the earth. All the time.

Rilla Askew

THE GIFT

THE CABIN SITS far below the rim of the hill. The path is steep. The boy can see black tarpaper peeling in long curling strips from the roof and, below that, the winding green snake of the river. It is too far, the path too steep. He will lose his footing, tumble and roll down the mountain, earth and rocks hurling up to meet him, a soft mass of legs and arms, spiraling, spiraling down the side of the mountain. He will plunge into the river and be drowned. His father laughs and pulls him up by the wrists. His arms could come loose from their sockets. Pebbles dislodge themselves and skitter down the path, gathering company, a miniature landslide. He wonders if they will be drowned in the river too.

Now he is riding under his father's arm. He can no longer see the river or the tarpaper roof. Now he sees two powerful thighs pumping up and down along the path. He sees the tops of his father's boots. His mother is behind him and he hears her laughter, high and thin in the weighted air.

The cousins gather all through the long sullen afternoon.

They come in twos and threes. Some stare at him from behind the door with their black glistening eyes. Some sit in their mothers' laps and hold their fingers in their mouths and watch him with no expression. Some make motions at him with their hands and eyes to tell him to come outside. He won't go. He knows what happens outside. They twist his arms outside and call him bad names. They spit on his hair. They make him walk in front of them down the long terrible path to the river. He sits on the floor beside his mother and holds on to a piece of her skirt.

There is a lot of movement in the room. The men are singing. Some of the women are singing too, though not his mother. The movement spills out onto the porch and beer bottles roll about on the wood. The trees are filled with cicadas. Their high rasping song rises and falls, rises and falls, in the air and the heat. He looks up at his mother. Her eyes are bright but the eyelids look sleepy. She is slouched in her chair, and the muscles in her throat and the bones at the top of her breasts are like sickles. She reaches a hand down to slap at his fist. He holds the skirt tighter. She isn't looking at him. Her head lolls back on its spidery neck and her pale hair inches down her back. She opens her throat and lets out a long, high, sad cry of celebration. His father gets up from the bed and comes toward them. His boots stumble on the slats of the floor. He puts an arm across her shoulders and she rises, prying the boy's fingers away from her skirt. Together they make their way across the rolling and pitching floorboards to the kitchen.

On the other side of the room an uncle is watching him. The uncle sits on the floor with his back near to the wall and his big hands dangling between his knees. His eyes are fine black slits. His hair is raven-black and shaggy, a ragged horsehair brush poking out in clumps beneath his hat. The uncle grins at him. His mouth is black too, a great black cavern filled with spit and rocks and salt. The uncle tells him, come over here, boy. I will tell you this one story. The boy hides his head beneath his arm.

The cousins holler on the outside. He can hear their war games and their shouts rolling up the hillside from the river. Beside the river is a bar of gravel. A long, flat bed of tiny rocks, the size for throwing. And for walking on. And for filling up your pockets and your shoes. The gravel bed extends for miles, maybe, along the side of the river, as far as the next bend, as far as anyone could see. You could walk for miles, maybe, along the side of the river and never have to touch the water, and never have to go in the woods. Maybe. Could be you could.

He is hungry. On the bed, an aunt is feeding her baby. The baby's face is turned away and the back of its head is an electric ball of fuzz, wisps of black feathery traces leaping in a circle to the air.

He tries to remember when it was that his father came and stood on the linoleum at the trailer in Tulsa. And then there was the long ride in the car and the bumps and the uncles with them and the smell of whiskey and sweat and the green dusty heat, and him on the armrest because there was nowhere else to put him and his mother in the front seat with her shoulder blades like sickles and her thin arms rising up out of no-sleeves and her fingers splayed apart on the hard ceiling of the car. And there were stops along the way and him left to be quiet on the armrest until they returned, and then the ride through the town and everyone said to shut him up, shut him up goddamn, but they weren't talking about the boy, and then they laughed. And then they stood at the top of the treacherous path that lurches away down the side of the mountain to the cabin.

The aunt moves her baby to the other side and for a moment the boy catches sight of fat solemn cheeks, brown solemn eyes, a wet tiny mouth, moving and moving.

He is hungry, and now the sun is slanting yellow through the porch screen and the cries from the river are far, far away, and his mother is asleep, lying sideways across the foot of the bed. Her yellow hair hangs down to sweep the slatted floor. The uncles are singing on the porch. The aunt puts her sleeping baby beside his mother and climbs down from the bed. She pads across the floor into the kitchen. When she returns she carries greasy sweet-tasting bread and gives him some and tells him come on out here, come outside, chooj, and pushes on the screen.

The uncles are singing on the porch, and their song is deep-throated and high and mournful. The cicadas answer back from all the trees. Below, the river has turned amber with the sloping of the sun. Soon it will turn bloody and then ease itself to pink and melt into the night in violets and blues. And then someone will light the lamp. And someone will tell stories. Could be.

His father leans against a porch post, holds it in his arms, and shuts his eyes, and sways and sings. The cousins' voices call to each other along the river. The trees are thick with leaves and hold the wetness and the heat in close and keep the cousins hidden. Only in the clearing and along the tilting path do the trees let the sun slant through to coat the porch in yellow and hide the corners in shadow. His father's face is distant, in the yellow of the sun.

And now the sound is of rustling and pebbles sliding down the mountain to their deaths and a hushed waiting in the air. The earth turns on a waiting and the uncles have stopped singing and even the cicadas have tamped down their song into silence.

Old woman comes between the trees and her skirt rustles in the sticks and grass and her feet stir up stones to fall down the long path to the river. She walks slow, coming down the path. The aunt pulls open the porch screen door and goes in the house. The uncles wait. Old woman does not look down into anyone's face. She holds her eyes to the river. Now the river is burning fire and bloody.

Old woman says, let me have that boy.

He wants to hold to old woman's skirts as they walk along in the creeping dark. He wants her to take him back to his sleeping mother. She walks in front of him, her soft feet making little scuffing sounds in the dirt of the road. When the boy starts to cry, standing still in the center of the road, she walks back to him and pinches him on the back of the neck. Soon he is moving again and his cries are swallowed deep in his belly, and his eyes are dry and open in the shuffling dark.

Old woman lights the lamp. The boy hears the wooden chair scrape on the porch, and then old man comes through the door and fills it up and moves on across the room to sit next to the stove. They talk to each other in words he doesn't know. The boy eats cold slabs of meat and kicks his feet on the rungs of the chair.

Later, he climbs up the ladder where old woman shows him and lies staring up into the black. He listens to the rustling in the hidden places over his head. An owl calls in a tree close by, and old woman and old man grow suddenly quiet. He can feel them watching each other in the silence. The boy turns over and puts his arms over his head. He thinks about his mother lying asleep, sideways across the foot of the bed.

In the daytime he follows behind old man, watches old man's boots step in the crumbling earth. He watches the plow's blade cut the green stems, shred the juice and the life from the plants, bury them deep in the brown broken earth. He watches the mule's white rump, its limp tail swishing at the black stinging flies. He smells the juice from the dying plants.

At night old man tells him stories. How the little people live far up the gorge in the rough craggy place. How sorcerers take the shape of owls, sometimes. Or a wolf, or a raven. How maybe in the night you can hear an owl and it wouldn't be no owl but a sorcerer, a Thinker of things, come to conjure your house. Come to make you sick. Come to do you some evil. Old woman does not tell stories. She sits close to the lamp and makes things with her hands, things to eat, things to wear inside your shirt. When it is time, she looks at the boy and nods her head. Then the boy climbs the ladder and lies alone in the dark.

His mother comes one time. She stands in the dirt yard with her elbows jagged in the air and shrieks at old woman. An uncle stands far back, leaning against the car, his jaw slack and his eyes almost closed. Old woman stands silent on the porch.

When his mother turns, her elbows fly out to the side. She weaves her way back to the car, makes a great circling loop to the far empty side, and gets in. The uncle and the boy's mother drive away down the road in the rattling car that belongs to his father.

The owl comes again. The boy can hear it in the trees far away, calling. Three nights the owl comes. The boy lies still, stares up into the black, listens to the soft *hoo-hoo-hoo hooo hooo*, the way it comes from far away above his head and then, later, answers itself, *hoo-hoo-hoo hooo hooo*, way off to the side or maybe from someplace distant where his feet are pointing.

Third night, deep in the night when the day birds are starting to sing, old man calls the boy. He stands beside the ladder, calls, you, chooj, come on down here. The boy opens his eyes. He listens to old man's voice wobbling in the air of the room. He climbs down and stands close to the stove while old man makes the grease hot. He sits at the table and watchs moths dance and dive, singe themselves brown, curl quickly and die in the heat of the lamp while he eats dark bread made from beans and the hot grease poured on top. Old man does not eat any but waits beside the door. His hair is white and stiff in the flickering light. His eyes have disappeared beneath the folded lids. He waits, and when the boy is finished he opens the door and moves outside. The boy gets up and follows him.

It is wet under the trees. He can feel the cool and the damp creep up through his feet. He follows close behind old man, tries to keep the dark shambling form just in front of his face. But he will not reach up and hold onto old man's shirt. The sky has turned from black to deep glowing blue. There are now stars. Once, when they come through a cleared place between the trees, he sees the moon. It is large and hangs low on the horizon, reflects back the light of the coming-close sun, glows white and luminous in the brightening sky. It is the shape of his mother's shoulder blades. The shape of his mother's bones at the tops of her breasts. The hot feeling backs up in his throat and he hurries to catch up with old man.

They stop someplace, deep in the woods where trees crowd in close all around. But overhead, light from the turning-blue sky reaches down. Old man kneels beside a clump of a plant with flat spreading leaves. When he tears off a leaf, the boy smells something bitter and sharp. Old man stands up slowly, saying words the boy cannot understand. And then old man walks off through the trees.

The boy must run quickly, tripping over roots and stumps, pain stabbing his chest, silent fingers and feet reaching out for him from the trunks of the trees. When he draws close, he slows himself to match the walk of old man. He wants to take hold of his hand. He wants old man to stop and bend down for him, lift him up to his shoulders and carry him through the clutching trees. But he walks in silence, holding his own hands close to his body, watching old man's dark moving legs.

Water is running. He hears the sound of it rushing away. The sky is turquoise. The moon has grown sickly and pale, fading away into the lightening sky.

Old man stops beside the water. It is not the winding green snake below the cabin but a different water, rushing and singing over a bed of stones, white where it swirls away from the rocks. Old man faces away from the moon, toward the place where the sun is coming. He holds the torn leaf in one hand, shredded now into tiny pieces. His other hand moves over the pieces of leaf, kneading them, rubbing them in a slow circle. He spits on the leaves. He speaks, half singing, half talking, saying the words the boy does not understand. Many times he says the words while the sky where he watches grows pink. When the fiery edge of the sun shows itself red and huge at the top of the far hill, old man lifts his hand high, holds the torn bitter leaves to the sun, sings high and mournful with his throat moving and his eyes closed.

All day, old man does not eat. He sits by the door and stares in front of him. Old woman feeds the boy but she does not look at old man, does not give him food to eat.

Twice more he takes the boy back to the water. In the middle of the day, when the sun is small overhead, burns down yellow and hot on the rocks by the way, when black flies whip through the still air and cicadas whine in the trees, he takes the boy back to the water and rolls the crushed leaves, now dried-out and faded from the heat of the sun, and sings the harsh songs. Again, in the evening, when the sun is one more time big, going down in the place where the moon disappeared, he walks back to the water and the boy has to follow.

They return to the house in the long purple evening. Old man stands the boy in the yard, tells him, "Wait." He goes into the shack at the back of the house and stays a long time. The boy slaps mosquitoes. He watches the trees on the far side of the road going black in the twilight. When old man comes out of the shack, he carries a pipe. He stands close to the boy and puts the brown crumpled leaves in the bowl of the pipe. He uses a thick match to light the leaves in the pipe; his lips pull on the stem, leathery cheeks fill and collapse. Smoke rises and stands in the air, not bitter but sweet.

Slowly, old man and the boy go in a circle around the house. Always he pulls on the pipe, and the smoke stands in the air behind them. Four times he stops and faces a corner of the earth and blows out a great puff of smoke, to the place where the sun rises, to the place where it sets, to the north and the south. Four times they encircle the house, and each time old man pauses to face four directions. When they are finished, the first stars have appeared. They go in the house and old man lights the lamp.

The boy lies in the dark and listens to the small scratches and scuffles over his head. He holds his eyes open in the deep purplish black and listens for the owl. He remembers what old man said, after the meal. How he leaned his chair back on two legs while they sat on the porch. How it was dark on the porch and old woman sat with them, her hands empty and still in the folds of her skirt. How old man said: "He will not climb over, this night-walker-about. This Thinker of me will not come over the circle of smoke. His soul itself will be broken."

The boy lies in the dark and listens.

Far off, he hears it. Faint, like the muted soft sound of far-away crying. *Hooo hooo. Hooo hooo.* And closer. Almost near now. *Hoo-hoo. Hoo-hoo.* Quickly, quietly, he climbs over the ladder. His bare feet move lightly on the wood of the floor.

On the porch, old man sits smoking in the farthest corner of shadow. His chair stands back on two legs against the wall of the house. He does not turn his head to look at the boy.

It sits high up in the trees on the far side of the road. The boy can hear its fluttering call. He waits, holding fast to the porch screen behind him. He tries hard to see. He tries hard not to break, not to run like a rabbit back through the quavering room to crawl shamed and afraid under old woman's covers.

It cries and cries, this night-walker-about. This Thinker of things. The boy waits, and his breath is a hard aching knot in the front of his chest. It won't come. It won't climb over. The boy speaks to himself. Its soul will be broken in the gray ring of smoke.

Old man stands up and his chair scrapes on the porch. He moves down the steps and into the yard. He moves toward the trees. His white hair has turned to the color of sandstone in the frail light of the moon. The boy follows on tiptoe, the hard little stones in the dirt of the yard bumping under his feet. He stands far back behind old man. Old man is waiting in stillness and silence, holding himself in the air of the yard, watching the black trees on the far side of the road. The boy creeps forward. Closer and closer. He comes near to old man's comforting legs.

And it happens.

Silent as death, the owl swoops from the black, talons extended, wings sweeping the air. It comes for the boy.

The boy cries out and falls to the ground, covers his head

with his arms. The owl shrieks, not the soft one-note flutter, but a high piercing scream. The boy hears the quick heavy flapping, the sound of his grandfather singing the words. He hears the owl scream. The scream fades in the blackness to a feeble low wail. And when the boy looks up, uncovers his hand for one frozen moment, he thinks that he sees, believes that he sees, the owl tumbling to earth in the shape of a man.

All is silence. The night creatures have ceased their continual thrumming, their chirring and creaking and calls in the night. Old man picks up the boy and carries him into the house.

When his mother comes, long days and nights later, long time after the night-walker-about, she brings with her a man in khaki tan clothes with a gun on his hip. They come in a white car with red lights on top. The man gets out of the car with the boy's mother and walks beside her when she crosses the yard. He stands to the side, arms folded over his belly, and looks up at the porch.

The boy's mother talks. She shows old man and old woman a paper. Her eyes are shriveled and pale in her face. Her hair is tied up in a tight yellow knot. When she talks, the muscles in her throat move up and down. The bones jump out above the scoop of her blouse. The paper shakes in the sunlight when she holds it out toward old man.

Old woman puts her fingers on the back of the boy's neck. She talks to old man in their unknowable language. Old man leans forward and stands his chair down on four legs. He gets up and moves slowly down the steps, goes slow and deliberate around the side of the house, It is silent in the yard, just the sound of cicadas crying in the trees. The boy looks at his mother. She is not looking at him but has her eyes on old woman. Her lips are buried in one narrow slit.

Old man comes into the yard from around the corner of the house. He motions the boy to come down off the porch. When the boy is beside him, he puts a ragged piece of red cotton into his hands. Through the material, the boy can feel something slender and hard.

In the back seat of the car, sitting close to his mother, watching the tangled-together trees rush by on the hillsides, he thinks about the trailer in Tulsa. He thinks about the yellow linoleum on the floor, the other trailers crowded up so close on every side. He can't remember what it feels like to live there.

He turns himself more toward the window, pulls his feet up onto the seat, hides the front of himself away from his mother. He takes the red piece of cotton out from under his shirt. It is warm from where it has been close to his skin. His fingers play over the material, caressing the long hard shape of the stem, poking into the bowl that holds the powerful leaves.

Rilla Askew is a native Oklahoman. She lived many years in the Western Cherokee capitol of Tahlequah and the surrounding countryside, and still considers that place on the earth to be her spiritual home. Her work has appeared in literary magazines such as *Carolina Quarterly*, *Sonora Review*, *North Dakota Quarterly* and the Oklahoma Indian Markings issue of *Nimrod*. She is the author of *Strange Business*, a collection of Oklahoma short stories published by Viking Press. Currently she lives in Brooklyn, New York, with her husband, actor Paul Austin, and is at work on a novel.

Marilou Awiakta

RED CLAY: WHEN AWI USDI WALKED AMONG US

Reunion of the Cherokee Councils of East and West

"I FEEL WHAT'S HAPPENING at Red Clay, but I don't know how to take a picture of it." The veteran news photographer shakes his head, folds his hands on top of his camera.

I show him my blank notebook. "The energy field here is too strong. I've never felt anything like it. It's so peaceable."

We smile, wander on, he toward the West Knoll, with its crest of trees faintly tipped with leaves. I toward the amphitheater tucked in the lee of a wooded hill. Weeks of chilling rain have left earth and air so sensitive I can almost touch the sunlight, the pungence of loam and pine carried by brisk wind. I am in my native mountains again, where my blood feels at home.

It's April 7, 1984 — the second and final day of the Eastern and Western Cherokee Council Reunion at Red Clay, now a state reserve nestled between steep ridges near Cleveland, Tennessee. This place is sacred ground, hallowed ground, a place that re- members. It was here in 1837 that the last council met, faced with the federal government's adamant demand that ancestral lands be relinquished; here in 1838 that federal troops began the Removal, the Trail of Tears that divided the people into what is now the Cherokee Nation of Oklahoma and the Eastern Band of Cherokee Indians, most of whom live on the Qualla Reservation in North Carolina. Other families and small communities are scattered along the Appalachian mountains from Virginia to north Georgia.

For the first time in 147 years, the chiefs and their councils have united to discuss mutual concerns about health, education, legislation, economics and cultural preservation. According to centuries-old tradition, the convening of the council is as much social and religious as it is political, and formal deliberations are being held outside, among the people – a crowd estimated, over- all, at twenty thousand. Five to six thousand are of Cherokee heritage.

We've gathered in a remote mountain meadow, its fingers wedged among wooded knolls and its palm sparsely dotted, as it was in 1837, with a cabin and other tenements made of weath- ered logs. In the center, near a deep limestone spring, is the rectangular, opened-sided council house. The amphitheater is concealed behind a hill. At the entrance to the Historical Area, shaded by pines, the museum and offices are housed in a low, fawn-colored wood building with a long porch across the front. Ordinarily, to walk onto the council grounds is to pass into another time, into a quiet broken only by songs of birds or occasional conversations of other visitors.

None of the planners had expected twenty thousand people. As April 6 drew closer, however, attendance estimates rose swiftly. "We don't know what will happen," said Carol Allison, assistant to the principal chief of the Cherokee Nation of Okla- homa and one of the organizers of the event. "We've told everybody – the media, the public – that this reunion is to be dignified, a historic council meeting, not a 'drums and feathers' event. But what if the non-Indians come expecting that kind of thing anyway and are disappointed with the Indians for *not* having it? It's still winter in East Tennessee—what if people swamp the motels and others are left milling around in the cold? We can't let this reunion get out of hand."

"We" included the principal planners—the Cherokee of east and west, the officials and citizens of Cleveland, the supervisor of the Red Clay Historical Area and his staff and their assistants, as well as unknown numbers of other people preparing for the journey. One thought united us all: a reverent spirit *will* prevail at Red Clay. For months we beamed this thought toward the sacred ground. Energies fused, creating a powerful field that ultimately would draw human currents from the Four Directions.

On the eve of the reunion, people were pouring into the Cleveland area by plane, by car, by camper, by train. Everywhere the friendly exchange: "Where're you from?" "Florida!" "Connecticut!" "Minnesota!" "Hawaii!" and points between. At the Chalet Motel, where many Cherokee were staying, the mood was happy, expectant, quiet. Around us the mountains seem frozen, their trees bare-limbed against dark clouds. In just such weather the ancestors began the Trail of Tears. We were thinking of them and asking ourselves, *What will happen at Red Clay?*

Now I'm in the midst of it all. From the beginning the sun has been radiant, the wind benevolent, though steadily rising. At the amphitheater in the lee of the hill, however, all is quiet. On the grass stage, where the final council session is in progress, Chief Robert Youngdeer of the Eastern Band raises his arms toward woods and sky. "When we came to Red Clay the trees were closed and cold. See in one day how the leaves have unfurled . . ." His unspoken meaning is clear:

Remember
how our Mother Earth has renewed
herself
how the people have endured
how hope has unfurled
invincibly!
Red Clay!

Something is moving among us. I feel it in many images—an energy as invisible and real as the atom's. Governor Alexander calls it electricity. A reporter, an aura. As I walk the council grounds, I gather these images as healing medicines for bleak seasons I know will come again.

The most striking image is the ceaseless current of men, women and children, moving peaceably among the knolls, over the meadow. Here pooling quietly for a ceremony, there running in rivulets among the food and craft booths that edge the grounds, pausing in eddies of conversation, then moving on, a constant lively contented murmur.

"I've never seen anything like it," an Anglo man observes. "Nothing seems planned but everything gets done! People just *flow* around."

The Cherokee set the tone for the crowd. Though visually they often may be distinguished only by a deeper tint of skin or hair, a bit of beaded jewelry, an occasional ribbon shirt or dress, they are still, as an observer of the 1837 council described them, "the decorous Cherokee," and they behave in keeping with the dignity of the occasion. There can be no drinking, no rowdiness. By immutable tradition, where the council meets is sacred ground.

RED CLAY IS GROUND THAT REMEMBERS

Maybe this is why so many people seem to listen inwardly to a different dimension. Even time images differently here. It is all of a piece, all in the present. I touch the railing of the open-sided council house. Once again it is the fresh of the morning, sunlit, chill with a light breeze. Paul, our son Andrew, age fifteen, and I huddle with about two hundred others waiting for the prayer ceremony that will open the reunion. Friends exchange news. Strangers chat like neighbors. The chiefs and councillors stand quietly discussing arrangements.

In response to a request for a photograph, a small wiry woman emerges from the councillors and stands apart. A blue kerchief is wrapped around her forehead and tied in back, in the traditional way. Her jacket and ankle-length skirt are dun colored. I recognize Maggie Wachacha, an eighty-eight-year-old member of the Eastern Band, scribe for the tribal council, and a "rememberer." I know of her through her grandson, who told me, "My grandmother heard her elders tell how they walked the Trail of Tears. When she speaks of it, we hear their voices. We feel their sorrow."

As she gazes unperturbed toward the steep ridge across the meadow, I study the seams of her face, the calm eyes, brown at the center, fading to hazy blue in the outer rims. Is she thinking of what an ancestor recounted, words recorded by George W. Featherstonhaugh, as the two men stood near the council house on that rainy August day in 1837?

> John Mason brought us greetings from President Van Buren. He said the president is guided by "justice" and is only concerned with our safety and well-being. He urged us to accept the treaty signed two years ago in New Echota [Georgia] and move west. He said this when he knows the signers were not authorized by the people. He told us, "In Oklahoma, the country will be yours — yours exclusively." We were not impressed.

Is Maggie Wachacha remembering this bitter sorrow? Or is she thinking of today, when the Cherokee diaspora has gathered from the Four Directions? As scribe of the Eastern Band, she knows the resolutions the reunion council will consider. Perhaps she is looking to the future, to the harvest that may come from seeds of unity.

Briefly her eyes meet mine, and I know. All are one to her: past, present, future, and the experiences they bring. I begin to understand the power that vibrates in this place.

RED CLAY IS STILL CENTER OF TIME

As the Reverend Robert Bushyhead of Qualla begins prayers to the Great Spirit in Cherokee, I think how at the council 147 years ago, similar prayers "soothed the spirit" of Featherstonhaugh, an English naturalist whose eyewitness account was used extensively in the modern reconstruction of the historic area. I hear his precise voice describe Red Clay:

> Rich, dry bottom of land . . . the irregular street of huts, booths and stores hastily constructed for the subsistence of several

thousand Indians . . . the hilly ground upon which the council house was built . . . the copious limestone spring . . . and the most impressive feature—an unceasing current of Cherokee Indians, men, women, youth, and children, moving about in every direction, and in the greatest order, and all, except the younger ones, preserving a grave and thoughtful demeanor.

How much is the same and how much has changed. "If we hold fast in the center," Maggie Wachacha's eyes tell me, "the good can be preserved and the grievous made well."

The youth reflect the wisdom of Maggie Wachacha. They too feel what's happening at Red Clay and respond energy to energy, a cloud of electrons orbiting the nucleus. They are the future gathering strength. Two merry teenage girls from Qualla sell red "Remember the Removal" T-shirts at one of the folding table "booths."

"Proceeds go to a joint youth project with the Oklahoma Nation," they explain. "This summer we're going to retrace the Trail of Tears so we'll understand our heritage better."

I buy two shirts. "I'm from the Far Away Cherokee Association in Memphis. We're going to host the group as you pass through. We'll be looking for you."

Beyond the line of tables small children run in the meadow, dart in and out of log tenements. In the barn loft they stick out their arms and wave through interstices in the walls. Laughter and calls of "Wait for me" drift over the grounds. A young couple is watching them. The woman's hands rest on her abdomen, which is stretched almost to term. "We're from the Nation in Oklahoma," the man says. And though I haven't asked, he adds, "My eyes are blue and my skin is light because every other generation my family 'married out.' My wife is full-blood. We don't know what our baby will look like. But it's what's in the heart that counts. 'There's power in the blood. . . .' "

"Wondrous working power." I finish the line of the old song, and the three of us smile. We are remembering that for more than a century the federal government subjected the Cherokee to a killing winter: divided the nation; forbade the teaching of language and culture; imposed the Dawes Act of 1890, which linked blood quantum to entitlement to land and federal services and which had the avowed purpose of fomenting "selfishness, which is at the bottom of civilization." Break up the land.

Break up the tribal system. Break up the family. The strategy succeeded brilliantly in both geography and politics.

Blood, however, flowed east and west and also into remote coves and valleys in between, secluding itself in the genes of families (some of whom have married outside the tribe and back since 1540) — and biding its time. Memory of language and culture spiraled in the cells of children, where the "remembers," including our Mother Earth, the greatest rememberer of all, have known how to call it forth. Although the quantum always has caused dissension, as it was intended, abetting the tendency of people to polarize into opposing groups, families have held fast. And now . . .

RED CLAY IS BLOOD CONVERGING

Within its watery nest
a baby listens
to gathering kin
to its own blood singing
— and slowly unfurls
invincibly.

This baby, like all our others, reaches toward us unaware of color — either of skin or eye, or of hair that may be straight, curly or wooly. The baby remembers only its blood-song. If the child looks "politically incorrect," will we cut it in pieces? Or will we say, "It's what's in the heart that counts. Sing, child!"

Today, in the warm peace of Red Clay, I dare to hope that we can help our children sing a bridge over all that is closed and cold, that we can help them by singing the bridge ourselves — invincibly.

Thousands of people here carry the image of an invincible singer — Nancy Ward, the last Beloved Woman of the Cherokee. She is pictured on the reunion's commemorative poster, which is reproduced on the program book's cover. Her grave lies twelve miles from Red Clay, but the sacred ground remembers her vision — and so do we.

During her tenure as Beloved Woman (1755–1822), Nancy Ward worked steadily and against increasingly desperate odds for mutual understanding between Anglos and Indian people. It was a concept of peaceful coexistence that she maintained in her own family. She had two children with her first husband, who was a full-blood. After his death she was married briefly to a white man, Bryant Ward, and they had one daughter. According to the Cherokee matrilineal tradition, the children took their mother's name. There was no thought of "cutting them in pieces"—part this, part that. Both privately and politically, this system was a matrix to nourish peaceful coexistence.

However, the patrilineal system of the Anglo culture provided no such matrix, and by the 1820s, when Nancy Ward died, the vision of peaceful coexistence and the matrilineal egalitarian culture that would have nourished it seemed to have died with her. In reality, the system used nature's oldest survival tactic—it adapted, went underground, preserved its roots. Today, Nancy Ward's vision, which was shared by many other Cherokee leaders of her time, is greening again. At the first session of the reunion council, which is composed of both women and men as in the traditional times, Wilma Mankiller presides. She is deputy principal chief of the Cherokee Nation of Oklahoma, the first women to hold high office since Nancy Ward.

RED CLAY IS UNITY BEING BORN

This unity is imaged by the principal chiefs—Robert Youngdeer of the East and Ross Swimmer of the West. Always accessible, they move easily among the people. But when they obviously are talking privately together, the crowd, including the national press, courteously avoids them. This unsolicited courtesy, in itself, is extraordinary. And I see it now, as the two men walk toward the West Knoll. They alternately listen, talk, sometimes serious, sometimes smiling. Weaving connections. Chief Youngdeer is medium height—sturdy, erect. His hair is white, his gaze often reserved and penetrating, though he is also noted for his compelling sense of humor. He is a master orator in the ceremonial tradition. Chief Swimmer is younger, tall and lithe, an attorney who moves astutely through the bureaucratic intricacies of Washington. His manner is urbane, firm, kindly. In both the Cherokee and dominant cultures, these men are highly respected for their knowledge, wisdom and governing skill.

Many things separate the eastern and western bands: twelve hundred miles, federal bureaucracy, lack of formal contact for nearly a century and a half. The Eastern Band numbers 8,882, is geographically enclosed, and has a low-income, tourist economy. The Cherokee Nation of Oklahoma owns several businesses, including a company that produces components for commercial and defense industries. Most of the Nation's 53,097 members are integrated into the dominant culture, although 30,000 of them live in the fourteen-county service area (not a reservation).

"But we have many points in common," says Chief Swimmer, "an ancestry, heritage, culture, and our outlook for the future. The future Red Clay brings is to renew tribal ties and family relationships that were ended in 1837. We will continue annual meetings, alternating locations east and west. (In June 1985, the council met in Tahlequah, Oklahoma.) We'll have opportunities to support each other on issues pertaining to one tribe and to strengthen our lobby effort in Washington on issues we have in common. Red Clay is not only historic but means a lot to contemporary Cherokees."

As the formal, major ceremony begins, Paul, Andrew, and I are part of the ceaseless current that has pooled quietly on the West Knoll. From our place midway, we can see the crest of trees, but can only hear the speakers as they step to the podium. As they speak, the images of Red Clay intensify – *ground that remembers . . . the still center of time . . . blood converging . . . unity being born* – and they seem to be slowly resolving into one. I feel what's happening, feel the expectant vibration in the crowd as whispers pass, "They're coming. The runners are coming with the sacred fire."

Young women marshals in traditional ribbon dresses have cleared a path for them that leads up to a monument of crab orchard stone, which will shelter the flame. In 1838, when soldiers herded Cherokee families from Red Clay, someone secretly carried the sacred fire, tamped and hidden in moss. The fire signified the spirit of the Creator, of the sun, of the people – and the Cherokee have kept it burning for centuries. In 1951 an ember was brought back to North Carolina. Now the young men have run 130 miles in relay from the Qualla reservation in the mountains of North Carolina, bearing torches.

The crowd is silent as the men run slowly toward the crest of the knoll. There the torches are joined together and passed among the council members before coming back to the chiefs for the ceremonial lighting. The chiefs invoke the fire's ancient meanings, and Youngdeer extends its light to include the present when he says, "The flame stands for freedom, and friendship between the whites and the Indians. We hold neither hatred nor malice in our hearts. We remember the past but look to the future."

I stoop to touch the path, where the earth has used winter rain to bring forth grass—thick, buoyant, rippling verdant, and sweet in the wind. I sense the people thinking with one heart, evoking the seventeen thousand who walked the Trail of Tears, the four thousand who died along the way, the small band that held out in North Carolina. We move with them through years closed and cold, through the slow-warming cycle of justice that restored many rights. Now, in the seventh generation since the Removal, we have come to Red Clay, where new leaves unfurl and a fresh, green path shines in the sun.

> We have survived.
> We thank the Great Spirit.
> We shall renew our strength and
> mount up with wings.

A powerful presence sweeps silently through the crowd. It is more than an "energy field." More than "electricity" or an "aura." Many who know his traditional story say Awi Usdi walks among us. Little Deer, a spirit of reverence and justice.

The Coming of Little Deer

From the heart of the mountain he comes, with his head held high in the wind. Like the spirit of light he comes—the small white chief of the deer.

> When one of his own is slain
> he instantly draws near
> and finding clotted blood on the leaves

he bends low over the stain,
"Have you heard . . .
Has the hunter prayed words of pardon
for the life you gave for his own?"
If the answer be "No" then Little Deer
goes—invisible, fleet as the wind—
and tracks the blood to the hunter's home
where he swiftly pains and cripples his
bones so he never can hunt again.

From the heart of the mountain he comes, with his head held high in the wind. Like the spirit of light he comes—the small white chief of the deer.

Once in a lifetime he may appear
to one whose spirit is deep
and a master's arrow may bring him down
so the hunter can take his horn
to keep as a charm for the chase—
a talisman reverently borne
for reverence alone sustains its power
and forestalls wrath and pain.
But the hunter must be swift of hand
for the arrow hardly strikes his throat
than Little Deer leaps for his ancient path
that slopes upward into the mist.

From the heart of the mountain he comes, with his head held high in the wind. Like the spirit of light he goes—the small white chief of the deer.

Some say he can't be here. That our high-tech age is "too advanced" to believe such stories. But Awi Usdi was in these blue-hazed mountains twenty-five hundred years ago, when the Cherokee named his spirit. To him modern arrogance is a mere drifting leaf.

He has come to Red Clay because the heart's blood of the Cherokee was spilled here. This is hallowed ground.

He has come on the hunters' behalf, because their descendants have prayed the words of pardon through their deeds. It has taken time.

Today Governor Alexander announces the formation of the Tennessee Indian Commission, a historic first for our state and an expression of the concern for Native American Tennesseans that has been growing for decades. The history of the Red Clay Historical Area exemplifies this slow, steady growth. In 1929 Colonel James F. Corn of Cleveland saved Red Clay from becoming a factory side by buying the land and giving it to the state. In 1973, archeologists began excavation and reconstruction, funded by tax money, not donations, from all of Tennessee's citizens. Locally, the Red Clay Association supported the project. When the work was sufficiently done, Jennings Bunn, area supervisor, invited the Cherokee to return, with the hope that "the reunion of 1984 will in some small ways help to heal this wound and reunite in oneness a great Nation. May the spirit of Awi Usdi watch over us all."

Because we have gathered here in reverence and love, Awi Usdi is watching over us, walking among us.

Swiftly, I gather his image: A peaceful power assuring all people that if justice and reverence prevail, in the fullness of time, sorrow may be eased, wounds may be healed. And within whatever morass we find ourselves, there is always a green path that leads us to the top of the hill, where the sacred fire burns for us all.

AFTER THOUGHTS

Experiencing a whole nation turning toward the east is luminous — beyond prose or photographs or poetry. Fifteen thousand non-Indians had come to witness the event. Why?

Without my asking, a couple with four children in hand — ages three to ten — told me the reason many people came. After the council meeting I was walking down the hill beside them.

"We have a little farm up in Minnesota," the woman said. "We drove all the way here in our truck."

The man said, "We wanted our children to see this. If the Cherokee can survive, so can we."

Of course, at Red Clay there had also been people who were "just curious" and a charlatan or two (isn't there always?). One of them was a man in a long feather headdress and pilot's sunglasses claiming he was a "shaman who had healing hands." The Cherokee quietly shunned him, although one of the chiefs re-

buked him indirectly by mentioning in a speech that the Cherokee did not wear feather headdresses. Although the only obvious security people were random park rangers, many others in
ordinary clothes roamed through the crowd, including tribal police ("Beauty is no threat to the wary"). But a greater power was
holding the twenty thousand people in check, and one expression of it came from those who live in the vicinity of Red Clay.

Before the reunion began, many of them had brought gifts
for Cherokee families who had traveled long distances and were
camped on the grounds. Firewood, jellies, fried chicken, cakes,
charcoal. Welcome notes and names were attached to some
gifts, others were left anonymously on the porch of Park Head-
quarters. At the beginning of the reunion, Chief Swimmer had
instructed a staff member to make a list of all identifiable do-
nors, so he could circle back letters of thanks on behalf of the
Cherokee. When the reunion was over, as the chief was getting
into his car to leave, a middle-aged man hurried up and thrust a
painting into his hands. "I made this for you," he said. "The
paint's not quite dry, but I wanted you to know how I feel about
you and your people."

> Harmony.
> Continuance in the midst of change.
> Peace.

The reunion at Red Clay convinced me that Homo sapiens
have a chance to avert Mother Nature's "pink slip" and create a
place where our children, the seeds of the people, can grow safe
and strong. By unweaving contemporary life back to our original error, we might be able to restore the balance and heal the
wounds. *"In the beginning, the Creator made our Mother earth
. . ."* If I could leave only one of my writings behind, it would be
the poem "When Earth Becomes an 'It.' " We must call Earth
"Mother" again, especially for the children. The baby who was
"slowly unfurling" at Red Clay is now nine years old. Her English name is Alayna. Her Cherokee name is Jigeyu – "Beloved,"
after Nanyehi, the Beloved Woman. She, children like her, and
those unborn are looking toward the future. They are expecting
the sunrise.

Winner of the Distinguished Tennessee Writer Award in 1989, poet/author Marilou Awiakta fuses her Cherokee/Appalachian heritage with the experience of growing up on the "atomic frontier" in Oak Ridge, Tennessee.

Awiakta has published in anthologies such as *A Gathering of Spirit*, *A Southern Appalachian Reader* and in Alice Walker's *In Search of Our Mothers' Gardens*. Other publications include, *Ms*, *The Greenfield Review*, *Parabola*, *Woman of Power* and *Southern Exposure*, which commissioned her essay on the 1984 reunion of the Eastern and Western Councils of the Cherokee. The Public Broadcasting System has made two documentaries that feature Awiakta and her work and an educational program, "Telling Tales," released in 1990, in which she was a principal storyteller. A collection of her poems and essays, *Selu: Spirit of Survival*, was published in 1993 by Fulcrum Publishing.

Through Tufts University, Awiakta is currently working with a team of national scholars to "develop a new model of American Studies, using black, ethnic and feminist perspectives to integrate the sciences and humanities." She has worked for many years in the Arts-In-Schools program in Memphis and has also conducted poetry workshops in the Women's Prison there. She was co-founder of the Far Away Cherokee Association, which has since expanded into the Native American Intertribal Association.

A magna cum laude graduate of the University of Tennessee, with a degree in French and English, Awiakta lives in Memphis with her husband, Paul Thompson, a physician. They have three children.

Betty Louise Bell

COMING TO *FACES IN THE MOON*

FROM THE AGE of six, I knew I wanted to be a reader and a writer. At the time it seemed like the most natural ambition but looking back, I wonder how it could have possessed my young mind and spirit: books were as rare as money for food at the end of the month. And books, even imagination, were unthinkable luxuries in our makeshift survival.

A Creek medicine man once said to me that all gifts and differences are present at birth. For him, the matter was simple: people are born with the seed of their being. The lucky few who trust and nurture that seed, without the need for evidence or explanation, live happy lives. His words, for me, are wise and true. The whys of our desires, ambitions, the way we do or do not love are mysteries that can be unraveled only so far before we begin to speak of dreams and hopes and other insubstantial but life-consuming passions.

I wish . . . I wish . . . I wish: to understand, to speak, in knowledge where there can be none.

The things I do know about my desire to write: I know I learned the agency of literacy from listening to my mother's pride in the accomplishments of the children she baby-sat. Those children, unlike her own, lived in large sunny houses where space and privacy were possible, even assumed. My mother did not resent her employers, the minimal wage, or the ways in which their luxuries were cheated out of domestic workers. My mother was captivated by the easy beauty of their narratives. And she would repeat, always with the familiarity of a family member, their stories of triumph or sorrow, exalting in their happiness or worrying over their unhappy moments.

I wish . . . I wish . . . I wish: to greet the rising sun in memory and anticipation.

But the stories that consumed my mother, before dawn as she dressed to take care of other people's children, circled around her mother. The light followed my grandmother into her home one cold March evening in 1932. Three days later, she was dead. Her daughters, ages nine, eight, and six, were left in the care of their new stepfather, a Scot with a mean streak and ugly desires. Here, at the edge of her mother's death bed, my mother planted all good and sacred memory.

She talked about being Indian, not because she knew anything about being an Indian, but because her mother was Indian. Her nostalgia for her Indian past was not the imperialistic nostalgia of colonial America but personal and dear. Her memories of her mother were all that she ever really owned and from that small space in her life, she created stories of hardship, suffering, courage and love.

Hellen Bell died young, but her spirit walked and laughed in our kitchen before dawn. After her death, the Scot forced her daughters from school, into the cotton fields, and into his bed. But this I only learned later, much later. By then I knew how to dream of my grandmother, how to bring my mother's stories of her close, so close that I felt her strength in my blood and made room for her in my home.

I have no daughter, no child, to wake at dawn and coax into my dreams. And so I write.

When I wrote *Faces in the Moon*, I knew I had to let my mother and auntie speak for themselves. Certainly, the stories of my grandmother belonged to them and could only be told through them. But more, their voices, holding lives and humor, *was* the story. The following is an excerpt from that novel.

BEAT THE DRUM SLOWLY . . .
DON'T . . . STOP . . . TOO . . . FAST

"YOUR GRANDMA was a full-blooded Cherokee," my mother said again and again, as far as I can remember. It was the beginning of a story, the beginning of a confidence, and I lean forward, knowing that in the next few minutes no cheek will be pinched, no broom handle swung, no screams or tears wasted, I listen and watch, grateful to be part of the circle. Her words come slow, a chant filling her sunken face and smoothing her wrinkles. Across the kitchen table, I never take my eyes off her.

I did not hate her, then. It was easy to believe in the photograph on Lizzie's bureau: a dark-eyed beauty with olive skin and black hair to her waist, shapely in a cotton housedress and holding a newborn baby. She stood forward in a new field, the baby close to her cheek, the woods far behind her. As a child I called the woman "Momma," slipping close to the photograph and tracing her outline with my fingers, whenever I passed through Lizzie's parlor. After my great aunt's death, it was harder and harder to put the pretty girl with the child together with the fat, beat-up woman who cursed and drank, pushed into her only threat, "Maybe I'll just run away and leave y'all to yourself."

Some tension had given, some spirit snapped in the space of ten years, and the pretty girl had swollen into fatigue and repetition. In her last years a big cozy mother appeared, in short housedresses with snaps down the front and letters sticking out of her pockets, letters written to me on scraps of paper, backs of envelopes, and carried around for weeks, even months, before she dropped them in the mail. Her running scrawl refused time, pushing ahead of it the events of her day and health, always confessing her secret love and pride in me, and arriving months after the fact.

But, long before the letters began to arrive, long before she knew she had something to say, she had already lost me to her stories. And there, I loved and forgave her.

"You was always her favorite. She was crazy 'bout you. I never seen her take to nobody the way she took to you. Ain't that right, Rozella? She was always too good for the likes a us. Uppity Indian. Her nose so turned up, her own shit don't stink."

"What did she look like?" I ask.

"Don't y'all member Lizzie?"

I shrug, my palms turned wide and open. I remember but I'm not supposed to remember. And I want to hear it again. I listen for Lizzie's name, watching as she moves before me in a calico apron and a tight face. She never smiles. Even as Momma and Auney move from laughter to tears, Lizzie stands silent and unamused.

"She was an Indian," Momma says. "She looked a lot like our momma, the same black hair and black eyes."

"Like us?"

"Y'all carry the Indian blood, that's fore sure. Your black hair and Rozella's quiet ways, ain't no mistakin y'all. I ended up with the Scotch blood. Don't look like there were a drop left for y'all. Member that woman ask me if I'm Irish? Black Irish, she says. I'm a thinkin she means nigger, and I almost give her a beating right in front of the chicken shack. I just look her in the eye and say, as cool as you please, 'There ain't no nigger in my woodpile.' But Lizzie and momma, they looked Indian."

"Indian," Auney says with a nod and a blow of smoke.

She was my spinster aunt, a survivor of four marriages, and my mother's chorus since birth. When one of her marriages broke up or she was looking for a new start, she came to us. And there, she was my mother's constant companion and an angel to me: silent and placid, she told no tales and didn't hit. And she gave me everything, except her bingo money. She drank and married hard-drinking no-good men. They almost killed her, more than once, but the closest she came to fighting back was to refuse to forget.

"I can forgive," she explained, "but I can't forget."

When she had had enough she came to us, put on her hairnet and went to work in the cafeteria with my mother, giving her slow attention to portions of corn and mashed potatoes. She never bothered with divorce, she simply lived in one married name until the opportunity for another came along. And like my mother, she just as easily switched from married to maiden name without consistency or legal considerations.

They were Evers, sometimes more, sometimes less, but always Evers. The daughters of Helen Evers and some no-account traveling Scotch preacher who never married their mother, turning up only to impregnate her a second time, and leaving them, finally, on the side of the road. The young Indian mother walked, carrying one baby and coaxing the other, until she came to a junkyard. There, she made a home for them in an abandoned car. There, until the rent money was saved, she left Gracie in the back seat to look after the baby, Rozella, while she walked into town and looked for work.

"You member, Rozella," my mother's mind fluttering from one story to the next, "the time I locked you in the outhouse?"

"I member."

Momma lit her cigarette from Auney's and spoke to me. "Your grandma used to have to go to work in town. Five miles there and back, she walked. Ever day, even Sundays. She was afraid someone would steal us, so she always locked us up in the house." Her eyes darted across mine, and she blushed with shame. "It was just an old shack, tar paper and cold in the winter."

"Cold."

"We was always up to no good." Her face lit up. "Still are, eh Rozella?"

"Yep. Sure was. Your momma was always the ringleader."

My mother took the compliment with a laugh.

"As soon as your grandma was down the road, we scrambled right out the window and back 'fore she got home that night. More coffee, Rozella?"

Auney was a strong coffee drinker. She'd been waiting for the offer for some time but instead of saying "yes," she looked down into her empty cup, took a drag on her cigarette, and came as close as she allowed herself to expressing want. "I believe so," she said in a slow and uncommitted drawl. She lived with us, on and off, for most of her life, but she never asked nor took without multiple invitations and assurances of plenty. That, my mother said, was the Indian in her.

Momma brought a new cup and the coffeepot to the table. She filled their cups and poured me half a cup. I wanted to smoke too but knew better than to ask.

"One day, you member Rozella?"

"I member"

"You went to the bathroom and I locked the door from the outside." Momma laughed, Auney blushed. "You didn't so much as raise a yell. I heard you try to open the door. But then you got real quiet."

"How did Auney get out?" I was the audience, and I held the story's cues.

"She did the durnest thing. I'm waiting out front, wandering when she's gonna start yelling, and here she comes around the corner of that outhouse. What a sight you was, Rozella. I thought I was seeing things when you come around that corner." Momma turned to me. "She was covered with shit and piss from head to toe. She crawled right out of that damn hole! And she stunk! Lord have mercy."

"Amen."

"Momma came home that night and whupped the living daylights out of me. She whupped Rozella too."

"She did. Yes, she did."

"She said the county'd come and get us if we didn't behave. They woulda, too. A young Indian woman with two little girls and no man around."

"No man."

"But she kept us together. I wander how she did it, Rozella?" The kitchen curtain flapped. Momma went to close the window and found it shut tight. "Witches, Rozella. You member them witches down there in old man Jeeter's river?"

"Sh-h-h," Auney said. "Y'all gotta watch who y'all call up."

Momma laughed and turned to me. "Your Auney were always afeared a them witches. Long afore our momma died, she'd a shiver and shake anytime she come near that water."

"Now, Grace, I weren't the onliest one afeared."

"That's true," Momma admitted, "true enough. Momma used to say only fools don't know what to be afeared of. And the good Lord save us from them. Eh, Rozella?"

"Ain't nothing scarier'n fool. The God's truth."

In the dream I'm being chased. Through city streets, down alleys, only a few slippery feet ahead of the monster behind me. I feel his reaching darkness, gaining and gaining, almost in grabbing distance. I watch the horror of running without moving, screaming without noise, the terror striking and missing, striking and missing, and I pull myself treading to the surface. Sweating and shaking, I lie still in my corner of the room. "Shoo," I whisper, "Go on."

"Those was tough times," Momma said. "The Depression and the wind blowing the topsoil clean outa Oklahoma. Times was rough all over. There was no welfare, no nothing for an Indian woman with two little girls to feed. Even ifn there was, she had that Indian pride, don't take nothing from nobody."

"Member she beat me fer askin Mz. Wilkins for that apple?"

"I thought she was gonna kill you."

"Almost did."

"Why'd Grandma do that? It was just a apple." The words slipped out of my mouth. I knew better. "I mean," I tried to explain as I watched the human drain from Momma's face, "why'd she have to be so mean?"

"What ya know 'bout it? It ain't ever just a apple. Things ain't never that simple. 'Cept you, sometime." Auney dropped her laughing eyes, and Momma commenced shaking her finger at me. "Missy," ya ain't but ten years old and you think ya know it all. Ya'll don't know donkey shit."

"I know something," I mumbled and pushed my shoulders back.

"Horse manure."

Auney laughed and gagged on her smoke. Through a fit of coughing she tried to say, "Grace . . . we . . . was . . . the same way."

"At her age Momma was dead and we was on our own with that old devil Jeeter. We had to grow up fast, it ain't the same."

I considered the distance from my mother across the table and gambled, "I can take care of myself."

"I wisht I believed it. I'd a take the first greyhound bus and leave youse to yourself. The trouble with you, Missy, is you ain't never knowed hard times. Ya don't know what it means to spend just as much time *not* looking hungry as being hungry." She was wrong, but I knew better than to gamble again. "I wisht I'd a had a mother to look after me. Maybe things a been different for me."

"Ya did your best, Grace."

"Lord knows I tried. I'd tried and tried till I'm a plumb tired out from trying."

"Plumb tired out."

"I tried to forget an' go on living. But those was hard times. Don't seem like there's a way a forgettin 'em. I member Momma like it was yesterday. I see her as clear as I see myself. I member her taking off down that road ever morning, walking those five miles to town to clean the Wilkins house and the Davis house . . ."

"And that one with the big white porch. The Johnson house."

"Yep. Those white women worked her to death, and the white men was always touching her up. Sometimes she'd come home crying. You member, Rozella?"

"I member."

"You member how we used to sit on old man Jeeter's back porch and watch for her in the moon?"

"I member."

"The day she died she said she'd be watching for us from the moon. You member?"

"I member."

"Used to be we'd see her. Most every night. All's we had to do was sit on old man Jeeter's back porch and watch for her. Soon those eyes a hers would be looking at us."

"Yep. Plain as day."

"We sit right there and talk to her like she could hear us. About old man Jeeter and the hard life we had without her." Momma laughed and shrugged. "Those eyes a hers would change. Looks like she were going to kill somebody."

"You member, Grace, what she used to tell us?" Momma and Auney laughed, and I saw Lizzie turn from her work at the sink and almost smile.

"I sure do." Momma leaned toward me, as if I hadn't heard it a hundred times before, and said slowly, "Don't mess with Indian women."

"Less you're a fool."

"Even a fool got more sense 'n that."

"Grace, you ever see Momma after ya left old man Jeeter's place?"

"Used to be when I ran away with that old man Baptist preacher, I'd see her. Now and again. You see her, Rozella?"

"Now and again."

Momma waited for Auney's words to clear the room. We waited for what Auney would not say. Then Momma laughed and said, "Used to be we believed indians went to the moon when they passed on." The joke passed through Momma's face before she spoke. "What y'all think? We gonna make it to the moon?"

"I can't see why not."

"Me too?"

Momma lit a cigarette. Auney said low and careful, "I believe so."

"You just tell them you're Hellen Ever's grandbaby. She ain't gonna let them turn ya away. They'd have a fight on their hands, sure enough. Wouldn't knowed what hit 'em. Ya member, Rozella?"

"I member."

"I remember."

Momma laughs, Auney stops mid-draw on her cigarette. "You weren't even born. How can you member?"

"I do remember."

My mother looks at me. The kitchen curtain flaps above my head. Finally, she says, "You musta dreamt it."
"Dreamt it."

Betty Louise Bell is an assistant professor in English, American Culture, and Women's Studies at the University of Michigan. She teaches courses in Native American literature and serves as the Director of the Native American Studies Program. Her first novel, *Faces in the Moon*, was published in 1994.

Charles Brashear

TRIPTYCH: THREE CHEROKEE WOMEN IN 1776

FOR SOME TIME, I have been working on a historical novel that deals with the overall transformations of Cherokee culture between 1763 and 1795. These three portraits of women show aspects of that transformation.

The events took place in May, 1776, shortly before Dragging Canoe's war of 1776. Henry Stuart and Alexander Cameron, the British Indian agents, had convinced Dragging Canoe and his followers to allow them to write a letter to the white settlers at Watauga, demanding that they withdraw from Cherokee land. Oconostota and Attakullakulla, the Cherokee leaders, decided that they, too, would send a letter. They asked Isaac Thomas to be their messenger.

1. SALLY CAMERON

Alexander Cameron, a stocky, sandy-haired man in his mid-forties, stepped out his cabin door in Toqua town, his suspenders still hanging down. He stretched to work the stiffness of the night out of his system, for he had to ride the three miles to Chota this morning to participate in welcoming ceremonies for Henry Stuart. He was trusted by both Cherokees and whites. He was the Deputy Indian Agent, whom even his enemies respected, and he was beloved of the Cherokee Chiefs, who had asked him to be their "linguister" and write their words on "the talking leaves."

Toqua lay before him, thin wisps of smoke rising from all of its chimneys, except where some warrior was still out on the warpath, or where the family had gone to another town to visit their clan. Most of the Cherokee houses nowadays were log cabins, some of them made of squared logs and chinked with mud and moss so that they were as tight and warm as any house you'd want. Each year, there were fewer of the traditional Cherokee houses of red clay plastered over reed and wattle frames and thatch-roofed with slabs of bark. Even most of those now had fieldstone fireplaces and blood-polished floors.

His wife came out behind him, still combing out her long, black hair. "Are you ready to eat, Scotchie?" she asked in Cherokee.

"In a few minutes," he answered in Cherokee. Then he turned to glance at her. "Sahti, Sahti," he said, exasperated. "When are you going to learn to wear clothes? You aren't supposed to go around naked."

"But this is a Cherokee town," she protested. "It doesn't make any difference when we're in a Cherokee town. We aren't at home, you know. Besides, I don't exactly have much girlish charm left — or hadn't you noticed?"

"I'd prefer it if you wore your dressing gown. Try to be a little modest. The white men of the trading houses, and even some of the half-breeds, aren't as indifferent as you Cherokees."

He turned to the wash-stand, a hip-high bench just outside their door and under the shed-roofed porch. He dipped water from the bucket, pleased that it was no longer freezing overnight, and washed his face in the tin pan beside the bucket. "And besides," he added, reaching for the broadcloth towel that hung from the end of the wash-bench, "we *are* home. This isn't Lochaber, I know, but it is *our* house. We've lived here almost as much as we have at Seneca."

Sahti stepped up to the wash-bench and splashed water, not only in her face, but on her chest, belly, back, and legs as well. She rubbed vigorously, washing her whole body. The chill bumps stood up on her skin.

"I've never understood how you Cherokees can stand so much cold," Scotchie continued in Cherokee. "You might as well have gone and jumped in the river."

"Then some half-breed or a trading man might have seen me," she teased. "And then you'd have had to challenge him to a duel . . ." She paused, toweling her body and trying to think of a better joke. "And then—you'd . . . Well, to speak honestly, Scotchie, I don't think you can shoot as straight as you used to, and I really don't want to have to train a new husband."

"You witch," he said, playfully slapping her on the buttock as they turned to go in. "I might just go off one of these days and find myself a Cherokee virgin—and train her to have less of a snake's tongue."

She turned in the doorway and caught him, her arms around his body. She kissed him on the bearded cheek, then on the mouth, clinging to his shoulders and pulling him into her breast. "Oh, Scotchie," she said, pouting, "I don't even like to joke about it. Too many women have lost good husbands to young girls no bigger than chickadees. Please don't ever leave me, Scotchie. I know it's not your English ways to walk away from a wife's doorway and still live in the same town. But I still worry. Don't leave me, like a Cherokee might."

"You have no need to worry, Sahti," he said. "You know me as a man of honor true to my word to Cherokee and Englishman alike. My words do not fall in the dirt, you know that, don't you?" He lifted her chin to look into her eyes.

"Yes, I know that. But—all the same—there are so many women with half-breed children, who have to live with their clan. Look at Wurteh. And Na'nyehi. And I don't know how many women that don't have the advantage of being related to Head Men. So many of the traders and soldiers have gone back to the settlements and have white families there and live in big houses."

"Aye. 'Tis true. 'Tis true," he said in his slight Scottish burr. "I am sorry to admit it of mi own breed, but 'tis true, 'tis true."

She twined her finger in the sparse hair on his chest, then kissed him again. It always reassured her when he spoke to her in English, which she had learned so that she and the children could speak both languages. She released him and went toward their bedroom to dress.

The house was large for a log cabin. The big room across the front was a combination living room, dining area, and kitchen. The two smaller rooms on the back were bedrooms, one for Scotchie and Sahti, the other for the children. They had skin windows in the big room, greased to make them more translucent, and sawed lumber floors, which they had rubbed smooth with a flat stone and polished to a fine dark sheen with animal blood. Scotchie had brought an upholstered settee, two armchairs, a lacquered table, and a roll-top desk from Charles Town. And they had a Franklin stove to cook upon.

Sahti put on her white, broadcloth blouse and her jumper dress that reached nearly to the floor. She buttoned her cuffs and her bodice and straightened her hair with tortoise-shell combs. She came back, looking like a tawny English lady who would not have to cook her husband's breakfast.

2, NA'NYE-HI/NANCY WARD

Isaac Thomas was a near giant of a man—six foot six, broad of shoulder and thick of leg. In his mid-forties, he was now tending toward paunchiness, so he weighed nearly eighteen stone. He had operated a trading yard at Chota for several years and spoke Cherokee well, which had earned him the trust of the older chiefs, though, because of his size and ferocity, he was feared by the younger men. It was an open secret that he was the paramour of Na'nyehi, the most powerful woman in the Cherokee Nation, whom the whites called Nancy Ward.

"Why you?" she asked in English, perturbed, as they got

ready for bed. "Why do they always choose you to be the messenger?"

"Oh, you know," he mumbled, sitting in a chair to take off his boots. "I go that way a lot. They think I can just drop off a letter on my way." Unlike most of the other traders, who got their goods mostly in Charles Town and Augusta, Thomas worked out of Virginia. So he often passed through the Watauga and Holston settlements. And he often brought back copies of the Virginia *Gazette* and other newspapers, which he willingly interpreted for the Cherokees.

They both knew that was hardly the reason Oconostota had asked Isaac to deliver the letters the Head Men and Henry Stuart were going to write. They choose Isaac because he was strong and dependable and fast on the trail; he could run sixty miles in a day, if need be, and do it again the next.

"Just the same, I'll miss you," she said.

Isaac looked at her where she sat on the bed, her dressing gown falling open as she combed her long black hair. At thirty-eight, she was still a handsome woman—a bit stocky perhaps, but the bloom was still on her round cheeks and her complexion was as fair as many Englishwomen. "Miss me? You? who can have practically any man you want, red or white? Don't tell me you'll be lonesome."

"Well, I will." She turned away, so he would not see her face, her dark Cherokee eyes. "I won't have anyone to help me read."

"Why, there must be twenty, thirty men within a day's walk of your house that can read and write. And another fifty that don't write enough to say they're literate, but talk the King's English well enough to be good practice. Take your pick."

Nancy said nothing. They both knew it was not just the language lessons that were involved. Nancy thought most of the white traders were crude and dirty and lived like dogs or savages. She wanted to be with a man who preferred eating his meals with a fork, who shaved his beard when it sprouted, and who kept up with affairs in the world outside. Too many of the traders had become like Cherokees themselves, even adopting Cherokee superstitions and clan politics.

To Isaac Thomas, Na'nye-hi, the Pretty War Woman of the Cherokees, was "queenly and commanding," as one white man of the time (Charles Robertson) described her. And she was civilized enough for any man. She owned this large, squared-log house in Chota, with wooden floors and glass windows with curtains on them. She had imported furniture for her living and dining rooms, as well as silverware, table china, and implements like butter molds and candle holders that few in the Cherokee Nation desired or valued.

From her second husband, Brian Ward of North Carolina, she had learned to raise and care for cattle, and she introduced the first drove into the tribe. For some fifteen years, she had kept and bred a large herd, so she and her family were never in want of meat nor leather, nor milk and cheese. She had become wealthy by white standards, at a time when virtually no Cherokee valued or even vaguely understood wealth, though everyone understood the concept of personal property. As she had told Isaac many times, she believed that the only way the Cherokees could compete with the whites and survive, was to adopt white culture. That was why she cultivated friendship with the Wataugans. "I wish I could go with you," she said. "You might need some protection on the path."

"You know you have your duties here," he said, shifting to Cherokee. "You might just have to lead a bunch to the water ceremony and jump in the river."

"Yes, I know," she sighed, answering in English. She stood up and put her arms around his naked body. "Well, I'll ride with you to Scotchie's house, tomorrow," she said. "I want to know what's going on." She pinched out the candle as they got into bed. "If my cousin who drags canoes is not too set on attacking the settlers, maybe I can talk him out of it."

"Ha! You know him. He's like a little kid – tell him not to do something, and that's what he'll want to do most."

3. WUR-TEH

Nathaniel Gist approached Wurteh's house cautiously, for some of her clan hated him. He didn't exactly want a hatchet in his hair today. Wurteh's house was a small, clay-plastered hut at the edge of Chota, nestled among a group of similar houses where many of her clan lived. They preferred these traditional houses and quiet streets to the log cabins and noisy town squares that some Cherokees chose these days. Though it was late in the day, Wur-teh and one of her clan sisters were grinding corn in their up-ended log mortar.

"Hello, Wurteh," he said. Then he shifted to Cherokee: "O-si-yo."

She looked at him a long moment before he saw the glint of recognition come into her eyes. She did not return his greeting.

"It's been a long time," he continued in Cherokee.

Still, she did not acknowledge him. She lifted the pestle with the same deliberate motion she always used and brought it down into the mortar with the same methodical force. Her clan sister backed away, not wanting to appear like she was listening. The other women, who were cutting meat for drying, or curing berries, or mending moccasins or dresses, also put down their work and silently went around corners.

He looked up and down the alley. A few children were playing down the way and a few dogs. A few old men sat on stumps under their porches and smoked their pipes. He recognized none of them. Wurteh continued her work. "You're looking mighty fine," he said in Cherokee. She wore a traditional deer-skin tunic, rather than a calico dress, which was more favored by progressive women. She had gained weight, was now a matronly-looking woman with a few strands of gray in her black, braided hair.

"What do you care how I look?" she said, turning away. "You never send messages. You never ask for news of me and Sequoyah. When you pass within an hour's ride of my door, you do not even stop. What do I care who you are? I have other men to walk through my doorway."

"Yeah, I know I haven't kept up."

"Kept up? Your son is sixteen years old and you haven't said sixteen words to him in his life. You keep up like a frog that doesn't even know which tadpole is his. You act like you don't even know which pond he's in."

"Well, uh—how is the boy?"

She turned to him and glared, her mouth clamped. She stared for a long minute, marveling at his audacity to ask, and trying to decide if she wanted to give this stranger any information. She hardly needed him. As a daughter of The Raven of

Chota, she was in a good clan and a good family. She and her son had never wanted for love and protection, or relatives to care for them. And now this – this storm from her youth was passing through her life again. And perhaps their son's life.

"The boy is slight and bandy-legged," she said, trying to hurt him, "and he keeps himself clean; not at all like you. He doesn't like to bully people around. Nor stink of old sweat and horses."

"Yeah, well," he said, shifting his feet. "A body do get a bit dirty on the trail." He slapped some of the dust from his buckskin shirt. "I s'pose I *could* use a bath. I've not crossed a river in several days."

Wurteh dipped the corn meal from her mortar into a clay bowl and put more whole corn in the mortar. Gist recognized that she was ignoring him. He gestured toward the small sweathouse that stood at the corner of her hut. "Well, uh – You reckon I could clean up a little?"

She made no reply, but lifted the mortar to crack the corn. He took that to mean that she didn't care what he did.

He went over to the sweat-house, took kindling from the pile, and built a small fire inside. He picked up an empty clay jar, got water from the nearby creek, and set it near the fire to warm. Then, when the fire had begun to make the sweat-house warm, he took off his clothes and crawled inside. He was soon sweating profusely. With his cupped palms, he put water on his head and shoulders, rubbed it along his arms and legs. It even felt good to sweat out the grime that had been collecting all winter. He'd be glad to rinse it all off with the warm water from the jar, but damned if he'd run and jump in the ice-cold river, the way the Cherokees did.

When he came out of the sweat-house, his clothes were gone. His rifle, powderhorn, and shot pouch, as well as his knife and beaded scabbard, were hanging under the porch beside Wurteh's door, where they were safe. Before he had finished rinsing his body, she came back from the creek, his leather clothes dripping in her hands.

"I washed them for you," she said. "I don't know why I bother, but I did." She spread them out on the hot sweat-house dome. She passed him, without looking at his nakedness. "Come on into the house," she said. "You'll have to wait for your clothes to dry."

When he went in, she was fluffing up a bear skin on the cane bench that also served as a bed. She motioned that he could lean against the back wall. "I'll see if I can find something for you to eat," she said. She built up the fire around a copper pot that contained steaming squash, then hung strips of venison on a metal rod over the coals.

"You don't need to go to all that trouble for me," he said. "I'd be content to eat pemmican and jerky."

"I know," she said, and lay fresh corn pone to warm on the flat stone beside the coals.

When the afternoon began to get chilly, she lowered the bear-skin over the door and weighted the bottom with stones. That left only the stark bar of light piercing the smoke-hole and the yellow light of the fire. When the food was ready, she brought him steamed squash, broiled venison, and corn pone on a wooden plate.

Gist leaned back and watched her while they ate. She sat on her folded legs, her hands at rest in her lap. She seemed to be studying something on the clay wall at his other side, her eyes fixed and far away. Was she on the verge of tears? He touched her hand, and she smiled briefly.

When he had first come to the Cherokee Overhills in the late 1750's, he had thought for a while of becoming a Cherokee. He had tried hard and learned the language fairly well, had accepted this Chief's daughter in marriage, had learned to dance and sing convincingly in most of the rituals, though he had always hated "going to the water." Then the trouble developed around the siege and destruction of Fort Loudon, and it was suddenly very dangerous for any white man, even one protected by his relatives, to be in Cherokee country. So he had abandoned Wur-teh and their son. He had gone back to Virginia, entered the service again of Colonel Washington, and finished the war in 1763 in the rank of Captain. By that time, he had the wanderlust and could not give up drifting.

In one sense, his going had not disturbed Wur-teh. She was the head of her household anyway and owned her own property. She was as well off without him as she had ever been with him. But she missed him. She missed his clever ways of farming. She missed the convenient gadgets he made around the house. She missed his skill as a hunter, who always brought home meat and leather. She missed the metal pots and spoons and needles he brought from Virginia. She missed his being able to read and write, which she had hoped he would teach their son. She missed his being a Cherokee.

When he had finished eating, she handed him an elongated white-clay pipe and tobacco. He filled the pipe and lit it. He puffed the smoke in the six cardinal directions: toward the Blue North for its advice about bad luck, toward the Black West for its respect for death, toward the White South for its nurturing power, toward the Red East for its power to bring about new things, then toward the Yellow Sky for its stack of Seven Heavens, and finally toward her, as a representative of the brown Earth itself. "Nice pipe," he said.

"Sequoyah made it," she said. "He is very clever with his hands. Like you once were. He fashions these pipes of clay, then hardens them in the fire. He also carves from wood and makes new things from silver."

"Well, I'm proud to hear it," he said, but knew nothing else to say. The bar of twilight at the smoke hole had grown dimmer.

Slowly, Wurteh stood on her knees, lifted her skirt, and drew her dress over her head. Her body was thick now, but still firm; her breasts sagged only a very little. Without a word, she made space on the bear skin pallet beside the husband of her youth and put her arms around his naked body.

It was what he wanted. He ran his hands along her hips and legs, played briefly with the clean silky hair of her pubis, then rolled her over and made love to her.

Afterward, he kissed her and fondled her breasts. She returned his kisses. "What in the world will happen to us Cherokees?" she asked. "You whites hurt us, and we never learn. You steal our land, and we thank you. You kill our sons, and we forgive you. We have every reason to hate you, but we come back to love you again and again."

Charles Brashear was born in 1930, on the south edge of the Llano Estacado in west Texas. "I have two strands of Cherokees in my family tree. I used to be very reticent about saying that, until one day a very good friend, a Cherokee woman, said 'Hey, Charlie; everybody's got to have a grandmother, somewhere.' So now, I take it for what it is. They say an ounce of gold can be drawn out into a wire fifty miles long. My Indian connection is like that: drawn out very thin, but still very real and shining to me, a conductor of valences."

He holds a Ph.D. from the University of Denver writing program, has taught fiction at San Diego State for twenty-odd years, and has published a dozen books, the most recent of which are *Creative Writing Handbook*, a text, and a collection of short fiction, *Contemporary Insanities.* His recent magazine credits include stories in *High Plains Literary Review Studies in American Indian Literatures, Four quarters,* and *Fiction International.* He is working on a collection of stories, tentatively entitled "American/Indian Interface," of which "Rough Creek, Texas—1888" is a part, and a documentary novel about the Cherokee war of 1776, from which he portraits of three Cherokee women of 1776 are taken.

E. K. Caldwell

BEAR DAUGHTER

KIYONA WAS BORN during a mighty snow in the Season of the Sleeping Bear. Her people lived at the edge of the forest on the bank of a wide river. It was a good place. And the people showed their gratitude at each rising sun, offering prayers and tobacco, singing morning songs. As each day reached twilight, they would gather again, and the drum would resound their collective heartbeat.

Time passed in its own way here, and as Kiyona grew with each passing season, she felt herself changing in ways she did not understand. She felt different and apart from the other children, always hanging back when the others played together. Sometimes her heart ached inside and she would wander silently into the forest. She especially liked to go there when the river mist was woven through the tree trunks and across the paths, lighted in places by muted sunlight. The silver green shadows soothed her.

Sometimes she would sing and listen to her voice as if it was the voice of someone other than herself. She had come to find a

deep joy in singing, although the other children teased her because her voice was much deeper than their own. Eventually she
sang softly when she was with the others, and expressed the
fullness of her range only when she had passed through the
forest to a secluded place on the river bank. Here the great blue
heron silently stood vigil for her as she sang with the river.
Forest and River. She was more at home here than in the noisy
circle of children playing back in her people's camp.

This year was going to be different than all the years that
had gone before. She didn't know why, but somewhere deep
inside her, she could feel the changes. She had tried to talk to her
good friend, Shona, about these feelings, but Shona had looked
confused, and even a little frightened. She told Kiyona that her
face changed when she talked about certain things, and that
sometimes her eyes looked too fiercely into Shona's heart. Kiona
didn't have all that many heart friends, and she didn't want to
scare Shona away from her. So she stopped talking about how
she felt. She secretly wished many times that the feelings would
just go away.

One morning she could hear the forest calling her. She felt
herself hurrying through her morning work. Her mother scolded
her lightly for not paying attention to what she was doing. She
wanted to tell her mother that the forest was expecting her to
come right away, but she thought her mother would tease her
about trying to get out of her work, and maybe even find an
extra chore for her. Finally, her work finished, she allowed herself to open her heart to the forest's call to her.

She hurried along the path and her heart was pounding in
her ears. A startled osprey lifted itself from the tall river grass
at her noisy approach. Her hand shaded her eyes as she raised
them in apology when the osprey's cry pierced her hurry. Kiyona
slowed her steps. The beginnings of disappointment stirred in
her heart. Everything looked the same. She did not know what
had carried her running feet through the forest and brought her
here this sparkling autumn day – whatever it was, she feared
she had missed it – that it had gone on without her. The sadness
welled up into her eyes and ran down her cheeks. She sat
hunched and forlorn, clutching her knees, feeling apart now
even from this secret place.

Kiyona did not look up when she heard the rustling grass.

She was shamed by her tears. She was, after all, a girl who had lived through nearly nine cycles of seasons, and crying was for younger children.

"Granddaughter, what troubles you so deeply?" The voice was soft and sounded like water running over pebbles. "Look at me, Child. There is no shame in giving water from your eyes. It is a gift to the earth. Flowers take their lifebreath from the tears you drop here. Tell your Grandmother. You shall be listened to and understood."

Kiyona shyly lifted her head and looked into the eyes of this grandmother. They were shining straight into Kiyona's heart. Her breath escaped her, looking into these eyes. She opened her mouth to speak and found her voice absent. When the old woman offered her hand, Kiyona silently accepted it and was momentarily surprised with how easily she was raised to her feet.

"Come and walk with me, Granddaughter. There are things we must talk about now. It has come to you at an earlier season than most, and your young heart carries great confusion and loneliness."

Kiyona and this Grandmother walked along the river, sharing many secrets. Kiyona opened herself and the words poured out like the river's white water. This Grandmother listened to them all without question or judgement. Time hung suspended between them. There was no hurry now.

"Ahead there is a place you will know when you come to it. You will rest there before you begin your journey home, Kiyona. It is one of the doors to the Dreamtime. It is in the Other World of the Dreamtime that you will find your destiny. Walk though this door with courage, Granddaughter. It is not my place to tell you what you shall find there, for each carries within them that which is from their own heart. That which you carry in your heart will be revealed to you there. Walk in a good way, Granddaughter. Know in your heart that you shall become someone you are glad to know."

Kiyona was again startled by the cry of the osprey and her eyes lifted to the west direction. The osprey circled for only a moment and was gone. She heard the rustle of the river grass, and realized she was alone on the river bank.

"Grandmother?" she called softly. Her only answer was the

singing river. She walked into the sun and the lengthening
shadows as the Sun made its westward journey across the sky.
Her mind was strangely quiet now and she moved soundlessly
into the darkening forest.

Her feet knew the way. They had traveled this path many
times. Suddenly she felt them changing paths, and felt the flick-
ers of fearful fire lighting themselves within her. This was not
the way she had come before. A fallen tree blocked the way. It
was getting darker. Where was that path?

And then she saw it. It led up a hillside studded with boul-
ders. As she threaded her way around these Stone People, she
was glad for their presence. Many relatives lived in the forest.
The Stone People would accept her presence as night came,
unlike some of the fourlegged relatives. And the Stone People
would not devour her. She clung to them as she pulled herself up
the hillside. Once the forest wrapped herself in her night blanket, Kiyona would have to stay in one place. All children learned
this. Choose as dry and sheltered a place as you could find, and
stay there. The night forest had fourlegged guardians roaming
through her. It was not the place for twolegged humans to be
wandering around, no matter how many seasons they had lived.

Kiyona lifted herself onto a ledge, and paused to catch her
breath. She looked around and saw an opening behind her,
lighted with the last of the day's blue time. It was a cave. She
felt her heart quicken as the Grandmother's words came back to
her,

"It is one of the doors to the Dreamtime . . . It is in the Other
World of the Dreamtime that you will find your destiny . . . walk
through that door with courage . . ."

Kiona did not feel the courage fire. She felt tired and frightened and hunger was gnawing inside her. As the first star
showed its light in the night sky, she wanted only to be with her
mother and her family and the people of her camp. She wanted
to go back to the beginning of this day when the forest had
called to her. She would pretend not to hear it. She would run
and laugh and make great noises with the other children. And
then she would not have to worry about being alone in the night
forest. She would be safe in the camp of her people, belly full, in
her own sleeping place.

A sigh escaped from deep within her. Her feet lifted themselves, one placed before the other, and she was moving towards the dark entrance. Shapes began to shift around her as she entered the cave. It was colder here. A shiver ran through her and she wished she knew how to warm herself with the courage fire.

As her eyes adjusted to the darkness she suddenly realized she was not alone! The cave was not wrapped in night's blanket. Long shadows painted the walls, drawn there by the reflection of a singing fire. The shadows belonged to those circled around this fire. They were waiting for her.

She stood at the edge of the circle, uncertain. This was that which she had asked within her heart so many times that she had lost count. This was that which she had seen in dreams over many years passing. This was that which she had called destiny. And now she hesitated, feeling her legs pulling her to run away – to run faster than she had ever run – with the wind at her back and no more thought of destiny and dreams.

The wind stirred and sparks lifted from the fire, Light Dancers. She felt her breathing begin again. Those seated around the fire did not look at her, yet her presence was felt in each heart. Each heart felt her in its own way. She was being considered.

Her mind was busy with its own thoughts. Uncertainty was, after a time, replaced with a quieting of her heartbeat. Her mind stilled and she could hear the singing fire. She witnessed its song in the leaping tongues of its chorus and inhaled its cedar smoked melody. Sweet fierce music.

Time passed and it did not. Her eyes lifted from the fire to meet another pair of eyes. The intentness of these eyes startled her, yet she could not look away. They entered her and held her. They searched every bit of her and rested longest in her heart.

One deep sound from the throat of these eyes and all faces turned towards her. She made only a slight attempt to distinguish their features. She felt the disadvantage of her youth in their presence. Her want to speak outweighed the wisdom of her silence and her voice burned in her throat. It refused to obey her when she commanded it to make breath into words. A low guttural growl lifted itself through burning edges of unspoken questions and she felt herself changing. The burning suddenly soothed and cooled into deep resonant growling.

She hesitated only a moment as this voice within her

stretched and she allowed it its range, feeling strong and welcomed into this circle. Her song lifted and mingled with the fire's song. Just as quickly it faded in her throat and the old fear brushed her like a sparking ember. As she waited for its sting against her skin, it extinguished itself without effort.

She lifted her hands and gazed at their sleek furred backs and leathered palms with the wonder of those who have truly been transformed. Her claws curved from them, shining in shadow.

And then she heard the voices, timbered and rich, speaking the words chosen for her.

"You have chosen this, Daughter. And on many mornings you will leave the Dreamtime and question your choice – crying out for the way you were before. You can try to return, and you will most likely make attempts, but it will not ever be the same as before . . . the path you walk will many times be lonely . . . you cannot have Solitude without her sister, Loneliness, as your occasional visitor. And in those times, you may not hear our answering song, but it does not mean we have abandoned you. It means only that it is your time to walk alone for a season, and to learn from that which you have chosen. Fear and indecisiveness will sometimes be your shadow. Know they are merely a trick of the light and the darkness and only your true shadow is worn by you. The shadow of Yona. Strong. Fierce. Not Without Gentleness and Knowing. Yona. Cutting through to the heart of the matter with sharpened claw and great intelligence. Friend of the Thunder Beings and the Going Within. These are the gifts you have been given. You will be a good friend to those who know you. Welcome your other relatives that come to stand with you. You will be a guest at their fires, and they will give you many blessings.

Now sit with us at this fire and share our salmon and our summer berries. You are welcome here as our daughter and our sister. We will share with you our ways and in time you will share these ways with other daughters who come to us in the Dreamtime. That is our way in these times."

She felt the earth beneath her haunches as she joined the circle. The smell of salmon brought water to her mouth even though her People had not met the salmon before and she devoured the feast before her. Sweet sun ripened berries stained her mouth and the juices ran freely down her chin. In their way, the others smiled at her appetite and their growls sounded approval in her ears.

The Other World was not reflected in the night sky here, and she felt it fading from her. All that is was in this circle. She belonged here. She wanted to roll and cuff and play. The words that had sounded frightening in her ears a moment before no longer worried her. They were part of the Other World and for this moment that World did not concern her. The others were tolerant of her youth and her inexperience and knew that, in time, she would understand. For now, she was allowed the joy of transformation and newly belonging. And the song rose again in her throat, mingling with the night sky and all that was to come.

Time passed and it did not. A voice called through morning mist, "Kiyona, Daughter, is that you? Can you hear me, Kiyona?" Kiyona opened her eyes and saw the silhouette in the cave's entrance. She rubbed her eyes and stretched her muscles, trying to figure out where she was and who was calling her name. She did not feel afraid, just a little confused. "I am here," she answered when she recognized the shape as that of her mother.

"We feared for you, Kiyona. But the old ones said you were not harmed. At first light we set out to look for you." Her mother wrapped Kiyona in her arms and hugged her close. "When I looked in here for you, you were curled up like a little bear cub. For one moment I thought I had found myself a bear daughter in your place."

The sleepy eyed Kiyona was now wide awake and the Dreamtime meeting with the bear women flooded through her. She smiled at her mother with an understanding older than time itself.

E.K. Caldwell is of Tsalagi, Creek, Shawnee, Celtic and German ancestry. She is a poet/writer/singer/songwriter who lives and works in Depoe Bay, on the central Oregon coast. Her work is also included on Harbinger Northwest's cassette sampler, ''Lights''.

She is also currently associate producer/story editor for Whitewater Productions, a video production company, in Depoe Bay, Oregon.

Robert Conley

THE END OF OLD BILL PIGEON

Just the Way It Was Told to Me— More or Less

THIS IS ABOUT Bill Pigeon. He was an outlaw, you know. One way they tell it, he killed a man who was trying to steal his hog, and he thought everything was going to be all right, because all he'd done was to just protect his own property. Well, this happened back before statehood, and old Bill just figured he'd go to trial in the Cherokee courts, and he'd be acquitted. But somebody met him on the road when he was on the way to the courthouse, and they said that there was a federal lawman, one of those deputies from Fort Smith, waiting for him there at the courthouse with a federal warrant. It seems they had discovered that the man old Bill had killed was not a Cherokee citizen, and that meant that the trial would go to the U.S. court.

Well, old Bill didn't want any part of that, so he just turned around and rode on back home, you see. Anyhow, that's one way they tell it, but that's not the way I heard it from Andy Dick. What he said was that there was a deputy marshal riding along toward old Bill's house, and he was singing a song to himself as he rode. He was singing a song about killing a hog, but what he really meant by it was that he was going to kill old Bill. Bill heard him, and he knew what he was singing about, so just as that lawman rode up to his house, Bill stepped out his front door and shot that lawman dead. Well, either way, he was an outlaw. They were after him, you know.

Now, Bill was an Indian doctor, and some say he was just about the best there ever was. He knew that those federal lawmen would be after him, so he set about making medicine to protect himself right there at his house. Well, they never caught him. They came around looking for him, all right, but they couldn't even see him. You see, old Bill could make himself invisible. Anyway, that's what they say. He'd be right there looking at them, but they couldn't see him. Another thing he could do, he could turn himself into an owl or squirrel or just about anything he wanted. A crow maybe. Well, eleven years went by like that. It was 1897 when the federal lawmen finally closed the case.

Someone had found a body out in the country, and they called the law. The body was all messed up. It was decomposed, you know, and the hogs had been at it, but some deputies showed up and took a look at it.

"That there's Bill Pigeon," one of them said, and that was all it took to close the case. Just that easy. You see, they were tired out trying to track old Bill down, and they were embarrassed about it, too. All those deputies out of Fort Smith that thought they were hot shit couldn't catch one lone Indian at his own house. And after eleven years, people were laughing about it all over the countryside. So that body was just real convenient for the law. It got the newspapers and Judge Parker off their backs, you see.

Now, here's the funny part. Once those deputies stopped trying to catch him, old Bill decided that he just didn't want to live any longer. It was time for him to go. I don't know why he came to that decision. Maybe it had something to do with the way things were going for the Cherokee Nation. You know, they were talking about allotment and statehood and all that sort of thing, and the mixed-bloods had just taken over Cherokee politics away from the full-bloods. Old Chief Bushyhead, he was the last full-blood chief, and they had just kicked in the door of his office and carried him right out of the capitol building. Put him out just like that. And Ned Christie, he was a full-blood council member and a member of the executive committee, and they had made him into an outlaw and killed him back in '92. I guess it must have pretty much looked like the end was in sight, you know. Then again, maybe he was sick and nobody knew it. I don't know. Maybe life just wasn't exciting anymore once the deputies had quit chasing him, or maybe he felt like since he had already been pronounced dead, he ought to be really dead. Whatever the reason was, he decided to kill himself.

Well, he had two little girls living with him at that time. I'm not sure who they were, maybe nieces or something, but he gave each one of them a twenty dollar gold piece and told them they had to go away.

"I'm going to show all these people how a man can kill himself," he said.

So they left, and old Bill, he took off all his clothes, and he went out in the woods. He bent about halfway over, you know, with his head way down and aimed straight ahead. He meant to run his head real hard into a tree and knock all his brains out. Well, he took to running, but he just ran past all the trees. He couldn't seem to hit one. Besides that, he was getting all scratched up from the twigs and things, being naked like he was, so he just went back to the house to think it over for awhile.

The next thing he did was he decided to burn himself up, and he built up a big brushpile. He built it in a big circle, oh, maybe six, eight feet in diameter. Then he took off all his clothes again, and he lit that brushpile all around the edges so that he had a big circle of flames, and then he jumped over that fire and sat down there in the middle to wait. Well, that fire got closer to him, and he was just sitting there sweating more and more, and by and by, he got up real fast and jumped back over the flames, back outside of the circle.

Andy Dick came by to see him after that. The word had got around through the two little girls what old Bill was up to. And Andy saw the burned up brushpile and asked Bill about it. Bill told him why he had built it up and fired it. Told him what his intentions had been.

"What happened?" asked Andy.

"Too hot," said Bill.

Anyhow I guess that he'd had about enough of that fooling around, because the next time Andy stopped by to see him, there was old Bill just laying on the ground beside his front porch. His rifle was laying there close to him, and his whole face was just about blowed away. He had put the barrel of that rifle right up under his chin and pulled the trigger and had made that awful mess of his face, but it hadn't killed him. Not right off. Andy knew that, because he could see the bloody handprints there on the edge of the porch where old Bill had tried to pull himself up. Andy figured that he was trying to go after something to finish himself off with, something up there on the porch, but he didn't have the strength. He must have just laid there and bled to death. Anyhow, he finally got the job done. He's buried in that little cemetery behind the church just up the road from where his house used to be. There's a house there beside the cemetery. It's still there. That's where I was born, and that's why I'm so skinny.

THE ELECTION OF
'EIGHTY-SEVEN

TAHLEQUAH, the capital city of the Cherokee Nation, was a bus-
tling community in the late 'eighties. It was dominated by the
two-story, red brick capitol building standing in the square. In
fact, the town had grown up around the capitol square. The
Cherokees had established their capital shortly after the Trail of
Tears by laying off the square and erecting a huge shed or arbor
for shelter during national council meetings. In a few years they
had managed to replace the shed with a brick building. That had
been almost fifty years earlier. The town had grown, and so had
the population of the Cherokee Nation. The mixed-bloods, many
of whom looked more like whites than Indians, far outnumbered
the full-bloods, and there were large numbers of white people
resident in the Cherokee Nation. Some, having married Cherokees, were citizens. Some were renters, and some were illegal
squatters.

On January 4, 1888, business was going on as usual. People
walked along the board sidewalks of Muskogee Avenue, Tahle-

quah's main street, going in and out of business establishments. Wagons rolled down the street going somewhere, and men rode by on horseback. Those who had not been around earlier in the day to witness the atypical activities at the capitol and who had not yet heard the news, must have wondered at the sight, on a cold January day, of the bulky chief sitting stiffly in his solid straight-backed office chair alone beneath the giant lofty elm tree there in front of the big brick building.

Chief Dennis Wolf Bushyhead, three-hundred pounds and three-quarters Cherokee, sat in full view of the town alone in his bulk with his thoughts. In the cold air, his face burned, fueled by anger, frustration, humiliation and righteous indignation. Oh, that it should come to this, he wailed silently. And it had been a long road. Such a long road.

Sixty-one years old, he had been born in 1826 in Tennessee, in the old Cherokee Nation. His father, the Reverend Jesse Bushyhead, had been one of the most prominent men in the Nation. One of the earliest Native preachers, Reverend Bushyhead had led one of the Removal parties to the west. At the time of his death in 1844, he was Chief Justice of the Supreme Court of the Cherokee Nation. With a father like that, Dennis Wolf Bushyhead was bound to go far.

At the age of 13, he had traveled the Trail of Tears with his father. He had later attended college in New Jersey, graduating in 1847 at the age of 21. Why, he had even attended the 1841 inauguration of William Henry Harrison as President of the United States. At 23, a bold, young adventurer, he had journeyed to the gold fields of California with other 'forty-niners, and he had not returned home to the Cherokee Nation until 1868. Then he had established a mercantile business and had become a successful and respected local businessman, so much so that in 1871 and again in 1875, he had been elected to the post of Treasurer of the Cherokee Nation. No one was better known. No one was more highly thought of. No one . . . . He felt the skin of his face heat up some more.

In 1879, at the age of 53, he had run for the highest office in the Cherokee Nation, the office of the chief executive, the Principal Chief of the Cherokee Nation, and he had won. The Cherokee Nation, like the United States, had operated up until that time with a two party political system, but the Cherokee system had developed through decades of conflict and violence.

Back in the old Cherokee Nation before the Removal when the Ridge-Boudinot family and their followers had suddenly begun to advocate removal, the Nation had split into two factions. The majority faction had been called, after its leader, Principal Chief John Ross, the Ross Party. The other was also named for its leader, Major Ridge. When Major Ridge and his followers signed the illegal treaty of removal known as the Treaty of New Echota on December 29, 1835, the Ridge Party earned for itself a new name, the Treaty Party. By that time, the Ross Party was also going by another name. It had become known as the National Party.

There had been years of turmoil in the Cherokee Nation, domestic violence bordering on civil war. Following the Trail of Tears, members of the Ross Party had assassinated members of the Treaty Party. Treaty Party members had retaliated. Just as it appeared that things were about to settle down, the Civil War in the United States broke out, and the Old Treaty Party became the Confederate Cherokees. Then there were the interests of the Old Settlers to be considered—the Cherokees who had moved west early, before the Trail of Tears, and established what was known as the Cherokee Nation West. Their government had been absorbed by the government of Chief Ross after the Trail of Tears. When Chief Ross died in 1866, Cherokee politics changed. With no one possessing the qualities of Ross available to take his place, new party lines were drawn. William Potter Ross, nephew of the old chief, became chief by appointment of the council and continued to represent the National Party. However, Lewis Downing, formerly assistant chief under John Ross, left the National Party and with some other former members of the National Party and some of the old Treaty Party members, formed a new party called the Downing Party.

Bushyhead knew all of this recent political history, and he was very much aware of his position in its continuing development. Of course, he had missed almost all of the most violent times. He had been safe in New Jersey and then in California. When he had returned to the Cherokee Nation in 1868, Lewis Downing was chief, having defeated W. P. Ross in the 1867 election. When Downing died while still in office, the national council once again appointed W. P. Ross to fill the vacancy, but with the 1875 election, the Downing Party triumphed once again with its new candidate Charles Thompson, also known as *Oochalata*. Thompson, a full-blood and a preacher, had no stomach for politics. He served only one term and did not run again. Then for the first time since the Civil War, the Downing Party failed to win the chief's election, Representing the National Party, Dennis Wolf Bushyhead was elected Chief.

Sitting on the lawn, Bushyhead thought back over his eight years as Principal Chief of the Cherokee Nation. He had dealt with a number of difficult issues and had handled them, he was confident, like a true statesman. The most difficult issue and one which was continuing to grow in intensity was that of the allotment of Cherokee land. Bushyhead and his National Party were opposed to allotment. The Cherokees had always held their lands in common, owning as individuals only the improvements on the land they occupied. The United States Government wanted to allot a certain number of acres to each individual Cherokee head of household making them over into private landowners. The surplus land, left over after the allotment process was complete, would undoubtedly be given over to whites. While the more traditional full-bloods were opposed, almost to a man, many of the mixed-bloods, thinking more and more like whites, wanted the land, either to hold or to sell.

And Bushyhead had lost one of his most valued advisors. Ned Christie, a member of the Executive Council, a small advisory committee to the chief, had been accused of the murder of Deputy United States Marshall Dan Maples in Tahlequah in May of 1887. Christie had become a fugitive and had sent in his resignation three months later. Bushyhead had sorely missed the advice and counsel of Ned Christie, and the issues would not go away. The election of 1887 had been particularly hot. A little over five months had passed since the election, but its details were as fresh in the mind of Bushyhead as if it had been only a few days.

The Downing Party had put forth Joel B. Mayes, a man less than half Cherokee who had served as a Confederate soldier during the Civil War. Mayes was a Methodist and a Mason, and Bushyhead and the members of the National Party were sure that Mayes and the other Downing Party members were fully in favor of allotment. Eight years as chief had been enough for Bushyhead, and he had chosen not to run again. He had put his own efforts behind the choice of his party, Rabbit Bunch, a full-blood and an officer of the full-blood Keetoowah Society.

The election had been a close one, so close in fact that the results of the count had been inconclusive, and both sides claimed victory. In such a case, the Council should meet and make a determination to resolve the conflict. The Council, dominated by the Downing Party, refused to call a meeting. Their reasons, Bushyhead had concluded, were clear. An honest assessment of the situation would reveal that Rabbit Bunch had won and should be sworn in as the next chief. Under the circumstances it seemed that there was nothing for Bushyhead to do but stay in office until the crisis was resolved. He had posted a special guard at the capitol building and remained in office. And five months had gone by.

Then came the morning of January 4. Chief Bushyhead had been sitting behind his desk in the executive office on the second floor in the southwest corner of the capitol. He turned his head and glanced out the window just in time to see Hooley Bell with a gang of men behind him striding across the lawn toward the building. It was bound to mean trouble. Bushyhead knew Hooley Bell, only too well, he thought. A member of the Downing Party, Bell was another ex-confederate solider. He was also a member of the Cherokee Senate.

Soon Bushyhead heard the sounds of a commotion at the front door downstairs, and he thought about the guard down there. Then he could hear the sounds of heavy footsteps coming up the stairs. He got up and moved to the door of his office as quickly as he could, closed it and locked it, then went back behind the desk and sat down again. He drew in a deep breath and braced himself. He watched as the doorknob was rattled from the other side, and then he heard the angry voice of Hooley Bell.

"Bushyhead, unlock this door."

Bushyhead did not respond. Suddenly there was a loud smash accompanied by the sound of splintering wood as the door came swinging violently inward and crashed back against the wall. It was obvious to Bushyhead from Hooley Bell's stance and from the quick movements he made to recover his balance that the senator had just kicked in the door. Bushyhead sat stiffly, working hard to maintain as much dignity as possible under the circumstances. The office was soon full of men.

"What is the meaning of this?" said Bushyhead.

"Come on," said Bell. "Let's get him."

Bell and two other men moved around the desk and took hold of Bushyhead. They tried to pull him to his feet but with no success.

"Give us a hand here," said Bell.

A fourth man joined them, and they grasped the arms of the chair in which Bushyhead sat. Still they could not lift him. Bell looked around quickly and formed a new scheme.

"Put this desk out of the way," he ordered, and two men moved the desk practically clearing the office. "All right," said Bell, "turn him over."

The four men around Bushyhead pushed the chief's chair over backwards, letting it down on the floor. The Chief, the back of his head resting on the floor, looked up at his attackers with rage in his eyes.

"Now," said Bell.

He gripped the side of the chairback just behind Bushyhead's right shoulder. Another man took the opposite side, and two others each took a chair leg in their hands.

"Heave," said Hooley Bell, and they lifted the chair containing the three-hundred pounds of chief off the floor. Their loud groans and the strain showing in their faces indicated desperation, so another man stepped forward, Bushyhead's feet almost in his face, to grab hold of a lower brace between the legs of the chair. Slowly, carefully, painfully, they backed out of the office, and as they did a sixth conspirator got his hands on the chairback just under the chief's head. With much grunting and groaning they made their agonizing and tedious way down the stairs and out the front door of the building. Going a few more paces out into the yard, they put down their load, righted the chair and left him sitting there.

He had not spoken to them except for the one question he had asked upstairs. He did not speak as he sat there. He saw, though he tried to appear not to notice, when some others accompanied Joel Mayes into the building. Still he sat in silence, his face flushed in the cold air. So this is how it all ends, he thought. This is the way the mixed-blood puppets of the United States Government take it all over. The full-bloods are out. My own illustrious career has come to an inglorious end. He thought about his father, and he was glad that the Reverend had not lived to witness his humiliation. It had all been so simple and so direct. People came and went, though none stopped to speak to the suffering chief, now effectively deposed. After four hours had passed, and no one had come along to even think about carrying him back to his office, he got up and walked the two blocks to his house.

Robert J. Conley, born December 29, 1940, in Cushing, Oklahoma, lives in Tahlequah, Oklahoma, the capital city of the Cherokee Nation, with his wife Evelyn. Following a long career as a professor of English and of American Indian Studies, he is now writing full-time. He is the author of *The Witch of Goingsnake and other stories*, *Go-Ahead Rider*, *The Saga of Henry Starr*, *Killing Time*, *Colfax* and other novels.

Karen Coody Cooper

CICADA PIGS

I GATHER cast-off cicada skins, plucking them from the trunks of the trees in the yard. They become toys.

I an twelve-years-old. I wait for my body to reshape itself. Where are the breasts for me that some friends have? My grandmother tells me how blood will come. I wait for things to happen. I don't expect the blood to be pleasant, but I know if I don't have happen to me what happens to all others, then I will be different. And I don't want to be different.

I break sticks and twigs and make a corral for my cicada pigs. I play for hours with them. The world I make is measured and safe.

I catch a cicada. I have heard them whine every summer for as long as I can remember and I have played with their amber skins for years. Now one has fallen from a tree and before it can turn over and fly away I have pounced on it.

Grandpa tells me I can tie a thread to its leg and fly it around my head. Grandma gives me thread, clucking her tongue and shaking her head without looking at me. The clumsy cicada buzzes and struggles in my hand, but flies smoothly in the air. Before I let it go I look at its iridescent green coat, its bulging eyes, its clear, veined wings – it is so different from my lifeless pigs. Grandpa says they are the same thing.

Fifteen-years-old. The heat of summer has stilled the land. At night the cicadas drill into the blank deep. I could wear a dress backwards and no one would know. I have learned make-up and overpluck my brows. But still no blood. I shave my legs and wear a bra without contour. Still no blood.

Again, I catch a cicada. These massive, bumbling insects fascinate me. Their maddening whir has drilled through my libidinous nights. Together we have declared our insanity, our yearning, our discontent. Together we have struggled to climb, to change ourselves, to fly against odds.

Giddy, I attach a thread to my captive. It whirls and I laugh. The cicada flies and I control the flight path. Around and around. Getting nowhere. Struggling. Zoom. Zoom. Again and again. Giggling. Breathless. Falling down in dizziness. Laughing slowly until I regain my breath.

The cicada clumsily crawls across the grass. I reel it in and watch it struggle. On its back the legs flail and work to find a grasping place. Its sharp leg spines hook onto my skin and it pulls itself right. I grasp its thick body and remove the thread. It flies away and lands high above, hidden in leafy branches. It is the last time I will tie a thread to one. And it is probably the last flight of that cicada.

At fifteen I don't know that cicadas come above ground to mate. To produce offspring. To produce more cicada for the world's ears and earth. At fifteen I don't know that I will bleed in order to have children. That I will sing and fly in my own human way. I only know I want to bleed so that I won't be different. I don't think about shedding skins. And, I don't know about people with invisible threads.

THE UNWELCOME

"COOWEESCOOWEE."*

The crane heralded the morning – or welcomed me.

I smiled at my arrogance. What was I to her? This was her home. I was uninvited, unexpected – perhaps, unwelcome.

But, I was determined. I came to the wetland in reverence. "Cooweescoowee."

This little lowland area, remembered from my Oklahoma childhood, had recently kept recurring in my thoughts. After twenty years away, I had come back to search for something. I had been concerned that the area might have been overtaken by the waters of the new lake. So much had changed. Remembered roads didn't go through because the lake rose over them. But I found the place as if it had been a magnet pulling me to it. Once I spotted the old grove of pecan trees, I knew the land again.

But, this white bird with its black-banded face was new to me. I had never seen any waterfowl in this trough of water. "Cooweescoowee."

*(Cooweescoowee was John Ross' Cherokee name.)

I watched her as she preened herself. Lovely bird. Lovely song. Lovely name. But, I remembered, sadly, that her name had already been used by another. I couldn't have it. I had come here hoping to find a name for myself. Perhaps she could help me.

Talk to me, I said in thought to her. Tell me who I am. Who I am to be. Give me a name. Talk, and I will listen.

She pulled a leg up, folded it beneath her, and laid her head upon her back.

"Cooweescoowee," I whispered.

She opened her closed eyes. I looked at her expectantly, but she closed them again. She said nothing to me.

I sat still and studied the scene, hoping for an answer. A butterfly flew silently by. A brief breeze rippled the water and rustled the grass, and then all was still again.

I fell asleep in the tall grass, nestled against the ground like a deer. Clouds slid by. I drifted. I heard from a distance a trumpeting "cooweescoowee" and a crane's red eye filled the sky. I floated up into the black center and entered a white, feathered tunnel. It was pleasantly warm and soft and quiet. A purple light glowed at the end of the passage.

Suddenly, laughter and shouting and the sound "thud . . . thud . . . thud" awakened me. The scene had changed. The crane was on its side flapping a wing and flailing its head. Five young boys were throwing rocks.

I stood and yelled. The boys' arms froze as their faces pivoted in my direction. Then, as one, they threw their missiles at me. One hit me on the shoulder and I fell back. Another volley pelted around me and then I heard the gang run away clamoring excitedly.

Everything was quiet. Too quiet.

I left the violated trough. I never looked at the crane. I never went back. I took no name.

I had been searching for truth that day. And it had found me.

As an Oklahoma Cherokee I enjoyed a childhood filled with outdoor exploration. I spent hours alone in rocky hill country enjoying wildlife, trees, flowers, farmland pastures and fields, peeking in windows of long-abandoned shanties and farmhouses, and climbing in the rafters of barns. Marriage brought me to New England where I learned about Algonkian and Iroquois people and began my museum career focusing on informing the public about native life. I took up fingerweaving, continued my childhood interest in writing, and moved through museum jobs ultimately winding up at the Smithsonian Institution. As curriculum program manager of American Indian Museum Studies in the Office of Museum Programs, I have the good fortune of traveling across the United States managing workshops hosted by tribal groups. Until I finish my masters studies at the University of Oklahoma, where I am working on a thesis about American Indian influence on museum exhibits, my creative writing efforts are like severely pruned shrubs, waiting to sprout, bloom, and regain natural shape and form. It's not that I have stories to tell, but that there are stories to be told.

Robert F. Gish

FIRST HORSES

SHE SAT AT THE END of the red-topped, chrome-trimmed cafe counter stirring the thickest bowl of chili he had ever seen. It didn't look like the usual Bronco Cafe chili, with pieces of beef and cloves and garlic and succulent pinto beans floating in a greasy broth.

He liked to eat "Bronco" chili with cheese on top and with plenty of crackers washed down by a fountain coke with three squirts of syrup, and agitated by carbonated water shot hard into the ice and concentrated coke – and whatever other syrups whose handle he hit.

In front of the grill's business-issue crockery bowl was a ribbed-plastic glass still full of water. No ice. Next to that, resting on a small plate, and drooping over the edges, was a piece of still-steaming Indian bread.

Florinda was the girl's name, as he heard it, for the introduction was fast since Lucy did the honors:

"Gilbert, this is Florinda. Florinda Tenaja. She's from Isleta. She's the new waitress. First day!"

The boy, out of school for the afternoon, with books and notebooks in hand, and just through the side door of the cafe, stopped – politely, but still thinking about history class – and stood by the end of the counter looking at the girl and her meal.

Further down the counter sat Abran, in his usual place, making the moves on Lucy during one of his frequent breaks from his brother's body and fender shop across the street. Reuben, Abran's brother, was a cheerful guy, always clowning. Abran was different. He was silent, sullen, as if he were mad at himself; maybe mad at his thinning hair and almost bald head; maybe mad at his one-horse shop and at . . . "Todo el mundo, ese." He liked to talk with Lucy, usually in low, Latin lover whispers – and with one intense purpose.

One time the boy had come into the darkened cafe at closing time and found Abran and Lucy behind the counter kissing. Her thin, synthetic-blend uniform skirt was pulled up around her waist and the boy remembered Abran's dark, calloused hands holding Lucy through her pink underwear. Abran's hand now raised a cup of black coffee to his lips as he half turned his head and, with his still steely stare, acknowledged the boy with a look which glowered all the way back to that twilight interruption months in the past, maybe even back to the Mexican War and Colonel Kearny's invasion.

"Que dice, Abran? How's it going, man?," the youth almost yelled, with as much bravado and authentic Spanglish pronunciation he could muster.

"Hola, Mendigo Gilbert," was Abran's cutting reply.

Then, turning nervously, with feigned interest, to the new girl, the boy said, "Hello, nice to meet you." – rote words accompanying his preoccupied look again at the girl's rich, orange-red bowl of chili with its cleavered chunks of meat, and a base more the texture of morning Cream of Wheat than *his* kind of chili, the Bronco's kind of chili, the greasy-filmed cafe chili which he ate out of a soul-hunger as strong and ravishing as Abran's longing for Lucy; a hunger which even now he could sense in Abran's leaning across the counter and, with those same large, remembered dark hands, holding his cup out for a refill of "mud" and attention from la mujer, from "wisa."

A quiet "Hi," was Florinda's answer to the youth, and she slowly lowered her head and began stirring again, with the large, tarnished cafe spoon, the pieces of meat in the bowl – back and forth, back and forth. There was no garlic. There were no beans – only the creamed, orange-red chili with small, hard, yellowish pod seeds coursing to the top.

She was Indian for sure. Probably a couple of years older than Gilbert. Maybe seventeen or eighteen. Short-cropped black hair. Round, dark face. Bright brown-black eyes. He noticed too that her blue and white apron was embroidered in Isleta fashion – in closely stitched navy-blue thread – with delicate miniature horses, little Indian ponies, blocked and squared and stylized.

There was at once an ancient and a modern look, a timelessness about them – primitive, compelling: steeds from out of the annals of the Crusades and the epic deeds of knights questing, or jousting for a fair maiden's honor; horses from over the vast and rolling sands of Arabia; mounts heading west from Vera Cruz to Tenochtitlan or up the Great River with the conquerors Onate and Coronado, and other later-day vaqueros y caballeros; ponies on the great American plains in pursuit of bison or coup; wild, mountain mustangs, roaming proudly; thorough-bred racers galloping with sweaty, shimmering muscles, for the finish line at the state fair; quarter horses in rodeo regalia; stalwart workers pulling a travois across dusty miles or turning a grindstone at a picturesque riverside "molino de glorieta."

These little horses struck the boy hypnotically as quintessential, as essences rendered in the artistry of thread. Across the top of the bib of her apron was an elaborate edging of black thread, bridled and harnessed and controlling. It was a beautiful apron compared to Irene's worn, food-stained smoke, apparel that looked more like a grease-spattered dishtowel than anything else.

Seated there in her Indian apron Florinda Tenaja wasn't anything like Lucy. Not beautiful and alluring – able to flirt and follow through with even the toughest of the cruel teasers like Abran or the more benevolent ones like C.V. Hankle and O.D. Schmidt, the two owners of C&O Motors down the street. No doubt her social trial-by-fire (hotter than Hatch chili), with the whole gaggle of regular customers, came earlier in the day over all the Anglicized menu of dishes: maybe over mid-morning Farmer Brothers coffee and doughnuts; and at noon over meatloaf and mashed-potato plate lunches, topped off with an oversized piece of and Jill's Bakery pecan pie *a la mode*. Such was the boy's imagined guess.

Now the girl was on a late afternoon break. Buddy Tedrick, with his Buick roadmaster, his eye patch, and his Forrest Tucker good looks, was due about this time every afternoon. One of the reasons the boy liked the Bronco after school was because of Buddy, "Tooter" they called him because of the assembly of horns on his roadmaster.

He had taken a couple of air horns off wrecked semis as they came into the junk yard and mounted them, replated and gleaming, on his car. Then he had some musical-sounding horns under the hood which played a three note doorbell chime which he used as a finale. He even had a miniature siren rigged up to scare other drivers and pedestrians at special times. His car was spectacular: canary yellow, red leather upholstery, white top with a small izenglass rear window, four chrome port holes on each fender, and a couple of glass-pack mufflers that could purr or growl depending on how much boot he gave the accelerator. Everybody liked Tooter – and his car.

From the first top-down ride in the buick around the valley and across the Rio Grande bridge, Gilbert had wanted to be like Tooter. He knew what to say and when to say it – and he played lead guitar, a big blonde Gibson L-5, with the Sandia Mountain Boys, out at the Paradise Inn in Tijeras Canyon, at the Palamino Club on Coors Road and, every third Saturday night, at the rowdiest of all the town's cowboy clubs, the Hitching Post further out on West Central at the edge of the volcanoes. He had even been on local radio shows, and talk had it straight from Tooter than the band might even land a weekly television show with KOB, the NBC "affiliate," to quote Tooter's new radio lingo and voice.

He was a good friend, and lots of laughs, a guy with "personality." Gilbert wanted to line up some guitar lessons once he bought a guitar. He was always talking with Tooter about guitars. Gilbert knew how to talk with Tooter. But the new girl would need all the strength of her meal for her first meeting with Tooter and for his razzle-dazzle, drugstore cowboy charm.

Still thinking about Tooter, in his happy afterschool tones the boy spoke:

"Hey, Loosie Lucy, how about my Bronco burger like I like 'em? Make it stud. And a bowl of beans and red?" came his usual afternoon encantation.

"Wish and command," responded the waitress. "One bronco. Make your own suicide coke, cowboy," and she grabbed a generous pattie of meat out of the whale-sized Norge, peeled off the waxed paper, and tossed the red slab on the sputtering double grill. When she reached up to get the spatula to press the raw hamburger meat to the hot metal, he stared at the outline of her bra strap underneath her waffle-weave nylon/rayon/orlon uniform, and marveled at her full, heavy breasts and outlined nipples, and quickly glanced down at her legs showing long and smooth and bare beneath the elevated uniform hem.

Amidst his reveries and wonderment at the memory of her standing behind the counter in Abran's hands Gilbert knew something else — Abran was luckier than Lucy. And probably Buddy was just as lucky if not luckier than Abran. Buddy flirted like crazy with Lucy. Maybe it was the competition with Abran more than the desirability of Lucy, but one look at her disproved that theory. Buddy was 100% better than Abran in the boy's book, and he sensed too that Abran and Buddy only pretended to be friends.

When she turned her head away from talking to Abran to speak to Gilbert, at first he couldn't believe that he heard Lucy say,

"Want some, kid? . . . Want some of Flora's chili? She just made it. Plenty of chili. Plenty of flour. Plenty of *carne*. Light on the water! Get it while it's hot . . . and it's hot, c-a-l-i-e-n-t-e, HOT. Jalapeno/Ja*pa*leno hot! Think you can handle it? She made some Indian bread too. Beats a horseburger."

Brought partially out of his reveries, the boy replied,

"You bet. Give me a bowl. Nothing's too hot for a chili champ — prince of the pintos. Let me at it," he blared as he placed his notebooks on the shelves over the wooden crates of bottled soft drinks — the Nehi, the Orange Crush, the RC, the cokes — and walked behind the counter.

"Still go with the burger — and Indian bread and honey for dessert," Gilbert continued, and looked over at Florinda, and smiled.

He took down a large "Coca-Cola" glass with the white script letters scrawled across the bulged-out top, and with his back turned to the counter looked into the mirror behind the shelf of clean glasses to catch the Indian girl's eyes, looking at him — eyes that seemed tired as much as anything, but frightened and forlorn too, sad and injured in isolation; eyes that seemed to look at him and beyond and his strange familiarity and belonging behind this chrome and red counter, not yet claimed by her; much beyond the mirror's reflection of the cars moving back and forth on the pavement in front of the cafe, on the street which ran south all the way to Isleta and Los Lunas and Belen, or northeast, just across the bridge, to downtown — the street which Gilbert loved to cruise with Buddy, the street which would bring the bus to the next corner, in front of Old Man Terrell's Variety Store, later that evening, to take her back down Isleta Road, sixteen miles to the reservation and the pueblo. Where she belonged — or used to.

Lots of Isletans worked off the reservation — for the railroad in Belen and in Albuquerque; on the Doodlebug which ran back and forth between the two railroad towns; on the military bases sprawling at the foot of the Manzano mountains. Long known as the ancient hunting grounds of the pueblo, and protected as their exclusive domain, Hell's Canyon and much of the other reservation mountain land was now ironically bordered by Manzano Base and Sandia Weapons Center, the next links in Los Alamos Laboratory's atomic bomb supply chain, the much rumored but still secret, high-security assemblyline and storehouse for more advanced brothers and cousins of "Little Boy" and "Fat Man;" and their awesome hunger for destruction.

Old "I-Like-Ike" had alluded to the bases and their contribution to national defense and the growing "military-industrial complex" on his campaign stop in Gallup at the Indian Ceremonial. The boy remembered the words and the white convertible and Eisenhower in a corny headdress, making "HOW — ME IN-DIAN. ME LIKE IKE" signs in front of the Camino Real hotel, and waving to everybody along both sides of the parade route like they were troops celebrating victory in Europe.

The location and name of Hell's Canyon in the Manzanos now took on a new kind of irony; and Isleta was now a modern "island" of a new kind, little anticipated by the Spanish conquerors who named it—an island situated on longitudes and latitudes between the barbarism of wars past, present, and to come.

The pueblo women who left the reservation worked in town stores as clerks or as housekeepers and waitresses, like Florinda. Now and then young Isletans would turn up in the public schools. Gilbert knew one or two in his school. Lorenzo Jojolla was in his home room. Many more pueblo kids from up and down the Rio Grande valley and over in Navajo land went to the Indian School north of town. There they had room and board and could learn a trade and explore Central Avenue in courageous scouting expeditions to the El Rey and the Cortez, the Sunshine and the Kimo. There they could eat popcorn, watch Hollywood cowboys that looked a lot like Tooter ride horses, kill Indians, and shoot up the glorious, gory frontier in Saturday afternoon, black and white, grade "B" entertainment. There, on the screen during the "feature" and during the "March of Time" newsreels they could learn and relearn their place in history.

Gilbert wasn't anywhere close to thinking about the larger implications of history—world or Eastern, American or Western. He liked his class in U.S. History. At least he recognized that much. He recognized too that as he looked at Florinda he saw her not just through the reflections of shelf-mirrors and fountain-coke glasses, but through the words of Mr. Marez, his history teacher, and through the anecdotes and asides of other Spanish-American friends—like Abran and Lucy (Lucinda was her given name)—as well as Anglicized stories and myths (and jokes) told by his own family, especially his older brother, Clifford, who worked at the Covered Wagon Trading Post in Old Town and could relate an endless stream of "Yah te hey" accounts about all kinds of Indians—Navajo, Apache, Hopi, Pueblo, you name it—who came in to pawn jewelry and pottery and rugs, or trade for dry goods and other supplies.

"Hear the one about the cowboy whose truck stopped in the desert?," Clifford would ask. "Injun trouble! Get it?"

Clifford's hero was Kit Carson, of all people. In history class Mr. Marez gave a decidedly Spanish and European account of the settling of the New World, "Nueva Granada or New Spain" he called it. "The Pueblos gave the Spaniards a lot of trouble, kids, a lot of trouble.," and Marez would tell about the taking of

Acoma, the Sky City. And about Mexican and then American rule. Carson had his orders and good reasons with the Navajos at Bosque Redondo too, Marez explained.

"Listos! Bronco up and out. Chili on the counter. Off the grill and into your estomago," came Lucy's announcement as she reached over the fountain to the boy—her bosom blue-veined, full and bouncy—and placed Gilbert's order on the counter next to Florinda's food.

"Shoot that syrup, Gillie, and get your seat on that stool and your loving arms up to that counter. I didn't make this combo, Honey-bun, for it to get cold."

Now much beyond the ritualized steps of "crushed ice in glass" and "three squirts of coke," "one of vanilla," "one of chocolate," "one of rootbeer," he thrust forward the long, black handle on the carbonated water spigot of the fountain, causing ice and water and syrup to splash out of the glass and on the young girl. She flinched back and touched her shiny black bangs with a paper napkin held in her turquoise-ringed fingers and looked up, smiling.

"Ooops! Sorry!," and he pulled the fountain handle toward him to lessen the pressure. "I shouldn't do that but I like to. Misjudged the range. Didn't think about you there, that close."

He said "Sorry" one more time, stirred the concoction with a long ice-tea spoon, and sat the coke on the counter beside Lucy's scrumptious-looking, made-to-perfection Bronco burger. Then he walked from behind the fountain, wiping both hands on a towel, and mounted the round, vinyl counter stool next to the girl as if it were a nervous bronc ready to spin and buck its way out of the shoots.

She moved her still-waiting glass of water to make room for his customized cook, scrunched into herself and slid further over toward the end of the counter.

He took a bite of the hamburger, the tan and toasty bun still hot and greasy; the lettuce, pickle and tomato slices fresh and tasty, and coated with generous swipes of cafe-staple mustard. Then he gulped down some of his icy drink and picked up the waiting spoon for a dive at the thick Indian chili. He filled the spoon and crammed it all, meat and thick porridge-like liquid, into his mouth. He knew immediately, even before the spoon passed his lips that he had too much, had gone too far for a first taste. His mouth flamed open, spewing out the spoon and its cargo, and he reached rapidly, frantically again for his coke. He swallowed most of it before he started to feel any cool relief on his tongue and along the sides and roof of his scorched mouth.

It was the hottest damn chili he had ever tasted. Hotter than a jalapeno bitten down to the stem! His mouth was throbbing—felt not just baked but blistered.

"What kind of chili is this? What do you put in it to make it this way?," he sputtered between gulps of coke.

"Just Indian chili that my father raised and roasted at the pueblo," she said. "Everybody at Isleta likes my dad's chili—and his Indian bread. It's not hot for me. I'm used to it, I guess. Isleta chili is the best."

"There's no damn such thing as Isleta or Indian chili," came Abran's words from a few counter stools away. "Only Spanish chili. We developed the damn chili pepper. We invented Spanish chili in the old country and raised it down in Cruces or Hatch. Go down to the Hatch Chili Festival, ese. *Diego Grande* variety from the Jorado Farms; that's the best Goddamn chili. I know my chili and, ese, there ain't no such thing as *Isleta Chili*. There plain ain't no such vegetable."

Gilbert found no words to reply. And just as the girl started to say something, a loud motor rev, a truck horn blast, and then the familiar door-bell chimes, announced Tooter's arrival. His glasspacks. His fanfare alright. The front screen door of the cafe flew open to frame him and, behind him, his big white-topped convertible roadmaster Buick. As he took off his cowboy hat and ducked under the door frame he bellowed—

"The waiting's over, people. Rooty, Toot, Tooter is here."

He had on his pilot-style Ray Bans over his eye patch. And a fresh, white tapered western shirt with the two top snaps undone—one of his special trademarks. He wore high-waisted Levi's which advertised his commodious maleness, accented by a hand-carved belt, laced in white and buckled with a big silver and gold-inlay ranger buckle which allowed some of the tip of the belt to dangle down and off to the side, shadowing his Levis. It was one of the fanciest hand-tooled western belts in the valley and Gilbert subconsciously started to trace on a napkin the design of the lettering of Tooter's name dyed in yellow across the back, seraph letters complemented by a yellow "T" tooled and dyed on the tops of Tooter's tan dress boots, invariably shined to a waxy brilliance.

As Tooter strode with loping stride across the green tile cafe floor to the counter they followed each step with their eyes. He moved like a calf-roper sliding his hand down a dallied lariat heading for a record time:

"Hey Gillie you old picker, plunk in a quarter in that old juke box for 'I'm Ragged but I'm Right,' E-1 on the list, and they better not have changed it. That's my theme song, buckeroo. Or punch old slick-haired Faron Young's 'Live Fast, Love Hard, Die Young.' Hell's bells, even Bob Wills's 'San Antonio Rose,' or Merle Travis smokin' and strokin,' feelin' and fretin' the G-string on "Wabash Cannonball" would do me. Just pick out something lively there Gillie Byrd. Cup of your best java, Lucy my lady."

When he reached the counter he stood over Abran and patted him on the back saying, "Why if it isn't the viejo vecino, 'la luz de mi vida'. . . . Fancy seeing you here. First cup on you? Well, if you insist."

Abran's words sounded laced with old resentments: "Wrecked your Spee-u-wick yet, I hope, highpockets? I'm ready to pound it out for you and maybe even try to match the paint for extra dinero," came Abran's scorching hello, accompanied now by the glisando tones of guitar runs and companion strums behind Eddie Arnold's "Don't Rob Another Man's Castle," coursing melodiously from the big, red and yellow juke-box by the pin-ball machine – and augmented by a silly grin and a shrug of the boy's shoulders.

"Hey, Gillie, thanks for the song. Just what I *didn't* ask for, pecker-head. Who's your friend?" Tooter said, ignoring Abran for a time, and giving Florinda a quick salute as he removed the curved wires of his Ray Bans from around his ears to reveal his cool but somewhat comic black eye patch. Lucy said that Tooter had a cherry bomb explode in his face when he was a kid of eleven of twelve. Took only one eye when he reflexively jerked his head. Tooter never said anything about it to Gilbert.

"That's the new girl from Isleta," interrupted Lucy. "She's real nice. And Abran isn't helping things by criticizing her Indian chili, her father's specialty, and her pueblo. Are you, now, Abran?"

"I just said it's not the true chili. The Spanish brought that vegetable into this country, just like we did irrigation and everything else," came Abran's cranky voice as he looked up at Tooter and down the counter at the Indian girl and Gilbert.

"Hell, Abran," interrupted Tooter, "chili ain't even a vegetable. It's a fruit. And the only thing you Spanish chapitos brought out this way were the first horses, much as I hate to admit it. Columbus named peppers 'chili,' in another naming mistake just like calling the first natives he saw 'Indians.' That's the word ain't it Gilberto? And don't forget V.D. – who's responsible for that?"

"I don't know about the first chili . . . but, small horses were always here I think. And then they disappeared. First Columbus in Haiti, and then Cortez and other Conquistadors reintroduced them – only eleven stallions and five mares at first, sixteen horses – when the Spanish came up from Mexico. At least that's what I remember Mr. Marez saying in history class."

"You're damn right gringo. Big horses, small horses, vegetable, fruit. V.D., T.B., what the hell's the difference. I say that the Spaniards brought the chili on their horses and showed the Isletans and all the other Indios how to plant it, irrigate it, cook it, and ride horses up and down the river and over the plains to Kansas. They even introduced sheep herding and pinto beans and tortillas and most of what holds this place together today."

"My father's people saw the first horses and the next ones the Spanish brought. We were first before the first horses.," came the quiet, resolved utterance of the girl. "Isleta chili was here in the beginning and it's the best, at least the way I fix it it is."

Only the last chorus of Eddie Arnold twanging out, "Don't Rob Another Man's Castle/It's written thou shalt not steal . . .," could be heard filling the pervading silence in the cafe.

"Put that in your hat and wear it, Abran," said Lucy as she walked over to the girl and reached across the counter to clear away her dishes. "Hand me your bowl of chili, honey, and hurry along now, Flora, or you'll miss your bus. That's enough hours for today."

"Believe what you will, all of you," said Abran as he slapped down a half-dollar, spun off the stool and stomped toward the door and his waiting wrecked cars.

"Take off that pretty apron, Florinda my lady. Ain't no bus

ride for you today. Gilbert, get your books and gobble down the rest of that Bronco burger. The three of us chili pods are off for a ride down Isleta Road. We'll out race the bus and the Super Chief and honk 'em hello/goodbye when we pass. I need to get me a bucket of that original, hot Isleta chili."

When Gilbert turned, smiling, to look at the girl, she had untied her apron and was pulling it over her head. Then he saw the smile now breaking behind her lonesome eyes and over her whole face and reflected in the coke-glass mirror, and he understood why she held her apron, with all its herd of prancing and parading little blue stitched horses, high over her head — lingering, stretching as if exulting not just in the end of her first work day but in the strange first feeling that maybe she and the first horses had marked out a small portion of the counter and the cafe as hers.

Sensing this in a way that flashed across his Indian talks with his brother, across his history classes with Mr. Marez, and even across his strained and tense times with Abran, Gilbert felt a big smug, even triumphant for the first time in his life and all he could do was wink at Lucy and say excitedly to the girl he would always insist on calling Florinda, her full name,

"Well, let's go, Florinda Tenaja. Tooter's got some horses of his own, not first but fast and fiesty, under that long, bright, musical yellow hood. We might even get him to put down the top and turn up the radio all the way."

"I'll see you later tonight, Lucy mujer," wafted back a sweetened request over Tooter's shoulder as he swept his long arms around the boy and the Indian girl and escorted them out the front door of the cafe to his beautiful buick.

Lucy said nothing but looked with special new feeling at each of the handsome hand-tooled letters in his belt and adjusted her bra to the tunes of Tooter's departing melody of horns and the screech of hot rubber.

Robert F. Gish is a member of the Cherokee Nation of Oklahoma and of Choctaw-Cherokee heritage, his parents both being born in Indian Territory. He is the author of *Frontier's End: The Life and Literature of Harvey Fergusson*, *William Carlos Williams: the Short Fiction*; and, most recently, *Songs of My Hunter Heart: a Western Kinship* (Iowa State University Press, 1991). He is a contributing editor to *The Bloomsbury Review* and on the editorial board of the *American Indian Culture and Research Journal*. He is professor of English and University Distinguished Scholar at the University of Northern Iowa, Cedar Falls.

Diane Glancy

A SENSE OF CONTINUITY
AND PRESENCE

CARS LINE THE DRIVE along the old road like they did when Harrison was alive and Elma made a dinner that everyone came for,
not just to sit at the table and talk politely, then leave, having
one's family obligation over with as they did at other houses,
but Elma made the meal, was the meal herself, talking and
laughing at her end of the table while Harrison, when he was
alive, snorted and put away enough to last several days.

"That's probably what killed him," Fillmore Running Bear,
his brother said, eyeing Elma for himself. "Heyye! What an
Indian he was." But Fillmore still had a wife, quiet and regress-
ing slowly into the grip of docility that always threatened her
and kept her from entering into a union like Elma and Harrison
had, or a union Fillmore assumed they had from what he saw,
but didn't know firsthand. And the children came willingly and
often, not to get anything, but to be there with them. How did
they do it? How did she do it now that Harrison was gone?
Fillmore's children ignored them or came out of duty when their

mother with her measly and peeling works made them feel guilty, and they knew they had to come or be removed from that part of the tribe that was decent folks, which standard had been instilled in them.

Cars never lined the drive of the other Running Bear house: Fillmore's and his wife's. Their three children were wooden, not lively like Elma's and Harrison's. Why was he still alive, and not Harrison?

"It's hard to understand all right," Harrison's oldest son said to Fillmore, his uncle.

"I know, Bill," Fillmore patted his back as they seated themselves at the dinner table, and Fillmore watched Elma in the large square kitchen of her house where they had come for some occasion. Did it matter? They didn't have to have a reason to come for one of Elma's meals. It was a pleasure for them to get together at her house—the house that Harrison and Fillmore and some of the men from the tribe had built room by room. It even seemed as though Harrison were still among them. Fillmore took his eyes off Elma as she came to the table.

There was some disagreement between Harrison's daughters. One snapped at the other as they sat down. Fillmore asked the blessing on Elma's meal as Harrison had done. They fought just as much as Fillmore's children. He also had heard fierce words from his nephews, and in front of Elma too. But they recovered, laughed together again. Fillmore's children bore grudges; always had, bitter as gooseberries.

And now, at her end of the table, Fillmore thought Elma looked small. He remembered Harrison before his death when he lost weight and still wore the large suit of clothes that had once fit him. Harrison had been in his sixties when he died.

"Too early to call in the cows," Bill said.

"But he did, he did," Elma shrugged as though it was his will that he leave her alone with the years to watch the sunlight crawl down the pawpaws on the print wallpaper and remember him.

"Elm," Bill said to his mother. "You know the shed out back?"

"Of course." She nodded and passed the bowls.

"There's room enough to make it into sort of an apartment. Lots of folks live in smaller places than that, and pay a lot for it too."

"Which one of you is it that wants to come back?" she paused. Fillmore sat on the edge of his chair as he spooned her green beans on his plate. "Or is it for me?"

"No, Elm. We're not putting you out yet."

"Deen needs a place," Bill's wife stated.

"He's always coming back to us, can't make it on his own. We haven't got room," Bill started to eat.

"The shed isn't big enough for the two of them."

"There's only one of them now," Bill's wife said.

Elma was silent. The table seemed frozen for a moment. "He lives with a girl for several years, causing us grief," she said, "and leaves her after that?"

Deen swallowed with effort.

"She left him."

"So you are pushing the responsibility of your abandoned son off on me?" she asked Bill.

"That's right, Elm. Though I don't look at it exactly like that—you see, he can help—"

"I won't have him." Elma interrupted her son. "Let him go back and to the girl and straighten out whatever is wrong."

"He can't." Bill's wife passed the relish.

"I've tried, grandma," Deen said.

"She decided she didn't want to be married after all." Bill dropped the spoon in his saucer.

"Isn't that too bad," Elma said curtly. "So I get Beets because no one else wants him?" Elma said that without thinking. Deen's red cheeks flared, and with his dislike of that vegetable, his grandfather Harrison had given him that name.

"You get Deen because you can do something for him and he for you—"

"Will you pay me?"

"No, mother, I won't. But as I started to say—several times now—I'll wire the shed and insulate the walls, install plumbing. It will raise the value of your property."

"That might attract another man for you." It was Deen's turn to speak without thinking. Bill's wife stared at her son.

Elma laughed. "What would I do with another man who wasn't your grandfather?"

Fillmore pulled in his wandering thoughts and gave attention to the conversation, while his wife, who never had made contact with herself, was left in the field.

"I could help you keep the back lot mowed," Deen said.

"Yes, you could," she said. "Whether you live here or not."

"Do you know, mother" — Bill always called her mother and not Elm when he wanted something — "you could even paper it the way you want."

"That's generous of you," Elma told him. "I could buy and sell my house and yours if I wanted and don't you forget it. I have the stability of the years behind me and you are an unsettled lot."

"You couldn't buy my house, nor yours again, and don't you forget it, mother," Bill corrected her. "You are an aging woman with a small pension and if you weren't so conservative and grew your vegetables and canned and kept your savings, you would be looking for a shed to live in yourself."

One of Elma's daughters frowned at Bill as they ate.

"I won't tolerate divorce and you know it," Elma said, "when there's no real cause other than it just doesn't suit a person to be married, or because it's a strain." Bill's wife looked at the ceiling.

"It's not religion, but economics. That's what kept us all together in our day, and it's about to come to that again. Our Cherokee tribe was relocated in Indian Territory just over 150 years ago. We lived here on the margin of subsistence for several generations. We finally keep what we got a little of by holding onto it no matter what!"

The others looked at one another, then back to Elma, knowing what they were going to hear. The daughters and their families wanted to get up from the table, go into the other room and turn on television, but they knew Elma wouldn't hear of it. Deen could take the boys out in the backlot to play ball. But they would have to hear what Elma had to say.

"Families are too fragmented." They'd heard it all before. "One is here, one is there," she said, "no one can be tied down. That's why there was stability in our family. Harrison made the living. I stayed home and cooked meals, sewed, mended, beaded, washed. I made everyone else free to pursue their own course." Elma continued eating.

"But one has to be sacrificed for it. And it was you, the mother," Bill's wife protested.

"The elm tree," Bill said. "They knew what they were doing when they named you."

"Do I look like I have been sacrificed?" she asked him.

Fillmore was on the edge of his chair. By thunder, no! He thought. Elma's face was lit like the old barnyard lantern on the farm; the only light on the whole dark, vast place when he went out at night to make sure the door was fastened. And she was talking, lighting up the darkness that engulfed in most of the time, her meal in his stomach, her light on his face.

"That's the way it was when we were young." Elma gave Fillmore and the others a sense of presence, of continuity. Everything was all right because she was there.

It had always been that way. The years they built what they now had—the men working hard at their jobs during the day, and at night they would put up a few boards for another room on their houses as the wives had more children, and often Harrison or Fillmore would get discouraged because they felt they weren't getting anywhere and Elma would always be there with a warm meal, humming and saying to them that they were. And finally, they had gotten somewhere, Fillmore thought proudly to himself. Though there was still an outside staircase that climbed Elma's house. Harrison had planned a second story, but it had never come about.

Elma was transition from want to security, as her mother had been transition from the terrible dearth after the removal. She was transition from whatever was dark and uncertain and painful to whatever was light and comfort. And because of Elma, Fillmore would see them all someday, he knew as he listened to her, all the generations that would come after them and all the generations that went back in time, as Harrison had known when he listened to her, and was numbered now among, since his death, though at the last he was not wanting to go, depressed like he got before a trip.

"It wasn't that bad to be sacrificed," Elma said to Bill. "Do you remember Broken Arrow, where we used to go visit your father's sister after she moved?" Elma seemed to trail off an another thought.

"I couldn't forget us fighting and Harrison cursing all the way and saying he'd never go again and us having to share a bed and hearing Harrison snore through the wall and thinking you

must be part deaf, Elm, to have slept with him all those years."
Bill stirred his coffee again.

"I got so tired of going there," one of Elma's daughter's
fussed.

Fillmore thought of Harrison's snoring as they talked.
Maybe even now the heavens sank and heaved with his breathing. It had the rhythm of the ancestral memories Elma carried:
the movement of the tribe through the winter months of 1839
and 40 when their ancestors marched from Georgia to Oklahoma. Their groans and steady trudging were like house-noises
that one gets used to. Fillmore wanted to dream the thoughts in
his head, but at the same time he wanted to listen to Elma.

He was in her old house with rounded doorways and long
halls and a breakfast nook in the kitchen that he had helped
Harrison build for her. The big square kitchen was awkward,
with everything away from everything else, and pots and pans
hanging on the wall near the wire hen with excelsior and wooden
eggs they used on the old farm, and outside, the stairway to the
second floor which they had never finished — as though it went
up to heaven — from which, Fillmore suddenly thought, Harrison
could reach back down with his arm thin as a beet root and
knock him in the head if he didn't stop thinking about Elma.

And she could make every day new though they had nothing
new and had not really been anywhere but Broken Arrow to
visit his sister after she married, and Fillmore had been in
Elma's house 1000 times before that day and the same people
were there with their grunting human natures and the same sofa
and chairs and dining table were always before him in her house.

Even when Harrison was an old man holding rein on Elma
because of his sickness, and he groaned with his fear of departing, she watched the light patterns on the wall and remembered
old trips to Broken Arrow and the sun on the pawpaws curved
into roads they had taken and she still could see the way.

They all listened to Elma then, her lively talk and laughter
holding them, her words like buffalo that roamed the prairie.

Those that came after her in all their seeking of fulfillment
would not know what Elma did in her sacrificing life. She didn't
have a job nor much time for herself as she saw children go, and
grandchildren come, and looked forward to great-grandchildren
with enlarged heads from all the knowledge and fulfillment they

would have in their own individual heads and would have to carry facts until they looked like the old car Harrison had, and ate Volkswagen soup, cooked with bark and tinder from linden groves and would have forgotten in the mechanized heads that they had once been a tribe of 17,000 Cherokees who crossed half of this continent on foot in the dead of winter and survived to build their lives again.

"AAmmmmmmmmmmmm." Fillmore cleared his head.

"And grandchildren studying computers," Elma was saying, "and not finding a place to live. I can understand that. Harrison and I didn't have anything either for years. But we stayed together and I won't hear of one divorce in this family. All that wasted money. Put it into staying together unless something is so terribly wrong that it can't be overcome."

Deen tapped his foot impatiently on the floor.

"We're not all like you," one of the granddaughters said.

"Then bring in the dessert, if you can't do anything else," she told them.

They got up gladly from the table.

"Character comes through grief and the grate of circumstance we can't get out of decently," she said. "Inner stuffing doesn't come through seeking of self, but in the denying of it. Then, and only then, something bigger than yourself comes into your pandering heads."

"Yes, grandma," the girls said as they brought in Elma's corn pudding for dessert.

"Ammm," Fillmore said.

The days of Harrison's sickness peeled off like old skin in the reptile winter they had when he died, cold and indifferent to human need, giving Elma a reason to cry when everyone was gone, regretting she had lived, for the moment, to old age and the grandchildren growing into the computer age and living with girls who weren't their wives and change so vast she was swept under by it, but held on to what she knew and the way she knew to live and would not let them forget what it was like when one had the responsibility put upon them and stayed with it no matter how uncomfortable it grew at times. Her life probably seemed dull to Beets and the granddaughters, the niece and nephews and young in-laws in both Running Bear families.

Nonetheless she would hold on to it so they would know how things had been, and probably still should be.

"It's all right, grandma," one of Bill's girls said. "I know what you're saying."

By thunder, Fillmore did too, and gave his wife an involuntary nudge of his leg in reflex to Elma's sermon, which held him captive, and nearly startled her out of her wits and she came alive, and looked at him shocked. A smile fluttered on her face in case something had been said she missed and should have reacted to. Fillmore wanted to nudge her again and wake her up and put into her the light Elma had. But he only confused her and made her seem more artificial in Elma's house, and it was why he came, why they came, not only for Elma's meal, for Deen was still having battle with the beets on his plate and raisins in his bowl and the boys were restless after they finished their corn pudding and needed, at last, to go outside, but it was why they all came, to hear Elma spout like a buffalo stuck in a mud wallow, and why cars lined up on the old road and they always would come to Elma's house to see her on fire, and to hear her speak with authority and experience so they, out of their confusion, would remember the way.

Diane Glancy teaches Native American Literature and Creative Writing at Macalester College in St. Paul, Minnesota. Her fourth book of poetry, *Lone Dog's Winter Count*, was published by West End Press in 1990. Glancy won the 1990 Native American Prose Award from the University of Nebraska press for *Claiming Breath*, a collection of essays. The book also won the 1993 American Book Award from the Before Columbus Foundation. Her first collection of short stories, *Trigger Dance*, was published in 1990 by The University of Colorado and Fiction Collective Two, and won the Charles Nilon Fiction  Award. Her second collection of stories, *Firesticks*, was published in 1993 by The University of Oklahoma Press, American Indian Literature and Critical Study Series. In 1995, TriQuarterly and Northwestern University Press will publish her third collection of stories, *Monkey Secret*. A first collection of plays, *War Cries*, is forthcoming from Holy Cow! Press in Duluth. Glancy received her M.F.A. from The University of Iowa.

Rayna Green

THE TRIBE CALLED WANNABEE: PLAYING INDIAN IN AMERICA AND EUROPE

'*It is very easy to make an Indian out of a white man*'
                                    — Weeatawash.'

ONE OF THE OLDEST and most pervasive forms of American culture expression, indeed one of the oldest forms of affinity with
American culture at the national level, is a 'performance' I call
'playing Indian.' Since the invasion of North America by those
'red hairy men' in the fifteenth century, non-Indians have found
the performance of 'playing Indian' a most compelling and obviously satisfying form of traditional expression. Almost from
their very arrival in the americas, Europeans found it useful,
perhaps essential, to 'play Indian' in America, to demand that
tribal peoples 'play Indian,' and to export the performances back
to Europe, where they thrive to date.[1]

This performance, or set of performances, with many stages,

performers, contexts, and variants, has its deepest roots in the establishment of a distinctive American culture. I would insist that it represents one of the ways in which we can demarcate the boundaries of an American identity distinct from that which affiliates with Europe. Curiously, perhaps, 'playing Indian' — since it is so well represented historically in England and Germany, and to a seller extent, in Russia, Poland, France and Italy — may be one of the ways in which Europeans affiliate with an America that causes them tremendous ambivalence.

The performance as significant historical roots and embodiments, some aspects of which (eg: 'white' Indians and stereotypes) have been well-described by myself and other scholars.[2] But we shall explore these many aspects as part of a cohesive phenomenon which renews itself yearly, takes on new versions and modes of expression, while retaining a performance core of versions from the past. These expressive complex of behaviours reiterates itself freely across boundaries of race and class, gender and age group, regional and other affiliative groups, to find its various expressions in a range of media from traditional orally transmitted texts (songs, stories, jokes, anecdotes) to formal, literary texts, to artifacts (clothing, toys, tools, drawings, paintings), to dramatic performances (games, gestures, dramas) and ritual enactments or reenactments. Some people wed to the roles of Indian play Indian for a lifetime; others for brief, transient staged performances performed only in childhood or erratically and situationally over a lifetime. For some, it is a hobby; for others a semi-religious passion; for others still, merely one of many reference points that root them in an American identity. The performance is, for the most part, one played by persons of Anglo-American or Anglo-European background, but persons of Hispanic, Mediterranean and African/Afro-American also play Indian in large numbers. Even Apaches, Sioux, and Cherokee 'Indians' play 'Indian.' Whether conventionally 'folk' or 'popular' in venue and form of transmission — even often conveyed through 'Classical forms' — the performance exists and thrives long after other forms (eg: blackface impersonation) of reiterating the cultural persona have long since been abandoned or fallen into disuse. For many reasons, we must look at this performance with critical interest. With the elaboration of those reasons to follow, let is suffice for the present to say that this

performance involves the reenactment of a script so deeply im-
bedded in and apparently necessary to the American persona
that to challenge its continuing reiteration creates a kind of
cultural 'identity crisis.' Thus, we must examine this performance and all the aspects of its artistic shape in order to com-
prehend the extraordinary consequences, historical, cultural,
psychological, and social, of its continued renewal and
survival – upon americans in general, on those Europeans who
cherish it, and upon those Americans most deeply affected by
the performance – the people called 'Indians.' For, I would insist
now, the living performance of 'playing Indian' by non-Indian
peoples depends upon the physical and psychological removal,
even the death, of real Indians. In that sense, the performance,
purportedly often done out of a stated and implicit love for
Indians, is really the obverse of another well-known cultural
phenomenon, 'Indian hating,' as most often expressed in another, deadly performance genre called 'genocide.'[3]

It is not coincidental that the earliest, most primary and
essential form of playing Indian belongs to Anglo male, military
behaviour, and extends itself through the four centuries of its
survival into the neo- or proto-military behaviour of games, political and social organizations, and sport. But, inevitably and
eventually, it draws women, even blacks, into the peculiar
boundaries of its performance, offering them a unique
opportunity – through playing Indian – of escaping the conventional and often highly restrictive boundaries of their fixed cultural identites based in gender or race. Playing Indian offers
this escape, of course, for all who perform the roles, however
brief or transient the performance may be, and thus, perhaps,
we can understand part of its contacts – between 1500 and
1600 – yields little to suggest that playing Indian had any significant presence on the cultural landscape. We should note,
however, that the Americas, or America herself, was understood
to have an Indian identity from the outset.

The iconography of the early Americas, about which I and
others have written previously, was distinctly tied to Indians
through the symbol of the Indian Queen, later to become the
Princess, who loses her Indian-ness as she transmogrifies into
the Anglo-European and neo-classic Miss Liberty.[4] That process, of altering the cultural icon so that it conforms to the

majority population's notions of itself, is certainly co-existent with nationalism and nationalization. Note, for example, the Nazi reinterpretation of their icons of origin via Wagnerian opera and Germanic folklore. Curiously and significantly, however, the Indian-ness of Americas remains premier in Euorpe, though it fades in the official iconography of the New World, and that primary identification reemerges in contemporary Euorpe through playing Indian as well as through other forms of fascination with Indians.

During this early period, nevertheless, Indians were dying in large numbers — some 10 million at the outside between 1492 and 1700 — primarily of disease introduced by Europeans.[5] Colonial Europeans were struggling to establish a habitat as well as a commercial, political and cultural presence on the american landscape. The removal of Indians, as obstructions to that presence, whether through military and political action, or through vigorous and destructive encroachment on the resource niches of Indians, was central to such an establishment. Indians were everywhere the physical problem for European settlers, and yet they had been the solutions to problems as well. America was still Indian country; yet Europeans had to be about the business of making it theirs. Both they and Indians were too busy fulfilling or resisting their destinies to permit the full impact of that destiny to spawn artistic expressions of it. In spite of the awful realities of the struggle for america, however, other realities — of cultural interaction and intercourse, affiliation and relationship, confluence and convergence — had begun to transform both Europeans and Indians into something other than what they were at first contact.[6]

While in this early period we have no specific instances recorded of the phenomenon of playing Indian in its true sense, that is, the artistic adoption of a dramatic role as 'play,' however culturally 'deep' or shallow that role or artistry might be.[7] Rather, we can see clearly the outlines, the structure of playing Indian begin to take shape and manifest itself in the forms which will later appear as the complex whole we describe. These initial shapes of playing Indian may indeed constitute some of the 'cultural origins of America' in which Europeans were transformed by Indians and Indians were transformed by Europeans into 'this new man' that St. John de Crevecoeur hailed.[8]

Still, Europeans were dramatically transformed in that first hundred years. While everyone in those early days of exploration, conflict, attempted settlement, and failed resistance was too absorbed with the serious business of survival to burnish the leisure-based artistry that playing Indian demands, the role had begun to overtake them unconsciously. The dreaded possibility that some aspiring colonists will 'go native' is ever the fear, much memorialized in Britain's relationships with India and Africa.[9] Perhaps it all began in necessity. Clothes wore out. Imported food supplies ran out. The Indians knew how to survive in their own habitats. Perhaps they offered more than shelter to these strangers in metal suits. Perhaps they showed them how to bathe regularly, even understandably insisted on it. They showed these French and English how to use animal skins, how to use their weapons, their moccasins, their snowshoes. Moreover, the Europeans are learning the language of Indian diplomacy, and adopting it for their own trade with Indians. Increasingly, this language – particularly of Iroquois diplomacy and, in the South, the forms of Coastal Algonkian diplomacy – becomes a part of their language. They learn to do business and politics Indian style. They have to. They are surrounded. And they are absorbed with dealing with the Indians. Even, perhaps, doing these things went beyond necessity. Maybe it was fun. For some – those who became translators and cultural brokers between the Indians and their own compatriots or other Europeans – it came to be natural, instinctive. Did they go on hunting trips and war parties with Indians, learn to walk, stalk game and enemies, move like Indians? Did they like the vocalizations – the yells and hollers – the dances and songs so necessary to Indian warfare and celebration? Perhaps, just more than a little bit, did they come to enjoy the loosening of European boundaries, the *frisson* that comes with acting out a different role? We do know they took to the role with alacrity and vigour.

Of course, for some – those captives of Indians about whom so much has been written, both in the past and present – becoming Indian was first a necessity; remaining Indian came to be a choice. As many early commentators like Franklin, indeed, Indians themselves, and later critics like James Axtell, have so abundantly and convincingly demonstrated, 'the Indians, despite all odds, succeeded in seducing French and English colonists in numbers so alarming to European sensibilities that the natives were conceeded to be, in effect, the best cultural missionaries and educators on the continent.'[10] The experience of Indian captivity, an utterly transforming one, involved the adoption of a tribal language, the clothes, skills, mores of these peoples. Even the rituals of captivity, quite different from those experienced by Indians in captivity to Europeans, were designed to convert Europeans into Indians. The first terrifying rituals of symbolic revenge on the captive, then symbolic new birth through adoption, name-giving, restoration to a new family, gift-giving, and affectionate welcome and integration into that family and the Indian society, created a process of change from which there was little comfortable return.[11] And, indeed, few did return, even when offered the opportunity to do so. The white captives did become Indians, and they and the successive numbers of whites who, in many ways, lived the Indian life, set the tone for everyone else. It is not precisely these total converts, those who became Indian for life, who interest us, but rather, those who became Indian in a non-Indian context. But it is these people who gave everyone else the pure model, and it is they who set the later example for being 'adopted' by the Indians and receiving an Indian name.

Of course, at the same time, Indians were changed by Europeans. Indians are beginning to wear items of European clothing, having begun the process of transforming themselves by the adoption of European goods and manners almost immediately. But Indians are doing very Indian things with European goods. They are working silver and old coins into jewellery, not using them as currency. They are combining items of military dress with their own clothes, transforming hat plumes into distinctly Indian uses of feathers, tying ribbons, medallions, and other items onto their hide shirts (signalling the eventual emergence of the ribbon shirt, a staple of Indian clothing to date). They are not, I believe, playing white, though they took apparently great delight in the dress of whites, particularly of wealthy whites and of military men. They appear simply to be engaging in readaptive use of interesting and convenient items they did not have before. In fact, they are making those items very Indian, as all the portraits of the figures painted in the eighteenth and nineteenth century will tell us.[12]

The beginning of Indians playing Indian takes place, not in America, but in Europe, and it is here that Europeans' expectations and role models for the future begin to take form and substance. In the very first return voyages, explorers take Indians back. The famous Squanto and Samoset from coastal New England, and the Powhatan pair from Virginia, Wanchese and Manteo, were 'accompanied by many others, often unarmed,' and it is they who are compelled to play Indian for European audiences.[13] While white captives were forced, by the circumstances of their need to survive and by the very imperatives of the Indian cultures into which they came, to *become* Indian, Indians, taken against or with their will, were forced to *remain* 'Indian,' acting out various aspects of their 'savage' lives for royal and groundling audiences alike. The same European instinct that created zoos and museums, indeed, the social scientific disciplines interested in 'other' human behaviour, was at work already, increating and feeding a perturbing curiosity about Indian clothing, Indian decoration, food, even sexuality. So the parade of Indian and Inuit visitors to Europe, those who came either as captives or diplomats, arrived to amuse and entertain in little tableaux and scenes created for interested Europeans. The demand was created for seeing Indians who remained, whatever their desires, in their 'savage' state, a demand that remains unabated to the present and is fulfilled in various ways by Indians who accede to playing Indian for such audiences.[14] The beginnings of this role for Indians stands, interestingly enough, in direct contrast to the demand by European Christians in America that Indians stop being Indian, that they become 'civilized' and Christian, eventually coming to be 'assimilated' into Anglo-American society.[15] It is precisely this contradicting which both hates and loves Indians, and enjoys them in their primitive role, that plants the notion that it is the role, not the real, which is to be enjoyed, and thus perhaps it is better for non-Indians to play it. Still, these early Indian visitors to Europe create the audience and define for themselves the role they will later play throughout the centuries of their relationships with those Europeans.

Two significant and instructive cultural 'origin' stories

emerge at this point, from the first two settlements at Jamestown and Plymouth: Pocahontas saving Captain John Smith
and The First Thanksgiving, or, Squanto Saving the Pilgrims.
'Nationalized' in the late eighteenth century by the mythologist,
Parson Weems, their signal emergence as *the* instructors of national identity points to the necessary, if somewhat contradictory, components.[16] In these stories, both the Indians save
whites. In the one instance, the Indian woman defies her apparently more savage (and in pictorializations, darker) brothers,
father and friends to 'adopt' the military adventurer, John
Smith, the significance of which – his ritual death as a white
man and his ritual adoption by Pocahontas as an Indian – is lost
on Smith and his faithful fans thereafter.[17] In the other story,
Squanto, the lone Indian, befriends the starving Pilgrims,
shows them how to survive, and they reciprocate with the boun-
teous feast so memorialized every November in American popular practice. Squanto becomes 'Christian;' Smith becomes 'Indian;' other 'Indians' are discarded; whites are saved; 'good'
Indians are isolated from their non-meritorious compatriots;
they will be alone, and eventually, dead; whites, having bene-
fited from their sacrifice, will take over their roles and will memorialize them in some significant way forever.

But increasingly, as more Indians die from disease or go
away because they are being displaced in their niche by the
increasingly horde of land – and goods – hungry Europeans, or
as they are driven away or weakened by armed confrontation –
in short, as the Indians become less of a problem, the seeds of
playing Indian burst into fully grown lifeforms. The first public
signs we see of it are in the early 18th century as the British and
French colonists begin to compete with one another for space
and – coincidentally – for Indian favour. In Jamestown and
other Southern settlements, in New England, the Canadian settlements, trappers, traders, soldiers speak Indian languages,
marry Indian women, live the Indian life when they are with
Indians, only to return to European clothing and manners when
they reach the settlements and towns.[18] Some, of course, did not
return to European manners and clothes; they cut, no doubt,
dashing and mysterious figures in their hide leggings, feathers
and moccasins. These people are not captives; they are 'Indianized' by choice. The numbers of so-called Red Englishmen, usu-

ally military men, and other 'white Indians,' have begun to proliferate, essentially growing in number and influence and
persisting really until the latter part of the nineteenth century.
In 1686, the Virginian William Byrd sent an English visitor 'an
Indian habit for your boy.'[19] As the formal portrait of Sir John
Caldwell, a British officer dressed in a Huron soldier's outfit, so
amply demonstrates, playing Indian for fun or ceremony is
early made a part of normative behaviour.[20]

The movements, the sounds and forms of Indian diplomacy,
those formalized speeches, have already come to be a part of
American discourse. Little books of Indian anecdotes, treaties,
items of linguistic discourse have begun to appear in speech and
publication.[21] The conventions of Indian interaction have become a part of American political interaction, so much so that
later figures of political prominence, such as Franklin, Jefferson, and others, utilize these conventions in their writings and
interactions, most notably in many of the documents that we
now regard as the cornerstones of American law and policy.[22]
Early plays, featuring strong American Indian characters such
as Pocahontas, Metamora, Ponteach (Pontiac) – played, naturally by white actors – begin to accustom an audience to the
costumed actors in their vaguely Algonkianized costumes, off-
set, of course, with some neo-classic draping.[23] The formal
staged tableaux work themselves down to the schoolroom level,
and these forms of playing Indian come to be a staple of the
classroom versions memorialized nowadays primarily at
Thanksgiving. The popular stage produces songs like 'Alkomook, the Dying Chieftain,' which underscore the real message
that Indians are disappearing.[24] Mr. Cooper's works, along with
those of the stage and Parson Weems, give Americans the artistic wherewithal to define good Indians from bad Indians, and,
as well, a great sampling of the vocabularly with which play
Indians will forever speak. The words and concepts of chief,
brave, warrior, princess, are intact; footgear is forever the Algonkian moccasin, and similarly women and children are Algonkian squaws and papooses, never mind the actual tribal words.
The taste, in fact, for Indian speeches, whether produced by
actual Indians or not, is already a part of the dramatic repertoire, and these 'dying Indian speeches' (only to culminate in the
19th century passion for the speech of Seattle) join the songs,

the dramatic presentations, complete with costumes, formalized speech and gestures (facing East or West, raising the arms upwards towards the sun) so familiar in the later Western movies. Within the increasing familiarity, however, another set of contradictions appearing in these publications and acknowledgments of Indian speech affects deeply the role of playing Indian. In these little books of sermons and anecdotes, and in the early plays, the eloquent, noble Indian is paired with a rude, pidgin-English speaking brother; the former is a *philosophe*, passionate and convincing in his judgments on the human condition, on European perfidy, on treatment of Indians; the other a clown. It is they, played on the stage by whites, and convincing in their printed versions, that give the language for fake Indian speeches later (were they already faked then?) and for the linguistic parts of the play Indian repertoire which put European words in Indian mouths, either as a form of critique of Indians by whites, or or whites by Indians.[25]

Beyond the dramatic presence of the white Indians, other forms have begun to develop at the folk level. As British and French colonists begin to compete with one another for space, and not coincidentally for Indian favour, we find British colonists mounting a minor, but highly ritualized raid on a French village, dressed as Indians. In like turn, French colonists then mount raids on British villages – often joined by their Indian allies – dressed as Indians. No one is fooled. Everyone knows they are impostors, but the impersonation strikes a happy chord.[26] Such events proliferate. Thus, in 1775, when colonists outraged by new taxes on tea, dress as Mohawks and dump the King's tea into Boston harbour, neither the act nor the impersonation surprise anyone. The village raiders have already institutionalized the form. All it required was the essential and one of the first mythic Americans acts – in separating themselves from Britain – to formalize playing Indian into a national pastime. By 1775, colonists knew how to do it. By 1775, it had become essential.

The Boston Tea Party signals the formalization of the role into the national consciousness and national characters. The deviants, white Indians, Red Englishmen and so forth, can now make collective their individual roles. It is not long until political organization makes itself felt in America, and those old 'Indian' raiders of the 18th century convert to newer, more sophisticated forms of political pressure than warfare. Again, whites dressed as Indians do what they could not do in their normative roles. Tammany Hall emerges in 1756 with its Indian characters, Old Tammany, or later, Saint Tammany, putatively the Delaware chief Tamanend. His chiefs, braves and warriors, and that 'old Squaw' of his fame in political cartoons of the Tammany Hall excesses, rule New York. Their corruption is swathed in 'Indian' garb; their predations on the Democratic process swaddled in mock-Indian language and war-whoops of victory. Tammany's visible use of the Indian metaphor then transfers to one of the proliferating social and civic clubs so common to the growth of smaller communities, best later embodied in the Elks, the Lions, the Kiwanis, the Society of Moquis and so on. The Improved Order of Red Men, with its pow-wows, victory dances, braves and princesses, signals the institutionalization of playing Indian through social organization, with its hundreds of chapters and persistence until the 1950's throughout the American continent. Most significantly, these clubs take their version of playing Indian to the growing middle class, and to the Midwest, now a part of the United States. But theirs too is the Algonkian version so common to the stage.[27]

From this point, the developing vocabularly, costume, and other paraphernalia of the performances are refined, in the East, to a vaguely Algonkianized/Iroquoianized performance that culminates and solidifies itself in Mr. Longfellow's poem (1855) of ancient and better times. Inspired by Schoolcraft's ethnologies, Moravian-Quaker theology via Reverent Heckewelder, and the literary form of the *Kalevala*, he offers up Hiawatha, an Algonkianized Iroquois god-hero taken from highly 'translated' origin stories and tales. A Hiawatha cult thrives both in America and in England, where recitations by costumed little girls and boys, in school playlets, in Sunday afternoon parlour performances, reaches its peak. A century of costumed Hiawathas, Minnehahas and Nokomis's speaking of Lake Gitchee-Gumee and Gitche Manito from the stage spawn jokes, name brand products, and operas, along with the linguistic and dramatic repertoire. The cult of the vanishing American, the vanishing noble savage is emblematically transformed forever as a named, tragic figure, just as Sitting Bull and Rain-in-the-Face are so personified and mythologized by the later Wild West Shows, and Sarah Winnemucca and Suzette LaFlesche by the reformist movement lecture halls.[28]

American primal myth is shored up by the Lewis and Clarke expeditions, who have another Pocahontas, the Shoshone, Sacajawea, to save the white men from her fellow savages, and to open up new Indian territories to the invasion of colonists. In the Northeast, where playing Indian has always been more deeply felt and more widely played out, real Indians are becoming a scare commodity. The Vanishing American cult among scholars, policy makers and ordinary Americans, signalled by the songs and laments (e.g.: the aforementioned Alkomook) of the late 18th century, thrives.[29] But westering whites still see the Indian as an obstruction to their 'pursuit of happiness' (read: land). Indian removal, the last barrier to white settlement, and the accompanying reservationization with allotments and leasing of Indian lands, ended finally in the 1880's with the ends of Indian wars.[30] And the phases and developments in the forms of Playing Indian are precisely consonant with those historical periods and consequences. Post-revolutionary America shifts into westward movement and prosperity, based often on land and land exploitation. Urban eastern America, exemplified by New York, Boston and Philadelphia, booms, Indians, in essence, disappear, or get pushed back beyond the boundaries of daily interaction with most Easterners. In the East, Indians are destined to be 'loved to death;' they have been replaced on the stage by play Indians. In the West, the Indian has become the primary metaphor of the Americanization process, and the metaphor signs the real Indian's death warrant.

Until this critical juncture, ideas about Indians had been primarily the province of philosophical, political and literary lights, but now the popularization of playing Indian—in the dramatic form—is joined by the growing body of 'American' scholars who are looking for their unique 'turf' in the separation from Europe. It is they who, with the later assistance of emergent museums, films and dramatic entertainments such as the medicine shows, Wild West Shows and circuses, Lewis Henry Morgan, with his Iroquois pseudonym (Shenandoah), and his Iroquoianist club of nascent archaeologists and anthropologists, begin a tradition that is to continue long into the twenti-eth century, best embodied then by the Zuniesque aspirations of Frank Cushing.[31] But Morgan's play-acting, intended to express the depth of his and others' knowledge about true Iroquois cul-ture, has the essential elements intact that will later so infuriate Indians, the elements characterized by the scholar's superior knowledge of the group, the rejection of their 'folklore' and 'un-scientific' knowledge, and the insistence of the 'objective' knowl-edge of outsiders to the exclusion of what they regarded as the impoverished and increasingly bankrupt Iroquois' own store of knowledge and behaviour. In essence, Indians become 'data' which only objective non-Indian scholars can interpret. And it is these highly selective scholars, like Frederick Jackson Turner of the 'frontier' thesis, who often become the key to the storehouse of images, through their writings and museum display, that Indians and non-Indians alike will draw upon for their play In-dian images. At this critical point too, Morgan draws Iroquois tribal people, such as J.N.B. Hewitt, the Tuscarora scholar, into his Indian club, so that they too, grieved and dispossessed by historical reality, can play Indian as well as the whites who train them.

At this juncture in the nineteenth century, Indian removal of the 1830's had reached its peak, the allotment and leasing of land had reduced Indians to a tiny foothold, and the end of the disastrous Indian wars of the 1880's had their inevitable end in the reservationization and depopulation of Indians. Depopula-tion (with Indians at their lowest population of 200,000 or so in 1910), reservationization, the official government policy of as-similation, and land allotment make real the Myth of the Van-ishing American, and for one brief moment in space and time, it appears to most Americans that, indeed, this species will go the way of the buffalo, leaving the stage clear for an unobstructed stage for playing Indian. White Indians, once captives, take on new life in the West; now as scouts as well as trappers and traders, they live with Indians one minute and fight against them the next. Sam Houston and Buffalo Bill personify the new breed of those playing Indian. They are 'adopted,' not abducted, and though living the Indian life while with Indians, they en-tirely submerge their Anglo identities to the Indian persona. They live a semi-Indian, but staged life, sensitive to popular representation. They, like the Indian hater, General Custer, are very aware of their roles in the public eye. Unlike the despised squaw men and half-breeds, their role is glamorized. And it is they who signal the presence of the Indian's oppositional role, the necessary nemesis, the Cowboy.[32]

It is here that the roles, both as Indians play them, and as whites play them, are forever fixed and sealed in both America and Europe. It is here that the Wild West Shows emerge, with the last of the old Indian warriors released from military detention to Indian hunters and white Indians like Buffalo Bill to play out the roles set for them. And it is here that Indians join whites in playing Indian. The Wild West Shows, with their remnant Sioux and Crow, travel America and Europe to enormous success.[33] These warriors, Lords of the Plains, forever mounted on their ponies, forever attacking wagon trains and hunting buffalo, become *the* Indian in the American imagination, and Europeans are assisted in their fantasies of these warriors by the writer, Karl May (the German Fenimore Cooper) whose tales of an America he never saw, tales of Old Shatterhand the Indian Scout, fuel the Western fires for German versions of playing Indian forever.[34] Hear Black Elk describe (to Neihardt) what he saw:

> We danced and sang, and I was one of the dancers chosen to do this for the Grandmother. . . . We stood right in front of Grandmother England. She was little and fat and we liked her because she was good to us. After we had danced, she spoke to us. She said something like this. 'I am sixty-seven years old. All over the world I have seen all kinds of people, but today I have seen the best-looking people I know. If you belonged to me, I would not let them take you around in a show like this.'[35]

European versions of the Wild West Show and circus abound. Whites even begin to play Indian roles in the European circuses and shows. It only took Western films to memorialize these Indians in the national consciousness forever, and it is here that the Plains version of Indians virtually replaces the Algonkian version in the American imagination. Only the Woodland fantasies of the Boy Scouts and Camp Fire Girls and the remnant social organization of the clubs retain their non-Plains versions. From henceforward, however, it is the Plains Indians whom people play, though I do not believe that the power of the Plains image is only a function of the Wild West Show complex; it is no accident that the last and most resilient enemy of Americanization comes to represent the most desirable form of playing Indian. In Arthur Kopit's play, *Indians*, Buffalo Bill and Sitting Bull (a ghost) sit on the stage, after the show is long over and Sitting Bull and his people are dead, massacred in Wounded Knee. His fictional words extend what Black Elk and others must have felt bout the shows:

> BUFFALO BILL: 'Oh, God. Imagine. I actually thought my Wild West Show would help. I could give you money. Food. Clothing. And also make people understand things . . . better. That was my reasoning. Or, anyway, part . . .' SITTING BULL: 'Your show was very popular.' BUFFALO BILL: 'We had . . . fun, though, you are I. Didn't we?' SITTING BULL: 'Oh, yes. And that's the terrible thing. We had all surrendered. We were on reservations. We could not fight, or hunt. We could do nothing. Then you came and allowed us to imitate our glory . . . It was humiliating. For sometimes, we could almost imagine it was real.'[36]

The Wild West Shows, with the sequelae, cemented roles for Indians who play Indian, or as Indians will later call them, 'show' Indians. As we have seen from the earliest of times, there was a ready audience for Indian performers in Europe, and the popularity of the Wild West Shows opened up the moderate thirst to a craving. The roles were developed by real and well-known Indians, like Sarah Winnemucca, the noted Paiute political leader of the late nineteenth century, who found that the role, if played to the satisfaction of whites, gave her a chance to carry her political message to a wider audience. Winnemucca, who became the darling of the reformist movement, which addressed Indian Rights as well as temperance and women's suffrage, began to speak on American lecture halls dressed in a fanciful garb which evolved into a more fanciful outfit as she became 'Princess Sarah' with her strong message for Indian rights. But white women who saw her and other 'princesses' of the day began to appear in number in similar costumes, performing little tableaux in various social and political settings.[37]

In these Indian roles, the performers speak in a measured speech, sometimes filled with treaty-language speech and with the Hiawathan metaphors now almost clichéd—of 'the Great

Spirit,' 'the big water,' the 'happy hunting ground' and so on, complete with the raised arm gestures, and often the accoutrements of Plains Indian costume and behaviour that accompany the role. Specific performances are called for, which flower in the 20th century. The persons performing are called 'Chief' and 'Princess.' They lead Thanksgiving and Columbus Day parades in full Plains regalia, on horseback; they perform 'America the Beautiful' or 'The Lord's Prayer' in Indian sign language; they entertain at schools or in social clubs or lodges with 'an Indian song' or dance; they stand in front of tourist sites out West (or even in the East), in full headdress or outfits, so tourists can have their pictures taken with them. They serve as the befeathered mascots of football teams, performing mock war whoops and victory dances when the team scores. No matter their specific tribe or affiliation, the dress is Plains; the gestures and accompanying parts of the act are those of movie Indians. For the most part, these real Indians – and the fakes who capitalize on their 'acts' – perform using translated, stereotypic names (eg: Bright Eyes) which appeal to the non-Indian imagination. There are a number of famous characters who made their living from these roles, but more numerous are the larger number who simply used these roles to supplement their meagre income and survive in the non-Indian world.

And, in this period of the Wild West Show, bolstered later by Western films, one of the primary folk forms of playing Indian emerges, the children's game of Cowboys and Indians. The game, requiring at most a toy tomahawk and paper feathered headband for the 'Indians' and a comparable hat and toy gun for the 'cowboys,' vitalizes the dying forms of playing Indian being abandoned to some extent by the Wild West shows, the social and civic clubs. The good, Algonkianized Indian made popular by Hiawatha and the Boy Scouts still must yield to the eternal battle played out in real life by settlers and Indians battling over the last land in the West, and Cowboys and Indians fulfills the need to allow bad Indians to stay alive. For the battle must endure, since it is the only cultural form that justifies the death of real Indians. Fully fleshed out, the game involves quintessential cultural roles, and it supplements the existing vocabularly of roles (brave, squaw, etc.) with an entire vocabulary of gestures and pidgin-English words. These, of course, transfer to normal discourse, and may be found throughout the American performance repertoire as a staple of transient performance. In the Cowboys and Indians game which best embodies the complete performance, the 'Indians' 'walk Indian file,' they howl and yell, putting their flattened palm repeatedly against their pursed mouths in an imitation of the shrill, ritual 'lu-lu' of Plains women or the battle cry of men. They greet each other with the upraised right forearm, saying 'how' in an abasement of the Sioux greeting 'hau.' They stand or sit with arms folded over each other in front of the chest, repeating the word 'ugh!' as a form of communicative discourse. They 'creep up' on the cowboys, who, of course, do not engage in such secretive behaviour, this embodiment left over from the shock endured by British troops when Indians would stealthily attack from the shadows rather than lining up and marching straight towards the enemy in a line of men, as characterized 17th and 18th century European warfare. In the game, Indians are allowed to 'run wild,' whooping, hollering, behaving in a completely unorthodox manner, while cowboys must behave scrupulously, not playing dirty, staying taciturn and calm. Their noise comes from their guns alone.[38]

The nineteenth century stage, and traditional folk, repertoire for playing Indian expands exponentially, with the spread of medicine shows which built on the idea of the Indian as healer.[39] These shows incorporated Wild West Show and circuslike performances, as well as more straightforward stage performance with Indian (or faked) song and dance, and, of course, the sale of Indian 'medicine,' mostly pure alcohol. Curiously, the presence of many Blacks in medicine show companies offered yet another opportunity for Blacks, as well as whites and Indians, to play Indian. European visitors and Americans alike saw the medicine shows, travelling throughout the country with their Indian snake oil salesmen, and yet another version of the old drama takes on new life. Certainly here, with the media-sensitive models of Buffalo Bill, the Wild West Show and other embodiments at hand, the role of playing Indian becomes a commercially viable, lucrative one, signalling to everyone that the role is worth more than attention. While the Indian had been a commercial symbol from America's beginnings, appearing as the graphic and sculptural huckster for tobacco products,[40] this

new embodiment demands real impersonators as Indian salesmen, and yet another significant development in playing Indian
occurs.

Another late 19th century practice in which the roles of Indian affect both Americans and Europeans is in spiritualism.
No doubt this is connected with several important notions: that
Indians inhabit the spirit world (certainly having vanished from
this one, sent there by whites), that Indians are wise and skilled
in healing, and that a medium directed by a guiding spirit of
some order can speak to or instruct others. In America and
Great Britain, many of the spirit guides are Indians. In the
accounts of spiritualist practice associated with the Chautau-
qua movement in New York, in diaries and autobiographies as
well as interviews of practicing spiritualists, story after story of
Chief So-and-So or Princess Such-and-Such appears. In the pamphlets handed out on the street in contemporary, urban Washington DC by Black palmists, readers and mediums, the message of spirit leadership through the Indian spirit guide is
offered to prospective Black clients. Spiritualist practice, as it
developed in the nineteenth century, contains the elements of
'guruism' that so characterize many of the successful 20th century versions of playing Indian.[41] Related to the 19th century
spiritualist movement was the earlier, but more restricted
Shaker fascination with Indian spirits. Late 18th century expo-
nents of the Shaker religion began in substantial numbers, in
their dances and songs, to be 'possessed' by Indian spirits, thus
to sing in nonsense syllables and use dance movements not char-
acteristic of their other dances and songs. Without doubt, the
'Indian' spirit guidance was associated with yet another way of
acting outside of the rules of conventional behaviour which so
distinguished the Shaker performance repertoire.[42]

The next significant emergence, in terms of additions to the
growing repertoire of ways of play Indian, comes with the Boy
Scouts.[43] Lord Baden-Powell's para-military outdoor education
movement merges with neo-French revolutionary philosophy,
and the French passion for the natural man comes to be embodied in the Indian, who will represent the Scouting ideal of
manly independence. Learning to walk, stalk, hunt, survive like
an 'Indian,' to produce beaded and feathered authentic outfits,
to dance and sing authentic music, to produce tools and weap-

ons, are the skills later to become fixed in the Order of the Arrow, Scounting's highest achievement.

> Most recently, in the *New York Times Sunday Magazine* column, *On Men*, a young writer tells of his own youthful 'Indian Ordeal,' where he and other young men of the community are given over to an Indianized river guide to spend the night, out in the forest, in silence, all alone in camp. In order to teach them self-reliance and to be one with nature, they must endure this masculine 'ordeal,' and for their persistence in learning these values, they receive the red tail feather of a hawk.[44]

The Scouting reification of the Indian, as Scouts played *him*, (note that, by this time, the Indian is a definitively male and be-feathered Lord of the Plains), affects more variants, some later practiced by the Girl Scouts and Camp Fire Girls, which concentrate, for their dramatic reenactments, less on para-military skill and more on crafts and nature-worship. The Boy Scouts' fixation on Indian singing and dancing creates, in its most pervasive manifestation, the hobbyist movement, with its passion for authenticity and perfection in dance movement, in costume. Special hobbyist pow-wows create a new venue for Indians willing to collaborate with non-Indians, spawning a reaction in the mid-20th century for so-called 'All-Indian Pow-Wows' where hobbyists are forbidden to participate.[45] And these movements burgeon into summer camping experiences for millions of children who attend Camp Gitchee-Gumee (or Camp Runna Mucka, as a friend would have it), and less institutionalized experiences memorialized in the writings of Ernest Hemingway and other men-in-nature affiliates. And still others experience the most recent phenomenon of the Y-Indian Guides programme, where fathers spend 'quality time' with the daughters through the Indian dramatic metaphor. The now familiar braves, chiefs and warriors take their little princesses to museum exhibitions, teach them Indian dances, make beaded objects, and otherwise disport themselves in paper headbands and paper feathers.[46]

> A colleague of mine, a Modoc Indian, met a neighbour, a Boy Scout leader, who proudly informed him that, on the next weekend, he and another parent would take several boys to the woods where they would like just like the 18th century Iroquois for a week. 'But won't their mothers be going?' the scholar asked. 'How can they live like the Iroquois if they don't

have the clan mothers and old women to tell them what to do, to elect their leaders, to give them advice?' Such a female intrusion on their reconstructed history was, naturally, the last thing desired by these scouts, my colleague reported. Real history and real Indians were irrelevant.[47]

Films, developed at the turn of the century, do little to implement or change the forms of playing Indian already developed. They took most of their simple cues from Wild West Shows, though plenty of their textual and stylistic references from Cooper, dime novels and stagey versions of Longfellow. They created a stage for a new type of 'white' Indian, the complete impostor, about which more will be said later, but at the same time, they offered a new stage on which many whites could play Indian. At first, films actually had Indians playing Indian on the screen. But quickly, whites invaded the screen the way they had invaded Indian Country, and many show business people — Jeff Chandler, Debra Paget, Michael Ansara and Antony Quinn, for example — made careers out of playing Indian roles, and did little to diminish the disappearance of real Indians where Indians most often played themselves, the pattern was for American whites or South Americans to take on Indian roles. The original movie Iron Eyes, for example, was an Arapaho Indian from Wyoming. But as these Indians were banned from the screen and stage due to racial bias against them (and Blacks, for that matter), whites (and more recently, Hispanics) took Indian roles and prospered. The rare Indian who actually played an Indian role, like Jay Silverheels, the Lone Ranger's faithful sidekick, Tonto, often suffered the fate of becoming a stereotype or negative role mod for young Indian people, the same fate often suffered by black actresses like Hattie McDaniel (Mammy of *Gone with the Wind*).[48]

And as part of the Cowboys-and-Indians cult, a more modern species of performance arises in the early part of the twentieth century. Built around the passion for organized sport, and institutionalized through interscholastic competition, the twenties and thirties brings us the new Indian wars on the playing fields. Mascots and team logos proliferate, using the Indian as the centre for ritualized reenacted battle. Where once real Indians like the Sac and Fox football player Jim Thorpe actually influenced the development of the sport, now and then, many

White and Black Braves, Redskins, Seminoles, Apaches, War-riors, and Chiefs battle on the playing fields. 'Wahoo-wah' be-comes the cry for schools as diverse as Dartmouth College and the University of Virginia, fans and official performers in vari-ous costumes dance for the assembled crowds at half-time and when a touchdown is achieved. Sammy Seminole at the Univer-sity of Florida, Little Red at the University of Oklahoma, Chief Noc-A-Homa for the Atlanta Braves, and the Washington Red-skins mascot (now dismissed along with the Stanford and Dart-mouth Indians), dance the victory dance and trumpet the vic-tory yell when the home team scores. Though these were a subject of enormous controversy in the late sixties when the American Indian Movement sued to dismiss the team names and logos, most persist today, unabashed at their presentation of Indian 'music' and dance. In many instances, of course as we have seen elsewhere, *the* single Indian on campus was asked to play the mascot, and just as often did so, some defending their roles to date. In a country where normally team logos involve aggressive large animals (Tigers, Mustangs) or, at most, extinct humans (Celtics, Vikings), it is ironic, but predictable, that the teams with mascots based on two living human groups are the Cowboys and the Indians. Of course, team members do not think of themselves as 'Indians' (any more than they think of themselves as Tigers) when they are on the playing field, but the mascots, logos, paraphernalia, clothing, and names accompany-ing their redefined acts of war root their acts firmly in the men-tal and cultural construct of playing Indian.[49]

> A Black friend, a columnist for a major newspaper, called me one day to discuss Indians' protest against the name and the mascot of the Washington Redskins, a team enthusiastically supported by the city's Black majority – even to the extent of dressing up in mock Indian garb for the games. 'But I always though having a team named for Indians was a compliment,' he said. 'We don't have any teams named for us.' 'Think about it,' I told him, 'do you really want to have them named for you?'[59]

It is at this period in the 20th century that American and Euro-pean hobbyists emerge, though in German and elsewhere the seeds of hobbyism were sown in the late 19th century with the success of American and European Wild West Shows.[51] European shows had 'disguised natives of Dresden' as Indians in the show, and carnival revellers in Leipzig began donning fanciful Indian dress as costumes in 1895. Modern clubs reenact the scripts given them by Buffalo Bill's Wild West and the novels of Karl May. A Hiawatha cult flourishes like the one in England and America, and German hobbyism culminates – at this level – in a passion for things Indian, including camps in the Black Forest or Thuringia where families can go, living the 'authentic' Western and Indian life for their vacations. A 1929 book on the noted imposter, Buffalo Child Long Lance, records that in his European visits he urged that 'our boys should learn to play their Indian war games in a proper manner . . .,' thus underlining the basic and continuing passion for the customs and costumes of one tribal group, primarily the Sioux. Contemporary hobbyist forms of play are elaborate – causing one German anthropologist (Feest) to refer to them (and their American hobbyist counterparts) as 'cultural transvestites.' It is in Germany that the most highly elaborated forms of hobbyism take place; yet, unlike in America, the hobbyist movement is accompanied by a passion for contemporary Indian politics and literature as well as for the material and dramatic culture of the Plains. So passionate is this movement in Germany that Karl May's books are kept in print, long after school-age Americans read Fenimore Cooper, and Germans make ritual pilgrimages to America where they visit Indian Country and are, inevitably, disappointed because Indians do not live, one-hundred percent of the time, as they would wish them to do. Moreover, because of tribal variation which does not exist in the sanitized Schwartzenwald versions, they are often very disappointed in Indians who do not act out the roles of Lords of the Plains. Germans, as well as Russians and Poles, invite numerous American political and cultural figures to speak, or to join them in their encampments, thus creating one of the primary markets for exploitation by whites and Indians who play Indian. A contemporary commentator described an 'encampment' thus: 'The aura of the historical figures impersonated by those people showed clearly that . . . the Western hobby is much more than a masquerade, it is an earthy philosophy of life.'[52]

Somewhat related to hobbyism, though at an entirely different level of feeling and attachment, are the 'Mardi Gras Indians' of Louisiana. A uniquely Black form of playing, these 'Indians' act out their roles during the annual spring carnival in New Orleans. At dawn on Mardi Gras Tuesday, troupes of elaborately costumed revellers dance and sing through the streets in Black neighbourhoods. The troupes, each of which has an 'Indian' name ('The Wild Magnolias') and is led by its 'Chief,' spend the year in creating their costumes and practicing their 'Indian' songs and dances. But unlike hobbyists who are directly imitative and passionately devoted to 'authenticity,' whether or not they achieve it, these carnival performances, dances and songs bear no resemblance whatsoever to any tribal tradition. Indeed, both costume and performance are inherently and definitively in the Afro-Caribbean tradition, though insistently described as Indian by the performers. They say that their performance is an embodiment of admiration for Indians, for their freedom, for their resistance to the white man's bondage. Thus, regardless of the real roots of the actual performances, the ideas about Indians conveyed by the performers and appreciated by the predominantly Black audiences root them squarely in the Boston Tea Party mainstream of masquerade for the purposes of 'acting out' roles rejected in the normative culture. They defy convention through 'Indian' behaviour, whereas 'African' behaviour might be disapproved by both blacks and whites in that racial climate. While this particular masquerade is unique to Blacks and, contrary to the Tea Party role, roots them in defiance of white America, it may as well bear some resemblance to the purposes served by the 'Indian' pose in Russia, Germany and Poland by hobbyists, in Italy by Marxist critics of the government, and in the US by hippies.[53]

In post-World War II America, new versions of the 'imitationist' performance continue to arise, seeds of which were sown in turn-of-the-century travel to the Southwest and in the new affluence of the middle class.[54] The phenomenon of wearing Indian-style fashion shares both an artistic and commercialized aspect with hobbyism, but retains little of hobbyism's frequent sincerity of depth. It begins in the Taos cult of the thirties, with Mabel Dodge Luhan, her 'guru' Indian husband Tony, her covey of displaced, hedonistic New Yorkers, and obeisance to the cult goddess, Georgia O'Keefe.[55] The Indianized Southwest becomes more than a canvas or a scene for the cameras lens; it becomes a

Style. At this point, fashion took an Indian turn, apparently consonant with a decided self-consciousness about American values, American styles and American economic support. The palette of colours begins to include 'earth' tones; the desert turns into a stylized scene for artists; elements of Indian dress are incorporated into clothes. In the thirties, the dancer Martha Graham created an American style in dance through the incorporation of neo-Indian dance movements into her modernist ballets. In the sixties, the counter-cultural hippies put on headbands, love beads and fringed jackets, carrying purses adorned with feathers. Young people, interested in Indian peyote cults and in a 'higher consciousness,' and inspired by cult books such as those of Carlos Casteneda, begin to show up on Southwestern mesas and reservation areas, begging to be 'inducted' into the natural way of life. And more recently, cleaner and wealthier Americans and Europeans, particularly the French, wear fashions derived form Western cowboy and Indian styles. Vaguely Hispanicized, since their aesthetic point of origin is in the Southwest, urban Jewish designers like Ralph Lauren and Calvin Klein create things made of hide, bone and shell to join the populist boots, bandannas, hats and denims in 'Indian' colours, with Indian design motifs. Santa Fe Chic, as it has been dubbed, shows up in furniture and other decorative objects as well, and the urban wealthy drape themselves in antique and 'designer' turquoise and silver ornament. Combining the hobbyist instinct with the ostentatious display of wealth, these play Indians are not concerned about authenticity as much as with style; both can rent an entire Indian village in Reno, Nevada, in which they can act out the fantasies of their drama.

Several other commercialized versions of playing Indian spring up at the turn of the century, and begin to make their presence felt in the 1920's. Particularly vulnerable as media for the representation are movies as the logical inheritors of their commercial precursors, Wild West Shows. In these versions, however, the performers do not engage in a transient 'imitationist' drama, but rather a lifelong impersonation. While white replacements for Indian actors have been of professional concern and while those interested in film are perpetually concerned about the misrepresentation of Indians in film, of more critical interest are these Indian poseurs who make their reputations

and livelihoods on playing the roles of Indians. Confined somewhat to movies and literature, the persona of Indian has always
been a compelling one, so much so that some have rarely wanted
to or been able to separate that persona from their reputations
and livelihoods on playing the roles of Indians. Confined somewhat to movies and literature, the persona of Indian has always
been a compelling one, so much so that some have rarely wanted
to or been able to separate that persona from their real bio-
graphical self. As early as the turn of the century, we find an
Englishman in Canada becoming Grey Owl, the actor. His biog-
raphies prepared by and promoted by his wife were bestsellers,
and he lived the role of the Indian, Grey Owl, until his death. Yet
another, a mixed-blood black man (as so defined by the time),
Buffalo Child Long Lance (or Silvester Long), appeared in
American films during the twenties and thirties, again creating
and maintaining the role of a Cherokee, then a Blackfoot, in
spite of his background of indeterminate racial and cultural origins and upbringing.[56] Literary imposters have been numerous
in the twentieth century, but we might note that two earlier
forms of impersonation or 'guruism' constitute major literary
forms in American and European culture. In the first of these,
faked speeches offered in the persona of a famous Indian leader,
such as the well-known speech of Chief Seattle, offered 'truth'
(often about the Indian condition or human condition) through
the mouth of a wise, old, defeated (and now dead) chief.[57] In the
second mode, best exemplified by John Neihardt's *Teachings of
Black Elk*, the old guru/master gives the teachings through the
'transcriptions' of a non-Indian student/savant. These forms are
somewhat similar to earlier literary forms exemplified in the
works of Cooper and Karl May, where Indian 'truth' and wisdom
is purveyed by the 'white Indians,' Old Shatterhand and Natty
Bumppo. And they are very similar indeed to newer literary
forms like ethnopoetics, where 'White shamans' like Gary Snyder or Jerome Rothenburg translate their translations of translations from the original native texts, or create new texts in the
primitivist mode for an audience which prefers the white shaman to the real Indian. In the second mode, the core of real
teachings exists, but the elaborations are quite often questionable. Still, the very common forms of fakery or literary postur-
ing, coupled with the outright bogus forms, cast a telling light

on the cultural need to have Indian wisdom purveyed in this particular mode of transmission.

In the commercial literary world of late, there continue to be notable impostors. They either write in an Indian persona, on Indian subjects, or in the most recent revival of the noted 'l'enfant sauvage' syndrome, best embodied in the Tarzan novels, they make their reputation by writing about putative Indian gurus who show them the true Indian way of life, healing them from the ills of civilization. In the first mode, writers (such as 'William Least Heat Moon' of *Blue Highways*) whose early work is not popular, drop their Anglo persona and take up an Indian one, finding a loyal and devoted following in the impersonation phase. As the phrase goes, Indian-ness somehow makes good press if promoted well, though it has rarely worked for Indian authors in that competitive business. Most notable among these has been the recently well-known and successful writer and critic, Jamake Highwater, who was recently revealed by an Indian newspaper to be of Armenian Jewish parentage. Specializing in costumed appearance in expensive 'Santa Fe Chic' clothes, he insists that he is Indian 'because I say I am.'[58] Of the 'gurus' species, two in recent years stand out because they have been so phenomenally successful—Carlos Casteneda and Lynn Andrews. Casteneda's very serious and authoritative series of works on the teachings of one Don Juan, an Indian mystic, were presented both as serious anthropology and as serious commentary on Indian life. The other, Lynn Andrews, capitalized on Casteneda's success and an interest in feminism, with her experiences in learning from her wise spiritual 'guide, Agnes Whistling Elk.' Neither Andrews or Casteneda pretend to be Indian by birth; they become 'Indianized' by introduction into the religious 'separate reality' by their Indian 'guides.' These works, along with Highwater's, have spawned huge and voracious audiences for 'Indian' religious experience, and, in turn, have enlarged the market for more exploitative impersonations.[59]

Fed by hobbyism, general cultisms (eg: the 'human potential movement'), and by a continuing revitalization of interest in Indians as the spiritual healers of European ills, the commercial exploitation of the seemingly fathomless hunger for Indian guruism has taken on new life. In these roles of playing Indian, some who are genetically and culturally Indian, but more who are quite marginal, and others who are neither, have developed a 'market' for Indian religious experience. Throughout North America and Europe, these 'masters' give spiritual counselling and religious advice. The ceremonies they conduct are often a hodge-podge of generic Plains ritual combined with holistic healing and 'human potential movement' language. None of the persons leading these ceremonies and providing these services is recognized by any tribe as a religious leader; in one instance, the persons providing these many services have simply declared themselves to be a 'tribe,' incorporating themselves as a legal entity.[60]

Finally, short of declaring oneself a tribe or member of a tribe and making a living from that identification, massive numbers of others claim to be Indian as part of their normative identity. Throughout the period of the last two hundred years in America, as a direct result of the significance of New World mestizoization, a cult for that process and its results developed. Hispanics call it the cult of *Mestizaje*.[61] The real new mixed-blood world, partly a result of those early white Indians' efforts to live in Indian country with Indians, created a curious form of racial politics in the claiming of 'Indian blood.' This is a fictional mixed-blood world, where those making the claim want to be rewarded in some way for their claim, though they reject implicitly any resultant negative treatment because of that status.

Whites simply claim Indian blood as a matter of casual conversation. Situationally, they usually make the claim to Indians as a form of affiliating, socially and for the moment, with the Indians to whom they are speaking. They appear to believe that Indians will think well of them as a result of the claim. So numerous are what I have termed my 'cocktail party relations' that it is, for most Indians, a barely tolerated exercise to be introduced to some new acquaintance. On a more serious level, some whites and Blacks introduce the notion of claiming their Indian blood as a precursor to a claim to the acquisition of land or government benefits that might accrue as a result of the claim. It is quite common still for someone to express a wish to validate their genealogy so that they or their children can claim putative scholarships which they believe are reserved for Indians, and they little appreciate it when told that both their claims to Indian blood and the existence of such scholarships are part of American folklore. Most often, however, their claim is simply one that creates interest in them as an individual, an individual with an admirable heritage. Many allege some relationship with a specific famous Indian, Tecumseh, or Quanah Parker, or, if they are from Virginia, Pocahontas. But most simply claim they are 'part-Cherokee,' as often through some distant grandmother who was, as the phrase always goes, a 'Cherokee Princess.' Whether a specific tribe or no tribe at all is specified in the claim, onlookers are encouraged to validate the claim by noting the 'high cheekbones' of whites, or the 'straight' hair or 'reddish cast to the skin' of Blacks.

For Blacks and Hispanics, both in and outside of the United States, the claim is deeply rooted in racial politics. In South and Central America, leftist political organizers decree that 'we are all Indian,' though it is rarely the case that political leaders in any of those areas are *mestizo*. In Mexico and in Mexican-American communities where once it was politically and socially 'better' to be 'Hispano' (or European), it is now common to claim 'Indianismo' in your family. When Hispanics in North America and Mexico assert their Indian-ness, inevitably they trace their lineage to the Aztecs, a claim somewhat similar to the relationships people assert to distant Indian royalty. The mythic pull of ancient power has its strength even today; no one says they are Tarahumara or any other group. Elsewhere in the Latino world, they are inevitably from a now extinct group (eg: Taino,) but rarely from a living and persecuted group (eg: the Maya).

The claiming of Indian blood is so common among Blacks in America that Langston Hughes, the poet, even devoted verse to it in his series of poems featuring the folk-philosopher, Simple, where Simple makes fun of those Blacks who need to claim Indian blood in order to relieve themselves of the burden of being solely Black, or, as in the case of most Black Americans, a mixture of Black, white and other races. Blacks also most often claim to have Cherokee blood, but as well claim Blackfeet blood (note the dual claim of Buffalo Child Long Lance). The assertion, unsubstantiated by any known familial or settlement pattern, simply appears to be a kind of folk alliterative device.

Both Blacks and whites insist, most often, on their Cherokee descent. When Whites and Blacks play Indian in the dramatic versions, they inevitably play Sioux, or some hybridized Algonkian in the earlier versions. But when they claim Indian blood, Sioux is the last affiliation they would claim. In the case of Blacks, Hispanics and Whites, the actual genetic makeup of the individuals making claims to Indian blood may actually include Indian genes. Certainly, the mestizoization of America was real and pervasive; certainly, more Indians and Blacks, for example, had extensive relationships in the Southeast than are documented. Still, this particular claim is important, not because it has a genuine basis in reality, but rather because it has a purpose and intent separate from its basis in reality or fakery. It is interesting because, like so many of the other forms of playing Indian, it has a formulaic, artistic quality in a role manipulated for specific purposes. Because of the peculiar racial climate in which America was born, with a concern about the percentage or quantum of 'Indian blood' or 'Black blood' (in folk terminology), Indians and Blacks responded to that racial climate in many ways. In the past, some light-coloured Blacks tried to, and many successfully did, 'pass for white.' Others bleached their skin and straightened their hair. It was clear that 'white blood' was a positive, certainly to whites. In the sixties, however, with the Civil Rights and Black Power movements, a new premium was placed on positive identification with African heritage and a consequent rejection of claims to and identification with an Anglo heritage. Indians rarely responded to a racially-based identification with an alteration of their cosmetic appearance. Still, the 'half-breed' designation implied an uncomfortable status for many; the presence of white blood, unlike for Blacks, was not mitigating. Open racist whites hated the Indian blood; yet liberal whites, led by scholars, insisted that mixed-bloods were not truly 'Indian.' Mixed-blood Indians are punished, in many ways, for being 'half-breeds,' yet a white claim to Indian heritage is viewed positively, as long as that claimant does not attempt to live out an 'Indian' life. Thus, it came to be that Indians who claimed white blood were bad; but whites who claim Indian blood are good. As in other arenas, for whites to play Black, the role must be very transient and absurd (i.e.: blackface comedy, minstrelsy). But the role of Indian may be more or less permanently and seriously assumed by whites. They may play Indian for any putative benefit that may accrue

as a result of their claim, while none of the negative consequences need be suffered.

Not surprisingly, then, it is the rare white person who ever
claims to be part-Black, and conversely, in the new racial climate, the rare Black person who comfortably acknowledges a
white heritage. But everyone appears to feel comfortable with
an acknowledgment of an Indian heritage, no matter how frail
their claim.

> I was at a cocktail party years ago, given in honour of a Black
> colleague. In the course of a very interesting conversation with
> a young Black woman, she asked what I did, and I replied that
> I ran an American Indian project at a professional association.
> She, looking at my light skin and blue eyes, said rather haught-
> ily, 'Shouldn't an Indian be running that project?' 'One does,' I
> replied. 'Yes,' she said, 'but you must be only part Indian.' 'Yes,'
> I answered, looking at her light skin and green eyes, 'in the
> same way that you're only part Black.' She angrily walked
> away, only to return a half hour later. 'I never thought of it
> that way until now,' she said.

So well known are these various forms of performance by
Indians and non-Indians alike, that tribal people have developed
a kind of metafolklore about them. For example, it would be
common in any gathering of Indian people for someone, in a
comic acknowledgement, to parody playing Indian, either in
gestures or speech. In affirmation of the truth of some statement, for example, I have for years raised my right hand in the
well-known 'how' gesture, and reassured onlookers by saying
solemnly 'Honest you know what!' Others will grunt meaning-
fully or make a fake sign language gesture to indicate their
feelings about a speaker or TV show.

> An Indian walks into a restaurant. The waitress sees him, and
> immediately raises her arm in the traditional 'play Indian'
> greeting. 'How,' she says. 'Black,' he replies, pointing to he
> coffeepot. (Or in another variant, 'Scrambled,' pointing to eggs
> frying in the pan.)

When speaking of a person with dubious tribal credentials, inevitably someone will respond to the question of 'what tribe is
she?' with the reply, 'probably a Cherokee Princess' or, if the
response is to me or another Cherokee, with 'probably one of

your relatives.' In fact, Indians have a name for those who play Indian. They are called 'Wannabees.'[62]

The enactments of the cultural scripts described here can be called stereotyping, at the simplest, and certainly, the ritual enactments themselves can be said to stem from a racist and racial consciousness that forever shapes the interactions of peoples. Like all such iterations, the enactments have a rich and interesting artistry brought to bear upon the texts. That is partly why they are so compelling, but more importantly, it is in their vary nature as compelling scripts that we must pay attention.

What are the stakes of playing Indian? In the commercial or professional role, certainly money is one of the biggest stakes. Rarely, however, has the role led either to big money or big reputation, but occasionally, the role has been lucrative. Still, I believe the biggest stakes, no matter what the longevity or depth of the performance, involve cultural validation, cultural approval for the second biggest role of all American roles, Indian. The other role is, of course, cowboy or some variant of it. The big bucks have been reserved for that role. But this most American of performances suggests that playing Indian is one of the most subtly entrenched, most profound and significant of American performances. Perhaps relief of guilt is an inherent part of the role, but, when taken in connection with other cultural performance epiphenomena of American life, I have come to think that cultural validation is the role's most important function. For in playing Indian, certainly Anglo-American players are connecting to the America that existed before European invasion; they are connecting to the very beginnings of the mythological structure called America (note the accompanying 'Mayflower' and 'Jamestown' complexes that exist with respect to American 'founding fatherhood'). And they are connecting to both the real and to the primally mythic shaping of the country, perhaps through the reenactment of conflict between Indians and their ancestors, perhaps through the affirmation of victory over Indians by their ancestors, real or spiritual. When Blacks, as opposed to Anglo-Americans, play Indian, perhaps they are connecting to a world that allows them to be first, to be other than Black, other than white, other than victims who did not fight their enslavement. When Europeans play Indian, perhaps they are affiliating with an America they 'lost' and, conversely, as represented by its Anglo power structure, with an America they don't like. Perhaps, all of them unconsciously know that the role of Indian is essential to the American identity, at least, and so, disappointed in the truth of what happens and continues to happen to Indians in America, they reconstruct the Indian presence in an acceptable version. Accompanied by some other adjacent and very comforting, if contradictory, myths (eg: the empty virgin land, the First Thanksgiving, the number of settlers who died by Indian attack in opening the 'frontier'), they reconstruct a good past. Who can say what each individual may think or feel, though the evidence for collecting feeling is quite powerfully articulated in the scripts.

But in the ritual reenactments of the scripts, however major or minor, however permanent or transient, two important points emerge. First, we forget, with respect to Americans, just how Indian they really are, from their food, clothing, landscape, architecture, material culture, and most profoundly, their iconography – an iconography which shapes the rest of the world and gives it shape in turn. But even more importantly, beyond the true Indian-ness of America, they play Indian roles depend on dead Indians. In order for anyone to play Indian successfully, real Indians have to be dead. Americans have to believe them dead or kill them off. The Cult of the Vanishing Indian was merely practice for the ritual reenactment. Note, for example, how important it has been historically in America to take fish, water, trees, buffalo and deer away from Indians in order to celebrate their oneness with Nature, their status as First Ecologists. If Indians were still in charge of the land, Americans could not lament their own impoverished stewardship of that land through memorializing the Indians they took it from. And so the iconography holds true. What could not be converted to a sterilized and non-specific American iconography from a very distinctly Indian one (eg: the Indian Queen conversion to Miss Liberty) had to be converted, by non-Indians, to one in which non-Indians played the Indian role, and thus could control the meaning. Not only is the impersonation of Indians essential to the American identity, but those who participate in these impersonations, for the most part, often believe deeply that in doing so they admire and respect Indians, the First

Americans, the Noble Savages, the First Ecologists. I think of all the children who come to public performances of Indian music wearing the paper headbands and feathers they made for Thanksgiving Day celebrations in school. Others, mostly the organized impersonations through social clubs, lodges, football teams and so forth, either actively despise or scorn real (read: drunken, welfare-dependent, savage) Indians. Curiously, their feelings about real Indians matter little, because their play Indian roles are not dependent on real Indians at all. For all of them, it is as if real Indians do not and need not exist.

These roles are no doubt connected to the 'Mayflower' syndrome (read: we were first), perhaps to the 'Anastasia' syndrome (read: we were noble), and certainly, more recently, to the historical reenactment (read: we were there) syndrome. Very popular and growing in America, England, Scandinavia and other parts of Europe and the Pacific, 'Living History' museums recreate as much of the authentic past as they can or dare to do, even with authentic animals, authentic smells, and authentic speech. But more at the folk level, reenactment groups take to the hills and plains on weekends, set up encampments, and reenact famous battles of the French and Indian War, the American Civil War, the English Jacobite Rebellions, or the South African Boer Wars. In New Zealand, new urban settlers play Maori just as the French and Indian war groups play Huron and Ojibwa, while others of their fellows play historic White roles.

> A French and Indian War reenactment group wants to perform a famous battle in which some Indians used their lacrosse game as a diversionary sham allowing them to attack a fort. The reenactment group wants to learn to play lacrosse, even to make the racquets. When asked why they don't simply get Iroquois or Ojibwa lacrosse players to bring their racquets and enact the roles for the battle, they reply, after some embarrassed stammering, that the point is to have them (the whites) play the roles.

The need to replay the roles, replay the battles, replay the historic scenes is there, especially when the distance of time has not resolved historical ambiguity about the actions of one's ancestors, or when the reconstruction of the past seems more glorious than the present. Perhaps this is why, like Sitting Bull in Arthur Kopit's play, even Indians play Indian. No wonder perhaps that German visitors to modern reservations and school-children visited by contemporary Indian speakers are disappointed when Indians wear three-piece suits, drive pickup trucks, and use computers. In that world, not only do Indians not play Indian, but the role for whites to play is not the one they want. They already know that role. It is the 'Indian' they want and want to be.

For now, I must be content with having described the illness, its etiology and epidemiology. I have no prescription, no pill for this disease, for this growing cultural epidemic which appears to get worse as people's faith in their national cultures gets worse. Should folklorists study the phenomenon in order to kill it off forever? A combination of non-Black racial consciousness and Black political power did kill off the offshoots of the minstrel show and its other blackface cousins. But the relative disappearance or submersion of American blackface impersonation has meant nothing to the persistence of playing Indian; the phenomenon has only grown. Whereas blackface has been omitted from the Philadelphia Mummers' Parade, for example, they still retain their costumed 'tribute to the American Indian.' Does one tell people that their folklore serves them ill when they appear to preserve that folklore out of a passion and need that bespeaks a dependent cultural persona? What would Americans or Germans play if they could not play Indian? What would Blacks do if they accepted racial realities, or is their myth tied of that of whites? Would Indians be freed to be something new entirely if they did not have the obligation to play Indian?

It may be too hard to face the consequences of history; it may even be harder to change them. As long as the substitute impersonation works to shield from truth, playing Indian serves its deadly purpose, and, as I have said elsewhere, Indians are in effect, loved to death through playing Indian, while despised when they want to act out their real traditional roles on the American landscape. For Indians to be Indian, or rather to be Indian in their some 200 distinct tribal roles, to be Indian in the historical future, non-Indians must give up the role. And they must quit asking Indians to *play* that role. For worse, I believe, and never for better, the role is so important and so diffused through many aspects of American life and culture that to challenge it anywhere creates rage and confusion – a kind of cultural identity crisis. Still, as scholars have operated to change other ideas in American culture, so we must act to change this one. As the Laguna poet Carol Lee Sanchez has said, 'we will all be rewritten.' So be it.

NOTES

1. I use the term 'Indian' because the essay is about stereotypes and images of the aboriginal inhabitants of North America. See Robert F. Berkhofer, *The White Man's Indian: Images of the American Indian: From Columbus to the Present* (New York: Alfred A. Knopf, 1978); Roy Harvey Pearce, *Savagism and Civilization: A Study of the Indian and the American Mind* (Baltimore, Maryland: John Hopkins University Press, 1965); Francis Jennings, *The Invasion of America: Indians, Colonialism and the Cant of Conquest* (Chapel Hill: University of North Carolina Press, 1975); for a discussion, and other references for the history of ideas about the 'Indian' and debates over the historical and philosophical use of other terms such as 'savage,' 'primitive,' 'redskin.' Also see 'The Indian in Popular American Culture,' in Wilcomb Washburn, ed., *The Handbook of North American Indians* IV (Washington, DC: Smithsonian Institution Press, 1988) for a comprehensive treatment of Indian stereotypes in oral tradition, popular culture, material culture, and classical literature related to the forms of playing Indian treated in this essay.

2. See James Axtell, 'The White Indians of Colonial America,' *William and Mary Quarterly* XXXII (January, 1975), 55–88; also Colin Calloway, 'Neither White Nor Red: White Renegades on the American Indian Frontier,' *Western Historical Quarterly* (January, 1986), 43–66.

3. Roy Harvey Pearce, 'The Metaphysics of Indian-Hating,' *Ethnohistory* IV (1957), 27–40.

4. See Rayna Green, 'The Pocahontas Perplex: The Image of the Indian Woman in American Vernacular Culture,' *The Massachussetts Review* 16, no. 4 (1976), 698–74; E. McClung Fleming, 'The American Image as Indian Princess, 1765–1815,' *Winterthur Portfolio* 2 (1965), 65–81.

5. This figure is generally accepted now by most scholars. At least 90% of coastal Indian peoples in Canada and new England were dead of disease by 1700. See Henry F. Dobyns, *Their Number Became Thinned: Native Population Dynamics in Eastern North America* (Knoxville: University of Tennessee Press, 1983).

6. The processes of interaction and transformation – of Indians and Europeans – into 'Americans' is best described in secondary sources by James Axtell, *The European and the Indian: Essays in the Ethnohistory of Colonial North America* (New York: Oxford University Press, 1981) and *The Invasion Within: The Contest of Cultures in Colonial North America* (New York: Oxford University Press, 1985); Neil Salisbury, *Manitou and Providence: Indians, Europeans and the Making of New England, 1500–1643* (New York: Oxford University Press, 1982); A. Irving Hallowell, 'American Indians, White and Black: The Phenomenon of Transculturation,' *Current Anthropology* 4 (1963) 519–31; In *American Indian Culture and Research Journal* 6, no. 2 (1982), see Olive P. Dickason, Jacqueline Peterson, and Alden Vaughan and Daniel Richter.

7. I am not concerned here to elaborate on theories of play or traditional linguistic/ideational/dramatic forms. Readers will be familiar with the signal works of Clifford Geertz, Roger Abrahams, Johan Huizinga and others which explore these concepts.

8. See Axtell 1981.

9. The Puritans in particular were much afraid, both of 'popish delusions' and 'white heathenism.' See Axtell, 1981; Jennings, 1975; Salisbury, 1982; also Richard Slotkin, *Regeneration Through Violence: The Myth of the American Frontier, 1600–1800* (Middletown, Conn.: Wesleyan University Press, 1973).

10. Axtell, 1975; Benjamin Franklin to Peter Collinson, May 9, 1973, in Leonard Labatree and William BV. Wilcox, eds., *The Papers of Benjamin Franklin* (New Haven, Conn.: Yale University Press, 1950–1978) 4, 481–82.

11. Axtell, 1975.

12. See any works on Charles Bird King, Karl Bodmer, Seth Eastman, George Catlin for samples of the kinds of paintings mentioned.

13. See David Beers Quinn, *Set Fair for Roanoke: Voyages and Colonies, 1584–1606* (Chapel Hill: University of North Carolina Press, 1985); for primary accounts, see the full bibliography of the early travellers and writers like Hakluyt, Hariot, White, Drake, Smith, etc. in D.B. Quinn, ed., *The Roanoke Voyages 1584–1590*, 2 vols (Cambridge: Hakluyt Society, 1955), 2, 918–46; for New England contact period narratives in the *Jesuit Relations,* the writings of John Eliot, Cotton Mather (ex: *Magnalia Christi Americana*).

14. For new and riveting accounts of the display of Indians in Europe, from the first voyages through the 20th century, see Christian Feest, ed., *Indians and Europe: An Interdisciplinary Collection of Essays* (Aachen, GDR: Edition Herodot/Raader-Verlag, 1987).

15. See Axtell, 1975; Salisbury, 1982; also Vine Deloria, Jr. and

Clifford Lytle, *American Indians, American Justice* (University of Texas Press, 1983) for a discussion of US policy connected to attempts at assimilation of the Indian.

16. Mason Weems, Jr., with his books of instructive tales for schoolchildren of the new nation, was one of the major sources of 'national' folklore, including the famous stories of George Washington and the cherry tree, Washington's casting the silver dollar across the Potomac, and others.

17. See Green, 1975, also Philip Young, 'The Mother of Us All: Pocahontas Reconsidered,' *Kenyon Review* XXIV (Summer, 1962), 391–415; see Frank DeCaro, 'Vanishing the Red Man: Cultural Guilt and Legend Formation,' *International Folklore Review* 4 (1986), 74–80, for a provocative treatment of the functions of legends such as the Lover's Leap and other Indian suicide tales.

18. See Jacqueline Peterson, 'The People in Between: Indian White Marriage and the Generation of a Metis Society and Culture in the Great Lakes Region, 1680–1830' (Unpublished Dissertation, University of Illinois/Chicago Circle, 1981); Jennifer S.H. Brown, *Strangers in Blood: Fur Trade Families in Indian Country* (Vancouver, Canada and London: University of British Columbia Press, 1981).

19. Marion Tinling, ed., *The Correspondence of the Three William Byrds of Westover, Virginia, 1684–1776*, 2 vols (Charlottesville: University of Virginia Press, 1977); also Christian Feest, 'Indians and Europe?: Editor's Postscript,' 609–628.

20. David Boston, 'The Three Caldwells,' in *The White Horse and the Fleur de Lys: The King's Regimental Booklet* (London, c.1975). An easily accessible portrait of Sir John Caldwell can be found in the Merseyside County Museums in Liverpool, England; a fine printed copy can be found on the cover of the exhibition catalogue, Ted Brasser, ed. *Bo'jou Neejee!: Profiles of Canadian Art* (Ottawa: National Museum of Man, 1975); Colin Calloway, 'The "Wild Indian Savages" in Leeds,' *Thorseby Society Miscellany* 16, no. 4 (1979), 305–315.

21. Such stories appeared first in the popular press, then in tracts. Jefferson makes famous the farewell speech of Chief Logan in his *Notes on the State of Virginia* (1785, Paris). See Ray H. Sandefur, 'Logan's Oration – How Authentic?' *Quarterly Journal of Speech* XLVI (October, 1960), 289–96; and Ed Seeber, 'Critical Views of Logan's Speech,' *Journal of American Folklore* 60 (1947), 130–46. Benjamin Franklin printed Indian treaties; the very popular anecdote books of the early 19th century put into print much that had circulated in popular and oral tradition in the previous century. George Turner, *Traits of Indian Character* 2 vols, (Philadelphia: Key and Biddle, 1836); Pishey Thompson, *Anecdotes of the North American Indian and Na-*

tives of the Natural History of the Immediate Neighborhood (Boston: John Noble, 1857); Harvey Newcomb, *The North American Indian,* 2 vols, (Pittsburgh, Luke Loomis, 1835); William White, *A Collection of Indian Anecdotes,* (Concord, NH: The Author 1837); see also Richard Moody, 'Indian Treaties, The First American Dramas,' *Quarterly Journal of Speech* XXXIX (February, 1953), 15–24; Lawrence Wroth, 'The Indian Treaty as Literature,' *Yale Review,* n.s. XVII (July, 1928), 749–66).

22. Franklin's and Jefferson's fascination with and use of Indian metaphors and other materials in the shaping of their thought has been widely commented upon – see Cadwallader Coldon, *History of the Five Indian Nations Depending Upon The Province of New York in America* (London, 1727); Recently, Indian historians (Deloria, Grinde) and others working with them have amassed considerable documentation on those direct and specifically Iroquoian influences.

23. See Arthur H. Quinn, *Representative American Plays From 1767 to the Present Day,* 7th ed. (New York: Appleton-Century-Crofts, 1953).

24. Austin E. Fife and Francesca Redden, 'The Pseudo-Indian Folk Songs of the Anglo-American and French Canadian,' *Journal of American Folklore* 67, Nos. 265 and 266, 1954; (July-September, 1954; October-December, 1954), 239–52, 379–54. Of course, the popular stage never quit producing fake Indian songs, right up through the 1970's with rock-and-roll (e.g., 'Cherokee Woman;' 'Half-Breed' by Cher). The twenties and ragtime produced many, the most popular of which were 'Tammany' and the 'Hiawatha Rag;' see Roger Hankins, 'Those Indian Songs,' *The Ragtimer* (May-June, 1970), 5–9; also popular stage opera gave us 'Rose-Marie,' with the famed 'Indian Love Call,' and country music included Hank Williams's notable 'Kaw-Li-Jah.' The Indian motif, though musically a stereotype unrelated to genuine tribal musical forms, is widely used in Classical and popular American music. See Joseph Hickerson, 'A List of classical American Composers Using Indian themes' and 'A List of American Music With Indian Themes,' Archive of Folksong/Library of Congress.

25. See Louis Jones, *Aboriginal American Oratory: The Tradition of Eloquence Among the Indians of the United States,* (Los Angeles: Southwest Museum, 1965); also Rudolf Kaiser, 'A Fifth Gospel, Almost: Chief Seattle's Speech(es): American Origins and European Reception,' in Feest, 1987, 505–526.

26. The accounts of white Indian raids are numerous. They continued even after Independence when numerous rural disorders plagued the frontiers. A note of their popularity may be found in Alan Taylor. 'Stopping the Rogues and Deceivers: A White Indian Recruiting No-

tice of 1808,' *William and Mary Quarterly* 90–103. For the Boston Tea Party incident, see Calvin Martin and Steven Crain, 'The Indian Behind the Mask at the Boston Tea Party,' *Indian Historian* (Winter, 1974), 45–47.

27. For Tammany Hall, or the Columbian Order, see Jerome Mushkat, *Tammany and the Evolution of a Political Machine, 1789–1865* (Syracuse, New York: Syracuse University Press, 1971); also Allen Franklin, *The Trail of the Tiger, being an account of Tammany from 1789; the Society of Saint Tammany, or the Columbian Order; Tammany Hall, the origin and sway of the Bosses.* (New York, 1928). There is little written on The Improved Order of Red Men. The 'Moquis' dress up in Indian clothes on ceremonial occasions, perform 'snake' dances and other rites. The name of the very large and important American civic club, Kiwanis, may have some Indian roots, but I have not been able to confirm that connection in more than the name, an Algonkianized word.

28. Henry Wadsworth Longfellow, 'Hiawatha' (1855); Stith Thompson, 'The Indian Legend of Hiawatha,' *Publications of the Modern Language Association,* 1922; Henry Rowe Schoolcraft, *Algic Researches,* 1839; *Notes on the Iroquois,* 1847; Reverend John Heckewelder, *Account of the History, Manners and Customs of the Indian Nations Who Once Inhabited Pennsylvania and The Neighbouring States,* (Philadelphia, 1819).

29. Leslie Fiedler, *Return of the Vanishing American,* (New York: Hill and Wang, 1968).

30. See Loring B. Priest, *Uncle Sam's Stepchildren: The Reform of U.S. Indian Policy, 1865–1887* (New Brunswick, NJ: Rutgers University Press, 1942).

31. Lewis Henry Morgan (Shenandoah), 'Letters on the Iroquois,' *American Review* (1847), Feb., 8–18; Mar., 242–256, 447–461.

32. Jack Gregory and Rennard Strickland, *Sam Houston and the Cherokees, 1829–1833* (Austin: University of Texas Press, 1967).

33. See Henry B. Sell and Victor Weybright, *Buffalo Bill and the Wild West* (New York: Oxford University Press, 1955); Don Russell, *A History of the Wild West Show* (Fort Worth, Texas: Amos Carter Museum of Art, 1970). For accounts of the European response to the Wild West Show, see Feest, ed., 1987; especially Daniele Fiorentino.

34. For various treatments of the Indian in American literature, see Leslie Fiedler, 'The Indian in English Literature;' C. Feest, 'The Indian in Non-English Literature' in Washburn, ed., 1987, also L. Fiedler, *The Return of the Vanishing American* (New York: Stein and Day, 1968); Albert Keiser, *The Indian in American Literature* (New York: Oxford University Press, 1933).

35. John Neihardt, *Black Elk Speaks* (Lincoln: University of Nebraska Press, 1971).

36. Arthur Kopit, *Indians* (New York: Hill and Wang, 1969).

37. See Joanna Scherer, 'The Public Life of Sarah Winnemucca,' *Cultural Anthropology*, 1988, see also Dorothy Clarke Wilson, *Bright Eyes: The Story of Suzette LaFlesche* (New York: McGraw Hill, 1974) for a popularized account of the beautiful and charismatic Omaha sisters who became the darlings of the reformist movement.

38. I have informally interviewed hundreds of current and former 'Cowboys and Indians' players throughout the US for their impressions of the game and what it involves. Most say that as children, most opted for the Cowboy role because they 'did not like getting beat.' Interestingly, whose who always opted for the 'Indian' role – a group which includes a much higher percentage of women than the Cowboy role players – are very clear about what attracts them, that is, the 'costume,' the yelling and 'acting out' which appears to accompany the role, and the 'underdog' aspects the role entails.

39. The last American medicine show, owned by a Black itinerant musician in North Carolina and still featuring 'Indian' medicine and performance, closed in the late 1970's. See Arrell Gibson, 'Medicine Show,' *The American West* 4, no. 1 (February, 1967), 34–39; and Brooks McNamara, 'The Indian Medicine Show,' *Education Theatre Journal* (Dec. 23, 1971), 431–449. So-called 'Indian' doctor products sold by the shows were followed by 'Quaker' and 'Shaker' doctor products.

40. See Green, 1988, for extensive references to the role of the Indian image in tobacco product advertising.

41. Little literature exists on the Indian guide phenomenon *per se*. I and my students have interviewed black and white spiritualists in New York, Massachussetts and Washington, DC. Only recently in England, I heard of the White Eagle Lodge, guided, of course, by Chief White Eagle.

42. For songs, see Edward D. Andrews, *The Gift To Be Simple: Songs, Dances and Rituals of the American Shakers* (New York: Dover Publications, 1962).

43. See Charles Alexander Eastman, *Indian Scout Talks: A Guide for Boy Scouts and the Camp Fire Girls* (Boston: Little Brown and Co., 1914) for an Indianizied inspiration for playing Indian to the Scouts; see also the European and international versions of the manual; as well as manuals for the Camp Fire Girls and the Girl Scouts of America.

44. 'The Indian Ordeal,' *New York Times Magazine*, 'On Men.'

45. William Powers, 'The Indian Hobbyist in America,' in Washburn, 1988.

46. I have derived my description of the programme from several accounts in the Washington Post, 1986 and 1987, and from several telephone calls to the American Indian programme office by 'Chiefs' wanting to arrange museum tours of Indian exhibitions for themselves and their 'princesses.'

47. Reported to author by Michael Dorris, Chair of Native American Studies, Dartmouth College, c.1982.

48. See Ralph and Natasha Friar.; also Raymond W. Stedman, *shadows of the Indians: Stereotypes in American Culture* (Norman: University of Oklahoma Press, 1982); Marsden, Michael, 'The Indian in Movies,' in Washburn, ed., 1988.

49. See Green, 1988, for a slightly more extended commentary on sports play; also 'Indians Open War on Redskins'; 'Redskins Keep Name, Will Change Lyrics,' *Washington Post*, July 15, 1972, p. 1, Section D; March 30, 1972, p. 1, Section A.; also Ralph Linton, 'Totemism and the American Air Force,' *American Anthropologist* 26 (1920), 296–300.

50. William Raspberry, *Washington Post.*

51. Colin Taylor, 'The Indian Hobbyist in America,' in Washburn, 1988.

52. In Christian Feest, 1987, articles by Bolz, Conrad, Vaschenko, Mulvey, Kaiser, Letay, Mariani 599–608; also *Akwesasne Notes*, 'Plastic Medicine Men.'

53. Stewart Brand, 'The Counter Culture and Indians, 1960's–1970's,' in Washburn, 1988, 'Happy Hippie Hunting Ground,' *Life Magazine*, December 1, 1967, 66–71; in Feest, ed., 1987, articles by Giorgio Mariani; Ewa Nowicka; Alexander Vaschenko.

54. 'Return of the Red Man,' *Life Magazine*, Dec. 1, 1967.

55. See Lois Palken Rudnick, *Mable Dodge Luhan: New Woman, New Worlds* Albuquerque: University of New Mexico Press, 1981); also Arrel M. Gibson, *The Santa Fe and Taos Colonies: Age of the Muse, 1900–1942* (Norman: University of Oklahoma Press, 1983).

56. See *My Life With Grey Owl;* Edgar Schmidt-Pauli, *We Indians; The Passion of A Great Race,* by Big Chief White Horse Eagle (London, 1931); Donald Smith, *Long-Lance: The True Story of An Impostor,* (Toronto, 1982). Contemporary films depend on one staple 'Indian' actor, Iron Eyes Cody, yet he, though married to a Navajo woman and enormously supportive of many Indian causes, is really of Mediterranean heritage.

57. In Feest, 1987, Rudolf Kaiser above; see also Ray H. Sandefur; Ed Seeber; Wilcomb Washburn on 'Logan's Speech' above; John Neihardt, 1971; Rothenburg; Gary Snyder.

58. William Least Heat Moon, *Blue Highways* (New York: Harper

and Row, 1984); Jamake Highwater, *The Primal Mind: Vision and Reality in Indian America* (New York: Harper and Row, 1981).

59. Carlos Casteneda, *The Teachings of Don Juan: A Yaqui Way of Knowledge* (New York: Simon and Schuster, 1969), and his succeeding volumes, *A Separate Reality: Further Conversations With Don Juan*, 1971; *Journey to Ixtlan* 1972; *Tales of Power*, 1974; Lynn Andrews, *Medicine Woman* (New York: Harper and Row, 1981); and *Spirit Woman, Jaguar Woman*, succeeding years.

60. References on Sun Bear, etc. *Akwesasne Notes* (Summer, 1987); 'Plastic Medicine Men' (Fall, 1987); 'Records of Councils Held by the Traditional Circle of Elders,' 4–6; Feest, 1987, 309–29.

61. See Peterson, 1981; Jennifer Brown, 1981.

62. See Vine Deloria Jr. *Custer Died For Your Sins* (New York: Avon Books, 1969) for references to such phenomena.

Rayna Green (Cherokee) is currently Director of the American Indian Program at the National Museum of American History, Smithsonian Institution. With a PhD in Folklore and American Studies from Indiana University, she has served on university faculties (Dartmouth, University of Massachusetts), in public service institutions (American Association for the Advancement of Science, the Smithsonian Institution), and on non-profit boards (Indian Law Resource Center, Ms. Foundation for Women). A writer with books (*That's What She Said: Contemporary Fiction and Poetry By Native American Women; Native American Women: A Contextual Bibliography*) and many essays on American Indians and American culture to her credit, she is also known for her work in museum exhibition, television and radio. In her dream life, she raises Westies on Wayna's Westie Wanch, is head chef at Bubba Sue's Bar and Grill, and chief writer for "Indian Saturday Night Live".

Catron Grieves

A MAN'S LUCK

MY NAME IS J.N. I am forty-three year old and have lived in the County all my life. Except when I had to go to Viet Nam or to the State Hospital up at Vineta. And I am a man who dranks now and then. They's no crime in that. A man's got to have somethin' to call his own.

I get drunk. I used to get real drunk and kick my wife, but that was ten years ago. Or was it fifteen. Anyways, she got tired and left me. Took my kid, too. My baby girl was nearly eight year old. A beautiful half-blood kid. Got all her Indian from me. None from her momma.

I am glad that woman left, though. She screamed and screeched at me night and day. I'd tell anybody, don't marry one of them white girls — you'll be sorry if you do. They don't have no respect for nothing. And I only kicked her now and then.

But a man's luck will change. I was sleeping with a girl down by Brushy, and she up and had a baby. Now her family — she never told me about the brother — was pleased to get the welfare check for the baby, but they done run me off. 'She's old enough to know her own mind,' I told myself. 'Hell, they ain't no woman a baby at fifteen year old.'

So, she and me took up again.

I was in town and getting real drunk. It was the twelfth of the month. And my disability check finally come from the V.A. Two days late. The money was gone like always. But I was feeling good.

The first thing I knowed, that brother I didn't know about was on me. Mad as hell. He was kicking me and hollering. Called me a bastard. I was drunk, and it felt better to just lay down. How was I to know he'd kick my head.

'Knocked up my sister again!' was the last I heard him say.

Epilepsy ain't that bad. But it bothers my momma. They give me pills for it at the State Hospital. But they can't give it strong cause my liver's getting swolled.

They said I was never to get drunk. The pills would turn to poison if I drink. But them pills don't work very good. And I get drunk once in a while just like always.

II

I always thought if I had been a better person, my dad could have had a better life. That somehow I could have helped him or changed things. My daddy was an alcoholic. When I grew up I talked my grandma into sending him up to the State Hospital. He went several times, but it didn't help him that much.

When he was in I got to know him better. We used to write. I have some of the letters. He couldn't write very well, but it meant a lot when I told him I was getting married, and he wrote back that he loved me and was happy for me. 'Seems like you'll do good,' he said. 'Marrying an educated man. When you went into town to school I hoped you'd marry good.'

I felt closer to him then. Not like when I was little and would hide from him when I saw him in town.

I told my grandma to leave him there, but she kept bringing him home. Every time, he'd get drunk first thing, and grandma would have to take him back.

I always wish that he could have come to my wedding. We

wrote about it, and he was going to help give me away. Him and my adopted dad — a dad on each arm.

Grandma brought him home for the wedding, but he got too drunk to come to the church. She had to take him back to the hospital in the morning before the ceremony.

He was really nice. I just wish it had been different. I'll never forget the time he saw me duck behind a car. I'll never forget the hurt look on his face — he just looked at me. I'll never forget. I never saw him after the wedding.

III

I am not a talker of English very good, so I had to say, 'I am J.N.'s momma' three times when I signed him into the hospital. It's only family can do it they say. But I took him out of the hospital when I saw it didn't do him no good. It was more like a prison than a hospital. It was too far from home to help my boy. So, I took him home to live with me and my husband.

The only thing I have is this old house and this woods. My allotment land. The government sends me two hundred-sixty dollars a month to live on. That's why I stay married. The men always buy the food, and I let them live with me. If one man don't work out I get another one. It used to bother J.N. when he was little, but he got used to it.

I never worked and got social security. That's for them white people and Indians that speak English. I can talk it some, but mostly I don't want to.

I forget what man was living with me the last time J.N. was home. But I had just throwed him out that morning, and was feeling mad. My boy must have felt one of them spells coming on, so he tells me, 'I'm going to the woods.' He's always been thoughtful. I don't like to see them fits, and he knows it.

IV

We don't get very many missing persons. Mostly kids run off to get married or city people drowned in the lake. The sheriff and me looked for that Indian two weeks. Off and on he always has been trouble. I never knew what my wife saw in him in the first place. But she's a do-gooder, and we all have to do one or two things to get forgiven for.

But I'm County Deputy, and my job says I got to look for missing persons even when I know they're just off drunk. I figured he'd got off down in the hollers and found a still and would get back home eventually. There's a lot of good people like to make their own mash up yet. I don't want to know nothing about it though. 'Just don't go too deep in the woods and never notice the smell of sour mash,' is my advice. I don't take no cuts, though. I am a deacon in my church, and I don't want no money from liquor. I just don't hold with that kind of thing. Besides the sheriff looks out after that end.

I had almost gave up on finding J.N. till he was ready. They'd had all the neighbors out looking for him more'n a week. And they'd not seen a thing. But my wife promised his momma I'd go look one more time. She is older than me and can be pushy when she wants something.

Anyway, I was out after morning church service in the four wheel drive instead of sitting down to my regular Sunday dinner. The wife had fixed me up with some fried egg sandwiches which I was eating as I went.

The clouds had been building for an hour or better. They looked as green as Easter basket stuff. If there's one thing I don't want, it's to be in the woods in a bad storm. There's a woodcutter's road through the woods, and I was hauling along pretty good when I hit a rotten old snag growed over with grass.

I figured I knocked a hole in my oil pan. So, I stepped out to look under the four-wheel, and that's when I saw him. He was off in the brush stretched out face down — like a man sleeping. He must have had one of them fits and hit his head.

I always say the Lord has a hand in it when a drunk dies sober.

Catron Grieves (Cherokee) has a M.A. in English and Creative Writing from Central State University, Edmond, Oklahoma. Now she is a graduate student at the University of Iowa in American Studies with interests in Native American Cultures, Literature and Cultural criticism. She also works as a poet in residence for the Iowa Arts Council. Her first book of poetry *Moonrising* was published by the Red Dirt Press in 1987. She was born in 1951 and raised on land settled by her family when they were relocated to Oklahoma during the Trail of Tears in the winter of 1838–39. Catron is trying to make sense of her cross-blooded

and traditional upbringing by writing her autobiography. She spent a lot of summer nights at Stomp Dances, is a high school dropout, and both her parents died under the care of Bureau of Indian Affairs hospitals and doctors for want of very basic medical treatment. She writes fiction and poetry, and teaches an occasional writing class. Presently, she is also collecting Native American oral autobiography and life histories of American Indian women. She lives with her fourteen year old daughter near Tahlequah, Oklahoma when she is not in Iowa City.

Raven Hail

CHEROKEE RELIGION

The Sun Goddess

TWO CHEROKEE WORDS, a-che'ra (fire) and a-gi' (she takes) are combined to designate The Cherokees as The People Who Carry The Divine Fire. The Sun gave a part of Herself to The People on earth in the form of fire.

The Sun—not the physical, visible sun moving across the sky, which had an entirely different name, but The Spirit Sun— was called Ghigau (pronounced geh'yuh). It is interesting to note here that the first Earth Mother Goddess in the mythology of the White-Eyes is named Gaea (geh'yuh?) or Gaia and that one of the environmental protection organizations of the present day is named for Her.

Ghigua (short for Agehyagugun) was translated into English variously as: The Beloved Woman, The Beautiful Woman, Ancient White, Ancient Red, Her Royal Highness, and Grandmother. It was often mis-translated, by missionaries and overzealous Christian men, as Grandfather. Also Sudalti (Sixkiller) has been mis-translated as The Spirit Sun. Such errors in the identity of The Sun and The Moon might be excused by the fact that the Cherokee language has a peculiar structure in the third person singular. Instead of the division into he (masculine), she (feminine), and it (neuter); the division is into animate, human (people, both masculine and feminine), and non-animate (neuter, like a stone).

Language usually reflects the thinking and culture of a people. It would appear that Cherokees (who did not domesticate and breed cattle, horses, sheep, chickens, etc.) were not particularly concerned with the he and she of it all. Not to be confused – I did not say that Cherokee people had no interest in sex – only that they were not overly concerned with the question of gender.

Since Fire was believed to be the manifestation on earth of The Sun, She (The Spirit Fire) always held the place of honor in the center of the Council House and also in the ceremonial dance ground out in the open. The Sun Goddess warned that The Fire must never be allowed to die. "So long as The Eternal Fire lives, as long will The People Live" is the ancient belief. This Fire still lives in the Eastern Cherokee lands, was carried along the Trail of Tears and also lives in the Western Cherokee lands.

Long, long ago, The Eternal Fire was entrusted to the keeping of a Priestess. The Priestesshood was to pass down through her to a daughter, for the Cherokees were matrilineal. They traced their ancestry through the feminine line only.

At the time of The Discovery of the Americas, the High Priestess of The Sun Goddess was the most powerful person in the Cherokee Nation. She was also called Ghigau, usually translated only as "Beloved Woman." This Beloved Woman was the "hot line" directly connected up through all of the Seven Heavens to The Almighty. Through her the wisdom of The Great Spirit was given to The People.

Another name given to the Sun Goddess by the Anthros was U-ne-hla-nv-hi, which is variously translated as The Creator, The Provider, and The Apportioner. "The Apportioner" more aptly describes the moon. When the New Testament of the Christian Bible was translated into Cherokee, by two Native

Cherokee speakers, the word U-ne-hla-nv-hi was used for the word "God."

In Genesis 2:27 it reads, "So God created man in His own image." To make a funny, I might suggest that those ancient Hebrews had the tail wagging the dog—they should have said, "So man created God in his own image."

DOUBLE TROUBLE

The Raven's Tale of the Ancient Astronauts

AHU'LI AND YAHU'LI were Twins. Everyone knew that they were fed only hominy soup and kept hidden from sight until after the first New Moon. And that their mother drank sumac tea. These were sure signs, they said, that the two would grow up to be witchs. Everyone was afraid of witches.

The Twins looked very much alike, except that one was a bow and the other a sifter. That is, Ahu'li was a boy and Yahu'li was a girl. They thought alike: often both said the same thing at the same time. They were inseparable companions. As soon as they were old enough, they were out roaming the countryside. They examined birds' nests and made friends with animals. Often they were gone from sunup to sunset. Sometimes they went out at night to hear the owls call and see the porcupines play.

One day Ahuy'l and Yahu'li were climbing among the rocks on the mountainside. It was the hour of sunset.

"I hear music," said Ahu'li.

"So do I," said Yahu'li.

"Shall we find out what it is?"

"Why not?"

And so they went looking. Suddenly, right before their eyes, appeared a Little Man. He was sitting high on a rock, dangling his legs over the edge. He was singing:

I come from the Red Star
  by way of the Red Lightning
    on the path of the Red Rainbow
I am The Beautiful
      Seven!

They stood quietly and listened, as the words were repeated over and over again.

When the song ended, the Little Man slid down from the rock and spoke to them. He already knew who they were, for he knew their thoughts. He knew they were looking for him. He invited them to dinner, and they accepted.

With the slightest touch of his hand, the Little Man pushed aside the rock, and behind it was the entrance to a cave. He went in and they followed. They came to a great cavern which appeared to be carved out of solid rock. It was bright as daylight and the air was cool and pleasant. There was a fire that burned without smoke, and an underground spring of clear, cold water. Many other Tsunsti, or Little People, were there, both men and women, but they were all the size of little children.

Dinner was almost ready. There was roasted deer and squirrel, corn and beans and squash. And cornbread, hot from the oven. There was hickory nut soup and wild grape juice to drink. All the bones from the deer went into one big basket and the squirrel bones into another. There was a basket for corncobs and one for bean hulls.

After dinner there was drumming and singing and dancing.

"How long have you lived here?" asked Ahu'li.

"For a long, long time — so many harvests that you could not begin to count them," answered the Little Man.

"Where did you come from?"

"From a distant land—far, far beyond the rising sun."

"Then how can you look just like one of us?" protested Yahu'li.

"I look like you expected me to look," the Little Man explained. "If you had been expecting something different, that's how I would have appeared to you. The food was what you expected to eat; otherwise you wouldn't have enjoyed it."

He went to one of the large baskets and took off the lid. A live deer jumped out. A squirrel hopped out of the second one. When they looked into the next basket, it was filled with corn!

"Ski-ghee'!" from Ahu'li.

"How did you do it?" asked Yahu'li.

"It comes from the power of thought," said the Little Man.

"Will you teach us? The two spoke as one.

"Anything in this world that you want to do, I will teach you how to accomplish it. To think it, is to cause it to be done."

"If it's that easy, why hasn't everybody learned? Have you told anyone else?"

The Little Man looked sad. "Who would listen? Nobody believes in miracles; they are only looking for magic!"

"We will listen," said the Twins.

"Then it must be tonight, for tomorrow we return to the land from whence we came."

All night long Ahu'li and Yahu'li listened and learned many wonderful things from the Little People, before they went away.

The Twins went home and continued living much as they had before. Only when they were alone, they sang the songs, chanted the chants, and danced the dances they had learned. And then some strange things happened. A widow there in the village found a freshly-killed deer at her doorway. An old couple went out one morning to find their corn crop had been gathered into the storehouse. A stolen horse mysteriously reappeared. The water in an abandoned spring started flowing again.

All the neighbors began to talk. They wondered who could harvest an entire corn field in a single night—without making any noise. For want of a better explanation, they thought of the Twins.

"Those two are surely witches," said one.

"Just as I expected," said another.

And soon everyone agreed that the Twins had supernatural

powers; they could take the form of animals or other humans at will. They could fly through the air or walk on a sunbeam. Whatever they wanted to be done, they had only to think it. Nothing could be kept a secret from them, for they could read one's every thought. And while others grew older as the years went by, Ahu'li and Yahu'li remained eternally young. At least that's what everybody said. It appeared that here was truly a miracle.

But The People only believed in witchcraft and magic.

NOTES

Ahu'li is the Cherokee name "The Drum" and Yahu'li is "The Drumstick" (made of hickory). Ski-ghee' is an expression of amazement, which might be translated as "Well, what do you know?" or "Fantastic!" "The Little People" are, of course, The Ancient Astronauts.

Raven Hail, Lecturer and Writer on American Indian Culture, was born on an oil lease north of Dewey (Washington County), Oklahoma, and lived on her mother's Cherokee Land Allotment near Welch (Craig County), Oklahoma, there going to school at West Anthracite and Prairie Center Elementary Schools. She attended Oklahoma State University, Stillwater, Oklahoma, and Southern Methodist University, Dallas, Texas.

On the roll of The Cherokee Nation of Oklahoma, and listed in *Ohoyo One Thousand*, Resource Guide of American Indian—Alaska Native Women.

Her poems and articles on Cherokee Indian Culture have appeared in

The Cherokee Advocate and *The Cherokee Nation News*, (Tahlequah, Okla-
homa), *Arizona Women's Voice*, *An American Indian Anthology*, *The
Clouds Threw This Light*, *The Remembered Earth*, *Poetry Dallas*, *The Texas
Anthology*, *The Blue Cloud Quarterly*, *Fiction International* (San Diego State
University), *Nimrod* (Tulsa University), *Cimmaron Review* (Oklahoma State
University), *Translation* (Columbia University), *The Little Balkans Review*,
The State (North Carolina), *The Archer* (Oregon), *Quetzal*, *Gray Day*, *Tosan*,
Indian Voice, *Daybreak*, *Lacuna*, *The Wayside Quarterly*, *The Herbalist*
(Utah), *The Herb Quarterly*, and *Bestways Magazine*.

Her record *The Raven Sings*: "A Cherokee Song" (Music for Turtle
Shakers) and "The Indian Christmas Carol" (vocal with guitar accompani-
ment) and her three-act play *The Raven and the Redbird* (the Indian Life of
Sam Houston and his Cherokee Wife) have been used in elementary schools
and universities in their American Indian Social Studies.

Geary Hobson

From
THE LITERATURE OF
INDIAN OKLAHOMA

A Brief History

THERE IS ANOTHER Oklahoma not immediately discernible to the traveler's eye scanning the Rand McNally atlas. Neither is it widely known even by most of the state's residents. This other Oklahoma, the original *Ogala-homma* ("the red people's land" in the Choctaw language), is the present-day homeland of approximately one-quarter of a million American Indian people from about forty federally recognized tribes (or nations, as most Indian people prefer to say). When the United States government, under President Andrew Jackson, made Indian removal its official policy in the first half of the nineteenth century, approximately sixty-eight Indian tribes and bands, numbering variously from sixty thousand to one hundred thousand, were forcibly relocated to the region "west of the Arkansas Line" and north of the Red River, which became known as Indian Territory. In 1907 that land, which was to remain Indian in its owner-ship for "as long as the waters run and the sun shall shine," became the State of Oklahoma. The Indian people had their parcels (which for the most part were soon lost to widespread theft and corruption) and were assumed by the U.S. government to be no longer Indians. However, matters did not work out quite like that. Indians, regardless of imposed land-tenure prac-tices and the government's bidding, remained Indians in the most important sense: namely, in their cultures.

Even before the removals, some of the tribes had already ventured far along on the "white man's road of acculturation" by adopting his legal and political systems and his educational, agricultural, and industrial institutions as well. Several emi-grant tribes from the Southern states had made such great strides in the white man's way that they (the Cherokees, Chick-asaws, Choctaws, Creeks, and Seminoles) were patted on their collective heads by paternalistic white Americans and called the "Five Civilized Tribes." The label persists even today, though now it is generally accorded that this says more about its users than about the people so designated. Be that as it may, these five tribes, and several others in Indian Territory/Oklahoma, have established at various times in the last 160 years more than sixty newspapers and presses, some of which utilize the native languages, and quite a body of literature has emerged.

Two years after the Cherokee Nation — for the most part still living in their traditional homeland east of the Mississippi River — had adopted the eighty-six-character Cherokee-language syllabary developed by Sequoyah (circa 1770–1843), a young tribal member later to be known as Elias Boudinot (circa 1804–39) published in Cherokee *Poor Sarah, or The Indian Woman* (1823). A later bilingual edition of the work, issued in 1833, carried the subtitle *or Religion Exemplified in the Life and Death of an Indian Woman*, which summarizes and identi-fies the content of the work as a tract for Christian conversion. *Poor Sarah* has been called by several scholars the first Ameri-can Indian novel, but due to the work's length (less than twenty pages) and its propagandizing element, it is by all accounts a religious tract set in an extremely artificial fictional mode. Boudinot is more widely known as the editor of the first Indian bilingual newspaper, the *Cherokee Phoenix* (flourished 1828–35) and for his political writings and translations of Christian gospels into Cherokee.

Tribal politics, Christian piety, and newspaper reportage, then, constitute the bulk of early-day Indian Territory literary efforts. The Choctaws, Chickasaws, and Creeks soon followed the Cherokees in publishing in the bilingual format. It was not until John Rollin Ridge (1827–67), Boudinot's nephew who often wrote under the name of Yellow Bird, published *The Life and Adventures of Joaquin Murieta, the Celebrated California Bandit* in 1854 that fiction made its debut in Indian Territory literature.[2] Called at first a biography, it is instead, most scholars now generally agree, a work of fiction. Ridge had left the Cherokee Nation for California during the Gold Rush of 1849. His literary output also included a book of verse, *Poems* (1868) — perhaps the first book of poetry to be published by an American Indian — as well as numerous journalistic and political articles written as the editor of several California newspapers. Two Creeks, Sophia Alice Callahan (1868–94) and Alexander L. Posey (1873–1908), produced the novel *Wynena: A Child of the Forest* (1891) and *The Poems of Alexander Lawrence Posey* (1910) respectively. Posey also wrote a series of satiric sketches, often in the form of "letters to the editor," for numerous Indian Territory newspapers under the pseudonym of Fus Fixico. These sketches were in the same vein of work as that produced by such American local-color humorists of the era as Bill Arp and Peter Finley Dunne. Never collected in a volume, the Fus Fixico letters deserve such preservation.

By the time Oklahoma had been a state for a quarter-century, Indian writing from the region often addressed a more generally American audience rather than specifically the state's Indian population. The great humorist Will Rogers (1879–1935), internationally famous as a vaudeville performer, movie actor, raconteur, and newspaper columnist, issued seven books in his lifetime. Although such titles as *The Cowboy Philosopher on the Peace Conference* (1919), *The Cowboy Philosopher on Prohibition* (1919), *Letters of a Self-Made Diplomat to His President* (1926), *There's Not a Bathing Suit in Russia* (1927), and *Ether and Me* (1929) do not on the surface appear to be "Indian," they nevertheless contain the kernels of an Indian humor often found in the Indian Territory newspapers widely available to Rogers during his Cherokee boyhood. Two other Cherokees, the novelist John M. Oskison (1874–1947) and the playwright Lynn Riggs (1899–1954), both friends and contemporaries of Rogers, wrote about the early days of Oklahoma in novels and plays often set on ranches and small farms. Though Riggs is more popularly known for *Green Grow the Lilacs* (1930), on which the Broadway musical *Oklahoma!* is based, his best play, and certainly his most "Indian" one, is *The Cherokee Night* (1933), a tragedy that is unfortunately little known. Oskison's three novels — *Wild Harvest* (1925), *Black Jack Davy* (1926), and *Brothers Three* (1935) — are good as local color for their time and place but appear very dated by today's standards.[3]

Cherokees were not the only Oklahoma Indians publishing fiction during this period. The Wyandot writer Hen-Toh (Bertrand N. O. Walker, 1870–1927) published *Tales of the Bark Lodges* (1919) and *Yoo-doo-shah-we-ah (Nubbins)* (1924), and the Osage novelist and historian John Joseph Mathews (1894–1979) produced *Sundown* (1930), *Wah'Kon-Tah* (1932), *Talking to the Moon* (1945), and *The Osages* (1961). All of Mathews's titles are maintained in print by the University of Oklahoma Press, a fitting tribute to this excellent writer. *Sundown*, with its theme of the mixed-blood protagonist within the context of a twentieth-century tribal milieu, prefigures more contemporary Indian novels such as N. Scott Momaday's *House Made of Dawn* (1968) and Leslie Marmon Silko's *Ceremony* (1977). As in these two novels, the protagonist in *Sundown* is a returned war veteran. *Talking to the Moon*, Mathews's philosophical reflections of a year spent in a hill cabin in the blackjack country of Osage County, has been called an Indian *Walden* by critics. It is in any case a truly overlooked American Indian literary classic.

Indian writing in Indian Territory/Oklahoma before 1968 was therefore concerned either peripherally with the tribal cultures of the writers (as with Rogers's, Oskison's, and Riggs's work addressed to the larger American audience) or was unabashedly romantic (as in the case of Callahan, Hen-Toh and Posey). Only Mathews seemed to write out of a strong sense of realism, which he combined with a genuine concern for his "Osage-ness" or Indian nationalist/traditionalist position, rather than disavowing or downplaying such matters, as earlier writers have been compelled to do. This was due, of course, to the times in which these authors wrote. From 1887 (the inception of the Dawes Severalty Act),4* to 1934 (the passage of the Indian Reorganization Act),⁵ Indian people underwent assaults on their cultural fabric that in retrospect seem just short of genocide. It is therefore not surprising that the best and the brightest literary lights of the tribes in Oklahoma at the time would mirror their awareness of the passing of their cultures and even of their race. "The Era of the Vanishing American" still prevailed. Nevertheless, although a Rogers or an Oskison could still write out of a sense of his Americanness, there is yet present in the work of each a strong, unmitigated pride in his Indian roots.

NOTES

¹The original Cherokee syllabary has undergone several modifications, some versions of it utilizing as few as eighty-five characters, others up to ninety-two characters. Cherokee is still a vibrant, thriving language in eastern Oklahoma. Contemporary native speakers such as Durbin Feeling, Adeline Smith, and Agnes Cowan continue to issue bilingual publications. Feeling has compiled several studies of Cherokee linguistics and at present is engaged in adapting a new version of the Cherokee syllabary to several models of computers and word processors. Several other Oklahoma Indian languages have tribal members who are similarly engaged.

²Joaquín Murieta (circa 1830–53), the Mexican bandit, has been the subject of numerous popular novels — so much so that it is virtually impossible to extricate the real Murieta from the legendary one, a process of apotheosis to which Ridge's book has been no small contributor. Of fairly recent date, Pablo Neruda, in *Fulgor y muerte de Joaquín Mureita* (1967), transforms the bandit into a Chilean, for which he claimed to have proof.

³The best source regarding early-day American Indian publishing and writing, particularly that of Oklahoma Indians, is *A Bibliography of Native American Writers, 1772–1924*, compiled by Daniel F. Littlefield Jr. and James W. Parins and published in 1981.

⁴The Dawes Severalty Act of 8 February 1887 — or the Allotment Act, as it is sometimes called — was one of America's more ambitious attempts to bring the Indian into the American way of life. Tribal landholding, communal by nature, was anathema to Americans, for whom individual land tenure was nothing short of gospel. All the

elected tribal leaders of Oklahoma tribes were adamantly opposed to the Allotment Act and to the termination of tribal governments it entailed, and they likewise expressed the consensus of the tribes' memberships. Needless to say, the American government felt it knew what was best for the Indian people, and the act became law.

The Indian Reorganization Act, also known as the Wheeler-Howard Act, was primarily the work of the Commissioner of Indian Affairs, John Collier, during the first term of President Franklin D. Roosevelt. Just as Roosevelt felt that America needed a New Deal, so Collie felt that Indian people were due one as well. The IRA represented a dramatic effort by the government to undo the catastrophic damage of the Dawes Severalty Act. In less than fifty years under the Dawes era Indian people nationwide had lost well over one hundred million acres of land through abuses in the allotment system. Native religions and languages were dealt irreparable damage in many areas throughout the country during this time. Many aspects of the IRA as originally envisioned by Collier have yet to be fully implemented; but the general impression of Indian people is that the act has been immensely beneficial, and Oklahoma Indians especially regard it so.

THE ODOR OF DEAD FISH

SOMETIME AFTER MIDNIGHT, two hours or so after the movie had ended, Frank Lawson was still walking the dark rainswept street of Oceanside which were now all but deserted. The shuttlebus, which would take him back to the base and to another week of Marine Corps duty, wasn't due to arrive until three-thirty, but he didn't care to spend the time waiting in the bus station. When he had gone to the station after the movie, he had found it crowded with Marines, young men like himself on weekend liberty and dreading going back to the base after their short tenures of freedom in the civilian world. Feeling the need for solitude, a feeling the depths of which he was certain was particular only to himself, Frank wanted to spend the remaining time alone in the town, as though to squeeze a last drop of desperate privacy from the fleeting holiday.

Oceanside is a beach town, huddled like a large parasite near the main gate and on the seafront border of Camp Pendleton. Its economy was based on the Marines who flocked in on liberty to wander aimlessly through the streets and bars and movie-houses, getting fleeced by the local merchants. There was no love lost between town and jarheads: at one time, Frank had heard, there used to be a sign on the City Hall lawn which proclaimed MARINES AND DOGS KEEP OFF THE GRASS. The sign had been removed, but not the sentiments it had contained. In the winter, seawinds sometimes slash and buffet the Oceanside coastline like a wrathful Dark Night of the Soul, their wind-driven sand, salt, and seawater wreaking an impervious and indifferent vengeance on the town and the land — except for when the sun shone, which seemed to be always. The sun made its mark, too, plying an equally indifferent judgement on the coast and probably caring even less about its consequences than the winter seawinds.

Frank was eighteen, but there were already lines of a perpetual sardonic scowl beginning to etch into the ordinarily inquisitive and expectant expression of his features. He had been in the Marines about six months and still retained something of the curious aura of naivete common to most boot privates, but a baffled anger, imposed by days of frustrating duty and organized stupidity, had started to take its toll on him.

As Frank walked along Hill Street, a few blocks from the ocean front, the December wind chilled him with thin sprays of rain and salt water. Drops of water matted in his crew-cut and trailed in rivulets down his face and into his shirt collar. The cold penetrated his thin rayon jacket with the glazed sharpness of frozen needles.

The streets were black and shiny, as though lacquered, from the night's alternating squalls of rain and sea-mist. Along the sidewalks gutter water glistened like oil, reflecting the neon lights of the stores and bars. Illumined titles — "Fisherman's Inn," "The Cozy Cove," "Tattoos — All Kinds," "Pete's," glared dully in the street.

He realized he was hungry. He had to think for a moment before remembering that he hadn't eaten since noon and then only a hamburger. Now, trying to recall the names of the films he had just seen, he found he couldn't remember them. He had sat through the double feature twice, allowing the hours to slip by, being by turns both interested and indifferent to the crap reeled forth on the screen. He knew he had been wasting time, but in the Crotch, as he had discovered, any effort of trying not to waste time was like hurrying through one long and tedious boredom only to arrive at the next. Besides feeling breathless and weary with the "hurry-up-and-wait" way of life, you felt cheated by it and soon you were almost unable to care anymore how you played the game.

Strong on the breeze of the seawind, a particularly rancid order of dead fish from somewhere down on the beach pervaded the streets like a black plague. It was an insistent smell, almost nauseating, and its scent had been there ever since Frank had been on the streets – and probably before that. It seemed to be growing even more pungent as the night wore on. A smell of tar and oil from fishing boats anchored at the pier mingled in the wind, but the rotten fish stench was stronger, easily superimposing itself over the other. Despite the smell, Frank was still hungry. All the restaurants were closed and there didn't seem to be any place to go. Except the bars. But most of them seemed to be closing, too. Anyway, being underage made him reluctant to try the hassle of ordering a sandwich. Besides, he was nearly broke.

As he walked along, he began to feel loneliness, something he had been able to ignore for the past few weeks. Now it began to rise again within himself like something rebellious and distasteful. He knew it was dangerous to indulge in this feeling. He had felt its tentacles of unrest before and he knew that it touched a dark well of lonesomeness and also a darker chasm of spiritual despair. So he chose to ignore its cold voice with a stoical bravado. He began to wish that he might meet a woman, lonely like himself, who would suddenly appear from one of the doorways seeking his assistance, perhaps to ask him for a match to light her cigarette, or directions to the bus depot, anything. The conversation could go on from there. Or maybe he might meet another kind of woman – he made this great moral distinction between the types of the sex – one of the sort that hang around bars and hotels, looking for men. If he should meet one of this kind, he wasn't sure if he would do what was expected of him, as Sloan and Jennings and the guys back at the barracks would do. They always talked about the women they had met under such similar circumstances. The possibility of such a meeting spurred him momentarily, and he felt his blood beginning to race. He brushed his hand over his crew-cut with a quick, self-conscious gesture and straightened his shoulders, as though making himself presentable should he meet her, this formidable lady of the night.

Then, as quickly as it came, his mood of expectancy melted away into loneliness again when he remembered Becky, his old girlfriend back home who had written him the Dear John two months before. For a moment he thought about home and his enlistment and how it all had brought him to California and now would soon be taking him to the Far East for a long tour of duty. Well, no use worrying about that now. That's over with. Gone and done with. He spat on the sidewalk.

He came to a USO establishment and stopped at the entrance. You could always get some coffee and sandwiches at these places, he knew, but he tried to decide whether or not to go in. He disliked going into USOs and Salvation Army halls because of the church-like atmosphere and the prayer meetings that were served along with the coffee and food. He particularly dreaded getting cornered by some old biddy about the importance of having his soul saved.

The wind was getting colder and the mist for all its heaviness could have been a constant downpour—the dampness had seeped through his jacket. Standing at the doorway, still deliberating, he listened to the faint wail of a juke-box coming from one of the bars up the street, barely discernable in the swelling road of wind and ocean-tide. Then, strangely enough, he could hear his intestines growling. Sounds like someone dragging a log chain across a board floor, he thought, remembering this as one of his father's favorite sayings.

A sudden gust of wind overturned a trash can. It clattered loudly in the alley as the junk and paper spilled at random. Up the street, a man and woman in heavy overcoats walked arm in arm. They looked around quickly at the noise and then at Frank, probably wondering if he had something to do with it. They hurried on and ducked in "The Cozy Cove." A scrap of newspaper went fluttering by in the wind; it was blown up an alley and lost from sight. Frank turned back to the doorway.

"Oh, what the hell," he said, opening the door and going in. Inside, the dimly lit foyer was crowded by wide stairs which faced the door. A large arrow-shaped USO sign pointed upward along the stairs. His footsteps clumped loudly on the wooden steps. The USO door was half-glass and half-wood and the frosted glass had been painted over with "Welcome GIs" in a crude effort to hide a former shoestring law office sign.

The place was lit up. At one end of the main serving-counter a group of homeless Marines and volunteer saints – mostly old women and one or two old men – sat in a cluster on metal folding chairs, chatting pleasantly. Several other people were grouped around an upright piano that was black and worn with age. They had just finished a song. Racks of religious pamphlets stood along the walls.

Frank wiped the dampness from his face and sat down at the counter. He watched the people at the piano as they began to sing another hymn. A gray-haired woman in a plaid dress was at the piano and a Marine corporal in uniform played an accordion. Most of the other Marines were in civies. The waitress, a slender young woman wearing horn-rimmed glasses, came over to serve him.

"Hi. May I help you?" she said, smiling at him.

"Yes, Ma'am. I'd like one of those ham sandwiches and a cup of coffee.'

"Coming right up." She got the sandwich and then turned to fill a cup from the urn. Frank watched her, allowing his eyes and thoughts to focus on her shapely hips. Not bad, he thought as interest kindled in him. She turned suddenly – too suddenly. He blushed thinking she knew what he was thinking.

"Here you are," said said cheerfully, unaware of his transgression. She moved away to clean the counter.

He made a mental note to check her hand for a wedding ring when she came by the next time. The sandwich was dry and sawdusty, almost lacking flavor, and the coffee was strong and bitter, even with cream and sugar. He watched the waitress for a while, now and then looking over at the group of singers. The hymn grew louder as the people at the end of the counter joined in.

". . . Though like the wanderer, the sun gone down,
Darkness be over me, my rest a stone,
Yet in my dreams I'd be, Nearer, My God, to thee,
Nearer, My God, to thee, Nearer, to thee . . ."

Frank finished his sandwich and coffee. The hymn came to an end and everyone smiled, pleased with themselves.

"Oh, how wonderful, Corporate Stevens. How truly wonderful!" one of the women, an old lady wearing a long string of pearls, was saying to the Marine who had played the accordion. He was a tall, gangling boy with a pimply complexion. He grinned proudly at the compliment.

While Frank listened to the group praising the tall Corporal, he didn't notice the old man who had sat down on the stool next to him.

"Iss not Corbal Steffens' playing vondeful?" the old man said.

"Oh, yeah. Yeah, I guess it is," Frank said, somewhat startled at seeing the old man sitting next to him. The old man was bald and redfaced and he had a kind smile. He was seedy-looking; he wore loose-fitting trousers and an old corduroy jacket, shiny at the elbows. Gray bristles of beard dotted his face.

"I nefer see you here before. You Marine like dees boys here?"

"Yes, sir," Frank said. He wondered where the old man came from.

"Vondeful. Like to see you boys come here," the old man said, smiling. "Grace, brink de younk fellow more coffee," he said to the waitress.

The waitress came over and refilled his cup. Frank saw there was no ring on her left hand. He smiled at her and she returned it. Just as he was about to say thanks to her, the old man asked him a question, which Frank didn't hear, and the waitress moved down the counter aisle toward the hymn singers. The old man repeated his question.

"I ast: are you a Chreestain?"

Here it was—the question. Now here comes the sermon, Frank thought. He began to feel uncomfortable, wishing to run out of the place, but not wanting to offend the old man with a rebuff. He had expected this, but the directness of the old man's question had nevertheless caught him off guard.

"I don't know. I guess so," Frank said.

"You guess so?" Don't you know?"

"I mean. I guess I am."

"Haf you accepted dar lort Jesus Christ as your personal Safior?"

"I was baptized once, if that's what you mean." Frank could feel himself resenting the old man's questions, resting his air of obsequious benevolence, as though he, Frank, were the prize customer of some crackerjack car salesman.

"Ven vas you baptize'?"

"When I was thirteen years old."

"You Prodastan', den?"

"I guess you could say that," Frank hoped this would end the discussion, but it didn't. The old man seemed to be just getting started.

"Do you still go to church now dat you in da serfice?"

"I go to church sometimes, but I guess that doesn't mean very much – I mean, just to go . . ." He remembered the Sunday mornings in boot camp and ITR when chapel services became the only real haven for anyone who wanted to get away from the yelling and bullying of the drill instructors and platoon leaders. There, at least, you could have a couple of hours of silence, except for the sermons of the chaplain, but these never seemed to intrude upon your thoughts of home, of the woods and the river, and family.

"You know, eferbody's gotta face Jesus sometime." The old man's eyes were looking intently at Frank. "Vy don' ve go inta von of da odder rooms to pray?" The suddenness of the suggestion surprised Frank. He looked down quickly at his hands to avoid the old man's gaze.

"No, sir, I guess I ought not to," Frank said. He wished he could be firm, but he didn't want to hurt the old man's feelings.

"Vy not? It do you good."

"No, sir – I mean, maybe in a little while, but . . ."

An awkward silence fell over them. Frank stared at the empty coffee cup in his hands. The old man regarded his closely, then said: "You Indian boy, iss you not?"

"Yes, sir. I'm Cherokee," Frank said, looking up to see what the old man's reaction would be.

"Vell, now, Jesus haf room for all Indian people, too. He iss da savior for eferbody." The old man sat back on the stool and spread his arm. "Ah, da vonders of Chreestianity! To t'ink dat it could grow into diss." He gestured his arms as if to indicate the room around him. "You know, ven da early Chreestins in Rome vent looking for each odder, dey hat no USO to go to. Dey hat to be careful. Dey vut draw pictures of fish in da dirt as a sign to each odder. But ven da soldiers of Caesar fount dem, dey vas kill't like dogs. Dey hat to be fery careful. Now, it's da Chreestians dat go after da soldiers!" He laughed as he pointed a bony, emphatic finger at Frank.

While the old man laughed, Frank looked back over at the singers. They had started another song and seemed to be enjoying themselves. The waitress, Grace, moved by quickly, her hands filled with dirty cups and saucers. Suddenly, the old man stopped laughing and looked closely at Frank as he had done before.

"Vat iss your name, younk fellow?"

Frank told him his name. The old man said he was glad to meet him and introduced himself as Mr. Paulsen. Frank said he was glad to meet Mr. Paulsen and began to feel more nervous and shy, as he always did when strangers sought him out. Mr. Paulsen said he was from Switzerland and had come to America during the Second World War. He had been a sinner for years, he said, but now he knew Christ and he had dedicated his life to spreading the word of the Savior. He talked about his work at the USO and his affection for young men such as Frank.

Suddenly, Mr. Paulsen said: "Haf you t'ought about vat vut happen iff you die tomorrow, Frank?"

Fidgeting nervously, Frank felt a moment of wildness, of carelessness. He felt like saying "Why, shit yes, I've thought about dying. Hasn't everyone?" But he was embarrassed when he thought the old man might know that he was mentally saying the word "shit." Then he thought of saying that if he died the next day then he wouldn't have to go on guard duty, or that he wouldn't have to go overseas next month and maybe get his ass shot off, that his military obligation would be up — some kind of joke that would relieve the tension he was feeling. Instead, he said: "Yes, sir. Sometimes."

"Haf you teclar't youself on da Lort's side? Are you really sure you vill be safed ven da time comms to answer da Lort?"

"No, sir. No, I'm not sure."

"Haf you t'ought aboud it much ladely?"

"Not much," said Frank. He remembered his Aunt Dinah and

her imaginative description of what happened to unrepentant sinners after death, and he saw himself as one of them—writhing in everlasting hell-fire.

"You know, der's always time to safe yourself," Mr. Paulsen said, his face filled with seriousness.

"Yes."

"Do you vant to go inta vun of da odder rooms now vere ve can pray? Perhaps I can show da vay to salfation."

Frank could feel himself getting trapped into something in which he didn't wish to become involved. Mr. Paulsen was beginning to probe that inner reservoir of darkness and doubt that he wished to keep buried within himself—at least for the time being. It was doubt not so much of a religious nature, but rather one of having to think seriously about any matter that might involve deep thought. Having tried—and failed—to set forth his mind of matters of God and death before his enlistment, he preferred leaving things alone. Since he might soon die with a gun in his hands, then why should he waste his time thinking about it. He thought of getting up and leaving, then he found himself looking at the waitress once again and he felt guilty. Suddenly, he seemed unclean to himself, hating himself for thinking of sex and religion at the same time. He thought, yes, with the way I think and act I need to be saved. He looked at Mr. Paulsen and the old man's eyes were glaring at him with such naked pleading that Frank had to look away. If the old man feels this strongly about the souls of others, then he must know something about it all that I didn't know, Frank thought.

"All right," he said.

"Dis vay," Mr. Paulsen said, a little too eagerly, and he pointed to a door at the left of the counter.

Frank followed him into the next room, a small and drab cubicle containing only two chairs, a table, and a small gasoline stove for furniture. Clothing hooks, spaced at ten-inch intervals, were bored into the walls. The room was lit by a single bulb hanging from the center of the ceiling, glaring nakedly at the end of a cord. Except for the small cheap paintings of Christ which hung on the wall above the table, the room reminded Frank of the cloakroom where he used to get whippings from the teacher back at the elementary school he had attended as a child.

He stood awkwardly by the table while Mr. Paulsen, kneeling and striking matches, tried to light the stove. The flame would not catch, and after a few attempts, the old man gave up.

"Ve nefer mind aboud da stofe. Ve don' neet it sinz ve haf de flame of Gott vit us,' he said, rising and smiling, holding in his hand a small pocket-sized New Testament which Frank hadn't noticed before.

"First, ve kneel and pray."

They knelt by the chairs and the old man prayed aloud. It was a prayer that Frank, the wayward one, might find himself here tonight and rededicate himself to the truth of the Lord Jesus Christ. When the prayer was over, Frank rose to his feet and the metal dog-tags beneath his shirt clinked together, like the prayer beads of a confused penitent.

"Now, I will read to you from da Holy Screeptures, vich vill show da vay to salfation."

Frank nodded, slightly embarrassed. He had expected they would talk, and he would ask Mr. Paulsen questions and that Mr. Paulsen would answer them for him, explaining that which he didn't understand. He didn't expect to be read to, and particularly, to have read to him verses he'd heard many times before as a child and still couldn't believe. The old man thumbed through the Bible and came to a marked passage.

"Ah – John t'ree-sixteen: 'For Gott so loffed da Vorlt dat He gafe Hiss only begotten Son, dat whosoefer belief-it in Him shoult not perish, but haf everlasting life!' You see, Frank, you see?" Mr. Paulsen's eyes shone triumphantly as he finished reading the verse.

"Yes, I guess so." Frank was looking down at his hands. He felt empty and without purpose, as if incapable of any sort of self-assertion.

"Vat you mean you guess so?' Don' you belief vat da Holy Vordt says? Don' you see dat dis iss da lort Jesus speaking to you?"

"I think so. You're probably right. But I don't know . . ." His voice trailed off and he shrugged his shoulders.

"You t'ink so! I *am* right!" He placed his hand on Frank's knee, grasping it. Frank looked up thinking for a moment that *this* was what the old man had in mind all along, getting him in the room like this. Frank felt a swift rush of disgust and anger, and just as quickly, as though completely oblivious of his offense, Mr. Paulsen dropped his hand and began thumbing once again through the tiny Bible. Frank felt ashamed of his thoughts.

"Yes, sir," Frank said, almost inaudibly. Old thoughts suddenly came to him: rural Arkansas in summertime, the Wednesday night prayer meetings, the Bible school sessions, the country revivals, countless other church socials which had been a part of his growing up—all as great sales-pitches to convert sinners to the way, all as near-frantic efforts to herd them to Jesus—as if those Indian-blooded people might backslide into a paganism that was really long lost to most of them. He remembered, among many things, an incident which had occurred while he was in boot camp, a couple of months before: a fellow private, whom Frank had known quite well, had gotten a discharge from the Marines after having passed himself off as a conscientious objector—even when Frank and the other men had known the claim was a lie—just so the man could get out of the service.

"Now dis prayer—haf you efer t'ought aboud vat da vordts mean for each of us?"

"Yes, sir. I've thought about it. I used to think about it a lot. But I can't believe in something just because it's in a book," Frank said nervously and was shocked to realize what he'd said.

"Vat! Dis iss not chust a book! Dis iss da Holy Bible!"

Now I've made him mad at me. Why the heck did I have to come here anyway? He looked at the door and clasped his hands tighter. Mr. Paulsen sensed his thoughts of flight.

"Vait! Dis time I read da prayer to you fery slowly, and you lissen to it, and t'ink of va da vordts mean. Den ve vill say it togedder."

Frank listened as Mr. Paulsen began reading again. There were things Frank wanted to ask about, to learn, so that he could believe as Mr. Paulsen wanted him to believe, but he couldn't. He was thinking of how it seemed that nothing is for certain and of how impossible it is to believe in something you aren't sure about, even if others were convinced of its truth. He tried to listen to the words as Mr. Paulsen read them, but he couldn't concentrate. His thoughts at first found no pattern. They were wild, surging thoughts, ranging from Heaven to Hell, from God to Satan, from Judgment to Salvation—or rather, they were a series of pictures, taken mostly from his memory of Biblical pictures he'd seen all his life, and were all the things the human imagination has yet composed of that black, fiery unknown void that was called Hell, of that bright, golden airiness filled with plumb, baby-like angels with silly pious looks that was known as Heaven. The old man's foreign-accented litany had become a drone. It seemed to Frank that everything was coming up against him—the night, the town, the old man himself. Frank's thoughts came to him like apocalyptic horsemen, riding roughshod and in absurd order. Then he remembered a time two years before . . .

. . . The Sunday School class was over. He and a dozen other teenagers walked out of the intermediate classroom into the church. The minister would begin his sermon in a few minutes. Someone called him.

Frank, can I talk to you for a minute?

Sure, Mr. Brantly.

You wasn't at church last Sunday or the Sunday before that either.

Yes, sir. I was —

The reason I called for you to come over here was this: I don't know how say it, but I heard that you been attending Catholic services in McAnnis with that Louisiana kid Bobby Orillion. That ain't true, is it? Somebody just talking, to be talking?

Yes, sir. It's true.

It is? Frank, you know that the Catholic faith ain't like the Baptist. You got your church and they got theirs. What do you want to go to the Catholic church for?

I wanted to see what Bobby's church is like.

But, Frank, that ain't right. As a Baptist, you got an obligation to your own church!

Why ain't it right, Mr. Brantly?

Well, because—because the Baptist faith is the only way to God. Why do you think the Protestant church broke away from the Catholic church? Because we saw that the Catholics was wrong, that's why.

I don't see it that way, Mr. Brantly.

Why not! It's—this is the right way!

I'll have to find that out for myself.

You're acting like a fool, Frank. Now go get a seat and let's forget all this nonsense about going to Catholic churches, you hear?

Yeah, I hear you, Mr. Brantley.

Good. Now, let's get a seat. Brother Mason is getting ready to preach. Frank — Boy, where're you going? Frank? Come back here, boy!

Frank Lawson closed the church door behind him and ran down the steps into the nearby woods . . .

Mr. Paulsen's face had a look of strained benevolence as he read. Perspiration formed in beads on his forehead. He was reading faster now, stumbling over the words. Frank watched a large drop of sweat form on the end of Mr. Paulsen's nose and then fall with a wet splat onto the Bible. As Mr. Paulsen groped for words, Frank began to feel sorry for him. He wished he could put the words into Mr Paulsen's mouth, the words the old man desperately needed to say to him to convince him. But what were the words?

"You see, you see? Does dis not proof dat Christ has died for us? Does dis not proof dat His vay iss da only vay?"

Frank felt a great dread at having to speak now. He wished more than ever for it to be over.

"No," he said.

"Vat!" Mr. Paulsen said, gesturing wildly. "You still don' see da trood of da Holy deaching yet?"

"No, I don't."

"Comm! Ve pray again."

They knelt again and prayed. This time the prayer was longer, and although Frank's knees were getting tried, he didn't notice it. He was thinking now of his rejection of Mr. Paulsen's words. He was suddenly jolted at the thought of nothingness, as it came to him now, so vast and unknowable. I'm going to Hell. I don't know if there is a Hell. God will probably strike me dead tonight for not redeeming myself in His eyes. When I walk out of this USO building, He'll probably strike me dead. But, God, I'm sorry . . . If there is a God. Why can't I believe in these words? Why can't the words have some kind of meaning for me? Did they ever have any meaning?

The prayer was over. Mr. Paulsen was sweating profusely. He tried to sound enthusiastic, but Frank could see the old man's defeat and disappointment as they sat down again. Frank felt a desperate empathy for the old man and was embarrassed by it. He considered, for a moment, that he could allow the old man to convert him since Mr. Paulsen seemed to be more defeated than he was. He felt as though he were on some high, bare wall, looking at the voids on either side, having to make a choice as to which abyss to jump into. He wouldn't choose a side now, and that, he knew, the decision of not choosing was in itself a choice. He knew the matter wasn't settled and probably never would be settled. In his half-awareness he knew he must live with what he'd now made for himself.

"Frank, don' you see? Da Lort Jesus is calling you to safe yourself. He forgiffs all. Remember dat dere are no at'eists in foxholes. You vill need Jesus. He *needs* you. Remember da Screeptures dat say a man vill be forgiffen sefenty times sefen times for all his sins iff he but repent dem?"

Frank nodded and the old man thumbed through the Bible once again. He read more Scriptures: Romans three-twenty-three, about everyone having sinned and coming short of God's glory; Romans nine-ten, and parts of Matthew, Luke, and Psalms. Frank listened, he felt calmer than he had felt in a long time. After awhile, he said it was time to be leaving, and rising, he looked at the old man and once again felt for him a deep, yet remote, urge of brotherhood. Frank could almost feel the old man's gaze on him.

"I'm sorry, Mr. Paulsen," Frank said, and was immediately beset by doubt and confusion again. In the brief moments they stood regarding one another, Frank found himself being frightened with fleeting thoughts of no afterlife, and then he would feel a momentary defiance at all those unknown and unknowable laws. It was as if he had been beaten all his life by overpowering forces, so that now, standing with his back against an invisible wall of his construction, he was not fighting blindly, resolutely. But he *was* fighting, and he knew that that was all that counted.

"Goot-bye. You comm again next Sunday night and ve vill talk some more. You vill comm, von' you?"

"Yes, sir, I'll be here," Frank lied.

"You comm den and you vill find da vay to Gott."

"Yes, sir. Good-bye, sir."

"Goot-bye, younk fellow. And Gott bless you."

Frank opened the door and walked into the hall. The singers were gone and the place was empty except for Grace, who was cleaning up behind the counter. Frank walked toward the main door, but almost as an afterthought he stopped and watched her as she wiped the counter. She smiled at him, warm and friendly. He smiled back.

"I want to thank you for the sandwiches and coffee."

"You're welcome. You haven't missed your bus, have you?"

"That's okay. They run every three hours. There ought to be one out there about now."

"Good. You'll come again, won't you?"

He nodded and they said goodbye. He stepped into the street, feeling tired and sleepy. He needed to piss, thought about going into the alley, but decided against it. It was colder now, the wind had died down and fog had settled like smoke over the streets. Eastward of the ocean-front, the pale gray light of false-dawn lay in a tiny strip, like a silken ribbon, above the ill-defined hills. The smell of dead fish, as old as the night, still hung heavily in the foggy air. Frank hurried along the street to the bus stop. The bus was waiting, the motor idling in a low diesel growl.

Later, as the bus sped along the highway through the hills toward Camp Pendleton, leaving Oceanside behind, Frank, half asleep, suddenly remembered that God hadn't struck him dead when he walked out of the USO into the street.

Geary Hobson (Cherokee-Quapaw/Chickasaw) was born in Chicot county, Arkansas, in 1941. He is Cherokee and English on his father's side and Quapaw (with French and Chickasaw mixed in) on his mother's side. He identifies more with both Arkansas groups of Quapaws and Cherokees than with the Oklahoma branches of the tribes. Served in U.S. Marines in 1960's; attended Arizona State University and received B.A. and M.A., and later Ph.D. from University of New Mexico. Currently, an Associate Professor of English at the University of Oklahoma.

He published *The Remembered Earth* in 1979 and *Deer Hunting and Other Poems* in 1990. He has three other completed books, but is too busy and gun-shy to deal with publishers at the present time.

Cynthia Kasee

TO MY NEW AGE "SISTERS" AND "BROTHERS"

PLEASE DON'T invite me to any more "New Moon Ceremonies." I cannot look the other way anymore when you try to tell me about my own Ancestors' religion. Please do not offer to let me attend a "smudging" with sage or sweetgrass or whatever and then explain to me how it's a sacred ritual for *all* Native Americans. Please don't ask me anymore to tell you about things *I* saw on *my* Vision Quest, because we don't all do that . . . remember how you laughed with me at your childhood myths about all Indians living in tipis and hunting buffalo? Think about how you said it was good that you didn't have any stereotypes about Indians now.

At first, when you came to me with these stories of having gone to a sweat lodge and purified yourself, I thought that you might have found one of the Old Ones who was willing to let sincere people of all backgrounds share in the beauty of an ancient faith. Perhaps not *our* ancient faith, but an aboriginal tradition, none the less. At *first*. When I later found out that you paid for your sweat with a Visa card, I was astonished that an Old One would do that. Then I was embarassed for you that you had been deceived by someone I had always said was a person to be trusted. Then I felt embarassed for my people, because I realized you thought this was OK with us, the way that Elders always passed traditions on.

I tried to tell you, in the gentlest possible terms, that you might just have run across a person who was unethical, or playing a trick on you to see if you were sincere, or some other excuse. Imagine my surprise when you began to tell me that I was the one who had no knowledge. In the gentlest possible terms, you told me that your "Spiritual Grandfather" (or some other metaphysical name) had warned you that "urban Indians" like me had no tie to our traditions and we're no more informed about Indian faith than you were. Or maybe it was the line about the Cherokee (they *never* use our name for our people, although they strive to make you use their correct tribal names) being just "red white men," people who became like Europeans a long time ago and therefore have no right to speak our prayers to a non-Christian God.

But we had been friends for so long, that I tried to ignore these words. You were the same person I had shared memories of stomp dances and Fall Festivals with, so I figured your heart was still friendly towards me. I know though that I have changed. I no longer tell you my dreams, for fear you'll explain the symbolism to me in your newfound code words. I let you in my world only so far as the mundane (job, family, neighbors, the latest movie I saw) goes, for fear you'll tell me I'm not "centered" or "empowered" or some other pop-psych ailment. I have begun to tell you more about the Christian upbringing I received, to see how you will respond to an alien in *your* territory.

You bet I've seen and felt things that would make the hair on the back of your neck stand on end. You bet things have happened to me without my bidding that scared the hell out of me. You bet I have felt touched by those that went before when I was in certain places, and you would have felt touched by them, too at an earlier time when you weren't looking for them so hard. I *have* known many moments of transcendent peace near these places and I did not have to fast and "cry for a vision" to do so.

Fast? How many times have I felt that special unity with my people and my God when we were feasting?

I do not tell you about these things, because if I do, they'll end up being retold by you as *your* experiences at the next Crystal Conference held at Chaco Canyon. And I do not go to those conferences with you because, aside from being saddened at the cooptation of our faiths, I never know how to act when I'm introduced with my seemingly Irish surname to your Euro-American friends with names like "Star Woman," "Medicine Eagle," and "Shadow Dancer."

This isn't to say that all you've been taught is wrong. Some of it *is* ancient, but in the old days, people didn't learn these things without years of study and symbolic payment was about all that changed hands. And some people who weren't Indians (I'm trying to get away from that cumbersome "non-Indians" word . . . you and I both know what I'm saying, don't we?) did believe in our ways from the times of early white settlement. Friend, I hate to say that you are not yet one of these. While I still care about you, I cannot deny that you have made me distrust my Elders, thinking one of them may be the next one to "syndicate." You have made me distrust words that I thought I understood the meanings of: "spiritual" . . . "traditional" . . . "visionary." You have made me wonder whether I have become less than my Ancestors would want, because you seem so much more *Indian* than I am!

I hope the time comes when you don't try to convince me that my people came from Atlantis. It raises a fear in me that this is just a way of saying that if my people are from some long-mourned mythic land, our dispossession here cannot be real. Please try to see it my way . . . first you wanted our land, then you wanted our lives, reduced to thin remnants, you wanted our cultures and languages, and now we must surrender our God.

HOMECOMING

THERE IS A Choctaw woman named Terry in Dayton, Ohio who is a close friend of mine. We have many things in common, not the least of which is that we are "urban Indians." Although she is Choctaw and I am Cherokee, we also have many traditional customs and historical events that we share. Her nation too was a "civilized tribe." In those days (that is, before the 1830's), our people must have believed that being considered civilized would save us from the forced exile to Indian Territory which many other Eastern nations had already suffered. Of course it didn't, and the removal of our nations provided us another commonality—our progenitors were split into separate entities . . . Mississippi Choctaws, Oklahoma Choctaws, Eastern Band Cherokees, Oklahoma Cherokees.

Add up all the roots to common vines, "remnant," "removed," "urban," and identity can be a confusing thing. Of course we must also factor in a plethora of non-Native ancestors and the relative cultural isolation of living in Ohio, and the fragmentation seems endless.

What this whole introduction has been leading to is my first trip to Oklahoma. I looked on it with trepidation, almost talked myself out of it a dozen times, and ran up huge long distance bills commiserating with Terry. Why was I so apprehensive? To understand the "race memory" of the Indian removals if you're not an Indian, try picturing yourself as a Jew visiting Auschwitz or a Cambodian survivor returning to Pol Pot's killing fields.

I feared how overwhelming that race memory might be when I first stood as my Ancestors had, looking into an Oklahoma night sky, remembering those who had not survived our version of the Bataan Death March.

Of course, I must also have feared how I would be received, although I didn't admit that to myself at the time. If the convolutions of Southeastern Indian history aren't confounding enough, my own background is more so. After the Removal Era was over, after the Easterners hiding in the hills had moved out to live in their mountain coves, 160 Cherokees from Indian Territory journeyed back to the Smokies at the behest of their North Carolina relatives (the US government soon got wind of this, stopping the repatriation tide at 160 individuals). I am a product of that repatriation, that comingling of refugee and exile. Some people couple that fact with my unlikely hometown of Cincinnati (hey, my Father had to find work during the Depression, didn't he?) and snicker loudly about "wannabees," "Five dollar Indians," and "Princess Grandmothers" (sorry, no royalty up my family tree, nor those trees of other Cherokees!).

Well, as you see, I can go off on tangents rather easily. To the point, dammit, I wondered if I'd be accepted! My run of luck that first day did not do much for my confidence. I missed my plane to Dallas, which meant I also missed my connection to Tulsa. Since I was staying at the Tsa-la-gi Lodge, or the Lodge of the Cherokees (which the tribe owns), they were sending the airport van to pick me up. What a great first impression I'm going to make, I thought. Three hours late, the poor van driver wondering where I am, and you can only get away with so much using this "Indian Time" excuse. I did manage to get a message to the Lodge when I got to Dallas, so at least they didn't send that driver out on the hour's drive into Tulsa too early. Even with that call, I still could feel my embarrass-

ment welling up as my plane touched down in Eastern Oklahoma.

The first pleasant experience for me was that "van." No
Chevy Econoline with "Cherokee Nation of Oklahoma" painted
on the side. It seems that, since I was so late, a Lodge em-
ployee had offered to pick me up on his own time . . . in his
sister's car . . . with his sister in it! It seems they were trying to
coordinate a Divorce Party for her for the next night, because
she had just received her Final Decree. A trip to Tulsa was in
order to inform friends and pick up supplies at the warehouse
supermarket, so getting me at the airport was fine with them.
They were a little hungry (so was I, but I didn't want to put
anybody out any further), so we all went to McDonald's. We ate
Big Mac's while we discussed Johnny Bench (an Oklahoma
Choctaw who played for the Reds) and where the hell was his
hometown of Bingor, Oklahoma anyway?

Before we arrived in Tahlequah, the capitol of the Oklahoma
Cherokee Nation, I knew all about the hated ex-husband and
they knew how the Cincinnati Reds were doing on their latest
road trip. Still, these were two very nice people and not neces-
sarily an indication of how others would be. I couldn't have been
more wrong. As I signed the Lodge's guest register, the clerk
told me, "Miss Kasee, please call your Mother back home. She is
so worried about you missing the plane that she's called here
twice."

This was just the beginning. Next day, I sat down to breakfast at the Lodge's restaurant, only to find myself sitting one
table over from Chief Mankiller, a person whom I greatly admire. Looking up from her plate, she smiled and nodded a "Good
Morning" to me. As I enjoyed my onions and eggs (we call them
ramps-n-eggs back East, something I had to explain to the waitress, who laughed goodnaturedly after she figured out what I
wanted), I began to feel a deep sense of belonging. Here I was
accepted, and here I accepted others, no longer feeling defen-
sive.

Finishing a sumptuous meal, I went to the desk to call for a
cab to take me to the Historical Society. The clerk told me the
Lodge runs a taxi for its guests and she would get it for me. As
my "cab" pulled up in front (a station wagon which was obviously someone's family car, judging from the toys and Happy

Meal boxes!), I recognized the driver as a maintenance worker from the previous evening. Although I'd seen him as I checked in, we hadn't yet spoken. You can imagine my surprise when he smiled and said, "Hey, you're the lady who missed that plane to Dallas, aren't you?" I couldn't help but laugh, as I wondered whether it had appeared as a feature article in the local overnight newspaper!

These were my initial experiences with Western Cherokees and the rest of the visit was just as wonderful. I excitedly called Terry the second night, telling her how it was like being the long-lost guest of honor relative at a huge family reunion. As I took a walk around the grounds that night, I looked up into that Oklahoma night sky without fear. We will never forget those who didn't survive that Trail of Tears, but we as a People have survived, in North Carolina, in Oklahoma, and yes, in Cincinnati. Feeling so safe and accepted, there was no overwhelming race memory of the devastation, just a prayer for those silent graves and the knowledge that we were still there, still a proud people. I laughed to myself as I thought of how Terry had reminded me of a phrase I had taught her . . . to be a descendant of a removed tribe is to be homesick for a place you've never been.

Cynthia Kasee lives in St. Petersburg, Florida. A professor of American Indian Studies for the Union Institute College of Undergraduate Studies located in Cincinnati, Ohio, she holds a Ph.D. in American Indian Studies from the Union Institute and has served as a co-convener of annual seminars for them on topics related to Indian Studies. In 1991 the theme was "Native American: the aftermath of the Columbus Voyages," and the previous year's theme was "Diaspora in the Homeland: Native American Dispossession (held in Miami, Florida and focusing on the Southeastern removals)".

Her poetry has been published in *The Eagle* and she has written sections on "Indian Participation in the Revolutionary War" and "Indian Wars of the West" for an encyclopedic series on American wars. Ethnologist for the

North American Indian Council of Cincinnati, her professional speaking engagements take her throughout the country where she has presented her professional research on issues related to Cherokee women's traditional and contemporary issues at such venues as the 1987 Symposium on the U.S. Constitution and the Cherokee Nation.

Wilma Mankiller

REBIRTH OF A NATION

A 1988 Interview with Wilma Mankiller by Marilou Awiakta

AT AGE 42, Principal Chief Wilma Mankiller of the Cherokee Nation of Oklahoma is the first woman to head a major Indian tribe. It's no easy task: her jurisdiction includes 86,000 of the 95,000 Cherokees in the country. In charge of a budget of nearly $50 million, Mankiller has compared her job to running a small country and a medium-sized corporation at the same time. But anyone who doubts that she can handle it need only spend a few minutes in her presence.

Like the mountains of her native eastern Oklahoma, the chief is staunch and sturdy; nurturing, yet not to be trifled with; and deeply calm. Running beneath that tranquil surface is a reservoir of humor that helps her keep things in perspective. She chuckles as she quotes what the Cherokee say about her:

"While other people get agitated and jump up and down, Wilma moseys on through and gets the job done."

Mankiller has defined that job on her own terms. Although her last name, passed down by her ancestors, could suggest that she's warlike and pushy, the opposite is true. The chief has an open-door policy and a philosophy of building programs from the grass roots up – helping people define their own needs and then developing systems to meet them. She always seems to have time for anyone who needs her.

Mankiller works almost around the clock, a cycle that includes making time for her husband of two years, two daughters, a grandson, and other family and friends. This is moseying, Mankiller-style, and last fall it not only got her elected to her second term as a chief but won her the Harvard Foundation Citation for Leadership and a *Ms.* magazine award as one of 1987's Outstanding Women of the Year.

One of 11 children, Mankiller was born on a farm in rural Stilwell, Oklahoma, to a Cherokee father and a Caucasian mother. When a drought in the late 1950s devastated the family's crop, a federal urbanization project for native Americans relocated them to San Francisco.

While living in California, Mankiller studied at San Francisco State University, married a wealthy Ecuadorean businessman, raised their two daughters, and became increasingly involved in Indian issues. The marriage broke up after 10 years, and in 1977 Mankiller returned with her children to the Nation and to her family's plot of land, Mankiller Flats. After receiving a degree in social sciences at a local college, she became a graduate assistant in architecture at the University of Arkansas. In the fall of 1979 she was seriously injured in a car accident. "That accident," says Mankiller, "changed my life. I always think of myself as the woman who lived before and the woman who lives afterward."

What were you like before the accident?
Mankiller: I had a hard edge. I spent a lot of time being angry at injustices against people in general and the Cherokee in particular. During the '60s and early '70s, I had an us-and-them mentality.
What happened to give you that "hard edge?"

It was an ongoing process: growing up Indian in an urban environment, feeling my family members were victims of ill-advised federal policies, and realizing the government had not honored treaties or policies for health and education. My father had always been active in Indian issues. But the protest at Alcatraz in 1969 against poor treatment of Indians was the catalyst that made me an activist.

And in 1979 the accident occurred. What happened?
One morning I was driving from Stilwell to Tahlequah. At the top of a hill, a car coming from the opposite direction pulled out to pass and hit me head on. The driver of that car was my best friend, Sherry Morris. She was killed instantly.

The doctors told me later that I was so mutilated they didn't know at first if I was a man or a woman. One leg was crushed, one broken. My ribs were broken; my nose and other facial bones were, too. All I remember now is how I felt.

I was dying, yet it was a beautiful and spiritual experience, warm and loving, soft. I no longer feared death. I saw how precious health and life are, how important it is to do something good with our life and to share. I realized how insignificant you are in the totality of things. It's a precious thing to be here and take part in the world.

How did the aftermath of the accident affect you?
I was incapacitated for almost a year. At home by myself I had time to examine my life in a new way – to reevaluate, refocus. But just when I thought I was finally getting well, my muscles began to weaken. I couldn't hold my toothbrush or my hairbrush, and I couldn't control my speech or my facial muscles. I had spells of not being able to breathe. Once, I fell and rebroke the bones in my face. I was very frightened and didn't know what was happening to me.

Then I saw a muscular dystrophy program on television that described a case similar to mine. I called a muscular dystrophy center and was referred to specialists. The diagnosis was moderately severe myasthenia gravis.

Creeping paralysis, the old-timers in Appalachia called it.
Exactly. Doctors removed my thymus gland and put me on intensive medical treatment. I'd suddenly gone from being an active, positive person to a person who was struggling to stay

alive. I was very discouraged. Sometimes I just wanted to roll over and play dead.

You've said that tribal medicine men helped you recover from the accident. What did they do?

Medicine men are healers and spiritual counselors. They help restore harmony from the inside out. They taught me to approach life from a positive, living perspective. Your chances of surviving are much better this way than with a negative outlook. I applied that concept to my work, too. What I really wanted to do was rebuild our tribe and our people.

Then I had the surgery. Afterward I was on a life-support system. Finally I got angry. I said, 'Get me out of here and off this stuff. I'm not going to take this any more. I'm going to participate in getting well.'

The doctors thought I'd have to stay on the support system for three weeks. Instead I came off it in three days. Once I took charge of my life, my body gradually began to heal. Last year I finally was able to discontinue the medicine for myasthenia gravis.

So the real turning point for your health, as well as for your vision of your work, was a change in spirit?

Yes. Illness had slowed me down enough to make me think, listen, and pay attention. The medicine men and the elders talked to me about how we should be as a people. They showed me the sacred wampum belts that teach the truths of Cherokee life: that we should have good minds, consider everything in the world – including nature – as brothers and sisters. We should not be judgmental, but accept all as family.

They taught me not to be dragged down by the negative. That divides people. I began to understand, to rethink. Out of all that, I grew determined to bring the people together as "we." In the old days, people talked about their problems and helped each other solve them. That was the genesis of my idea for the Department of Community Development. Instead of accepting the paternalistic approach that tells people what they need and gives it to them, we would define our own needs, develop resources, and do the work ourselves.

That reflects the principle of working from the inside out. Were there other ways that you changed inside?

Coming so close to death moved me beyond the ego to the calm.

I can't imagine what could rattle me now. I also became a lot tougher and firmer, without becoming mean-spirited. I don't worry so much about little things. I focus more on the good.

How has your experience influenced other people?

More than anything else, I give people hope. I'm a daughter of the Cherokee people and they know that, a woman from a poor family who landed on her feet. Last year, when I was on the Good Morning America television show, people back home said, "when you were talking it was like we were talking."

Whatever the subject, your theme is unity: sharing, consensus, cooperation. Is that the historical role of Cherokee women?

Women were the center of the family and the tribe. They trained the chiefs and had their own council. The head of their council had a powerful voice in government. Women sometimes went to war alongside their husbands and sons. In the early 1800s, for the sake of survival, the tribe adopted a system similar to the federal government's, which had no place for women. But underneath, the people passed on the tradition of nurturing and assertiveness to both genders.

That's why it never occurred to me that anyone would be concerned about having a female chief. My husband was as confused by the furor as I was. Tribal people think holistically. Whether you're a man or a woman, you do what needs to be done. The nurturing skills I apply to my family apply to the tribe.

What advice do you have for women as a whole?

Many women internalize the stereotypes of "the woman's place," passivity and so on. We need to rethink where we are – there's a lot of unlearning to do – and extend our ideas of home and family to include our environment and our people. We need to trust our own thinking, trust where we're going.

Then "mosey on through". . .?

And get the job done.

KEEPING PACE WITH THE REST OF THE WORLD

THIS COLD GRAY DAY seemed right for what Pearl had to do. It was a simple thing, really, taking her Grandma Ahniwake to the Indian Hospital, except that Ahniwake, at 68 had never been to an American doctor. She had always gone to traditional Cherokee doctors.

Ahniwake was ready when Pearl arrived. "Do you need help with anything?" Pearl asked quietly.

"If you can find my cane, I'll be ready to go. My legs are very swollen today and my left leg hurts when I walk.' She did not tell Pearl that she discovered her toes were purple when she woke up that morning.

As they walked to the car Ahniwake remarked, "You know, its been almost a year since I've been doctored. Not since Charlie Christie passed on. It will be good to feel well again." Pearl knew how long it had been. She had taken Ahniwake to other Cherokee doctors, and they had even gone to the Creeks and the Eucha but no one knew the medicine to help her.

"Grandma, remember last summer when we went to see that Creek medicine man and we had to wait all night for him to finish his clan ceremony before he could talk to us?"

"Yes. And when he told us that the Creeks had also lost the secret of the blood medicine, he seemed as sad as we were." Ahniwake looked out the window at the stark beauty of early winter and said, "He was sad, Pearl. Very sad."

Pearl drove on and Ahniwake continued speaking. "When Charlie Christie passed on, we lost many of our medicine secrets. Charlie once told me that many young people came to him and told him they were interested in learning about medicine but that he couldn't teach them because they weren't willing to accept the pure lifestyle of a Cherokee doctor. For some healing ceremonies, the songs will not allow themselves to be sung by anyone except the purest of spirits."

Although she had heard the answer many times, Pearl asked her grandmother, "Is everything Charlie knew lost?"

Ahniwake was quick to say, "No. The way it was told to me, as long as Cherokee people continue to honor our ancestors and our creator through good living and our ceremonies, the roots, herbs, and medicine songs will be available to us. When it is right, these things will be shown to our people again. They are never really lost, as long as we are not lost. I wish Charlie had passed on the medicine to help me, but when it is right his knowledge will be shown to our people again."

Again they rode in silence, each lost in her own thoughts. After a while, Ahniwake laughed and said, "I hope Maude and Thelma don't find out I've gone to the clinic. Lots of times we've talked about the way things have changed – about how our people don't plant big gardens anymore, put up food for the winter, raise chickens, hunt squirrel, rabbit, and deer, or go to Cherokee doctors. I told them I would never go to a modern doctor, an American doctor who did not know how to heal an illness, only how to cut it out." She continued fretfully, "I wish I didn't have to go. I feel almost ashamed."

The Indian hospital was just as Ahniwake had heard it to be. The hallway and waiting room were full of people. They reminded Ahniwake of cattle waiting to be herded through a gate.

When she and Pearl were seated, Ahniwake commented, "Most of these people don't much look like Indian people."

After hours of waiting, a nurse finally took Ahniwake and Pearl into a small white room. A young man entered the room, introduced himself and began to ask questions. Pearl let him know that Ahniwake did not speak English well, and Dr. Brown began to talk to Pearl as he examined Ahniwake.

Ahniwake thought he looked like a young school boy — except for his eyes. He examined her with cold gadgets that matched his cold eyes, occasionally asking questions which Pearl translated. Ahniwake noticed that he made hurried notes in his folder and she commented to Pearl, "He must have a poor memory."

After 15 minutes Dr. Brown said, "She appears to have severe diabetes, but we can't tell for sure without further tests. She also has high blood pressure and there's some indication of heart problems. We need to keep her in the hospital for more tests. It shouldn't take more than a day or so."

The doctor had already begun reading his next patient's chart when Pearl began to translate all he'd said for Ahniwake. He stopped reading to look up when Ahniwake blurted out, "No!" and started out of the room.

Pearl grabbed Ahniwake's hand and pleaded, "Grandma, it's serious. After these tests, a medicine will probably be prescribed to help with your legs. What else can we do? We've already tried to find a healer among our own. Where else can we go?"

Though Ahniwake was wary of the young doctor she finally agreed to stay. "I've gone this far," she sighed. "I'll see this through to the end."

While Pearl finished filling out papers, Ahniwake was taken by wheelchair to a room more spacious than the examining room but it too was colorless and cold. Pearl waited until the nurse helped Ahniwake settle into bed before asking her what she needed from home. As Pearl was leaving, Ahniwake called out, "And don't forget to bring my hairbrush." She liked to brush her thin, waist-length hair and rebraid it every night.

With Pearl gone, Ahniwake suddenly felt exhausted. She lay back on the smooth, soft pillow and fell asleep. She almost immediately slipped into a dream of her youth. She was dancing alongside her husband-to-be, Levi Buckskin, at a summer ceremonial dance. Everyone was laughing and happy. Levi and the other men sang ancient Cherokee songs while Pearl and the other women kept the rhythm with the sound of turtle shakers strapped to their lower legs. They all circled the fire, circled each other, circled the four directions of the world.

Suddenly, Ahniwake felt one of her turtle shakers slipping so she stepped out of the line of dancers and leaned down to tighten the straps. While she was stooped down, she felt chilled, the night seemed darker, and she was instinctively afraid to look up. When she finally forced herself to look up, all the other dancers had gone, the fire had died and the only person she saw in the moonlight was a young blond man wearing a white jacket. He moved toward her and she somehow knew she had to dance with him so she managed to shakily stand up and wait for him to join her. She linked her left arm through his right arm and they began to dance. But instead of the familiar Cherokee songs she had heard earlier, he sang a fast, loud cowboy song while twirling her around so rapidly she tripped and fell to the ground. She was out of breath, there were sharp pains in the left side of her chest, she could not get on her feet again. He jerked her up, laughing in a way that frightened her even more and told her that she had to keep pace with the rest of the world.

She was still twirling around in this terrible dance with the strange blond man when Pearl shook her awake. It took her a moment to shake off the dream. It left her drained and frightened. At home she never had bad dreams—her house was well protected against such things. Though Pearl stayed to talk until Ahniwake felt sleepy again. Ahniwake did not tell her of the dream. When she fell asleep again, she slept dreamlessly through the rest of the night.

The next afternoon, the doctor came in to talk to Ahniwake. He talked very slowly, and she understood part of what he said. ". . . remove part of your foot . . . possible loss of your left leg." Ahniwake merely stared at him till he finally left the room. He returned shortly with a woman who spoke to her in Cherokee. Ahniwake did not respond. She was looking out the hospital window at the parking lot. Pearl had just parked the car and was getting out. As Pearl walked toward the hospital, Ahniwake thought how like a very young girl she looked, tall and slim with long, straight black hair.

Ahniwake sat up and waited for Pearl while the translator explained that the doctor had to remove part of her left foot to save her left leg and ultimately her life. When Pearl entered the room and saw the three of them and noticed the look on Ahniwake's face, she asked, "What's wrong here?"

After the doctor had explained, Pearl turned to Ahniwake and was not surprised when she merely said, "Take me home." Though she knew Ahniwake would never consent to surgery, Pearl sat on the edge of the bed and dutifully repeated all that the doctor had said about her worsening leg.

Ahniwake was adamant. "Pearl, I have asked you to take me home." Pearl knew it was pointless to continue pleading with her so she helped Ahniwake get dressed and collect her things; together they left the Indian hospital.

Though she felt no better now than when she had left home the day before, Ahniwake told Pearl, "I am so happy to be home. I don't care if I can't walk again without a cane, I never want to go to that hospital again. I don't know why I agreed to go. That place may be okay for white people but it's not for Cherokees! What kind of medicine would require removal of parts of the body to heal an illness?"

While Pearl made a pot of strong coffee, Ahniwake continued, "I've heard of other people with blood problems like mine who were treated at the Indian hospital. First they had their toes removed, then their foot, then their leg, and later they died anyway." More to herself than to Pearl, Ahniwake added, "He did not know my clan, my family, my history. How could he possibly know how to heal me?"

There was one Seminole doctor Pearl had heard people talk about. It was said that he could heal almost any illness. She decided that she would try to get some sleep and then take a day or so off from work to go to Seminole and search for him.

The next morning, after checking to be sure Ahniwake had everything she needed, Pearl went to find the Seminole doctor. After many wrong turns and telephone calls to Seminole friends, she finally found Billy Joe Harjo's house. He seemed to be expecting her. After she explained Ahniwake's symptoms in detail, Billy Joe said, "I have doctored some people with your grandmother's illnes. Many of our people suffer from blood problems, but most get insulin from the Indian hospital so the need for my medicine is not great, but I do have some."

Pearl was very excited. "When can you see her? Should we bring her up here or can you go to her house," she asked. Billy Joe said he thought it would be better to go to Ahniwake's home.

Noting her relief and exhaustion, Billy Joe invited Pearl to spend the night. He told her to rest and that he would gather the medicine in the morning and travel to Ahniwake's house in the evening. Pearl slept well, woke up early the next morning, and began the long drive home. She stopped at her house, picked up a change of clothing and finally arrived at Ahniwake's house in the late afternoon.

When she entered the small, warm house she called out to Ahniwake but received no answer. She went to the bedroom and found Ahniwake sleeping soundly. Pearl called her name repeatedly, and finally began to shake her. When Ahniwake didn't regain consciousness she decided to get help. With mounting panic she went down and road and got one of her cousins to help put Ahniwake in the car. Not knowing what else to do she took her to the Indian hospital. Only after she got there and the interns and nurses began immediately to attach wires and cords to Ahniwake's body did Pearl allow herself to wonder if she had done the right thing. Her grandmother had told her she never wanted to come back to this hospital. "Maybe I should have tried driving back to Seminole," she thought. "But then I might have missed Billy Joe on the road," she realized. She consoled herself that she had done the only thing she could have under the circumstances.

One of the interns called the doctor who told Pearl that her grandmother was in a diabetic coma and would not regain consciousness until the insulin took effect. He advised Pearl to go home and come back in the morning. They planned to keep Ahniwake in the intensive care area and Pearl would not be allowed to stay in the room. Pearl looked at Ahniwake, thinking that she looked beautiful and untainted even with all the wires attached to her. Pearl hated to leave her in this unfamiliar place. She went into the waiting room for a couple of hours and then, finally, after another peek at Ahniwake, went on home.

Hours later, Ahniwake began trying to get through a veil of

drugs and illness to figure out where she was and what was happening. She felt strange, as if she was in a space between something incredibly beautiful and the present world. She knew she was on the edge of the most significant feeling a human could experience, more powerful than childbirth, or the love of young Levi, or the feeling after a cleansing ceremony. Yet she lingered there on the edge and did not go over quite yet.

Ahniwake broke through to see a fire in the center of a white room. After she was able to focus her eyes, she realized it was not a fire but a bright light. She was in that hospital again! There were tubes in her hands, on her chest. She tried to call out but there was even a tube in her throat. She managed to turn her head slightly toward the sound of voices. She could see two men in white talking by the swinging doors. One started walking toward her. To her absolute horror it was the same man who had appeared in her dream. The doctor walked behind him and said, "It won't do much good to try to talk to her even if she's conscious. She doesn't speak English." The young bad dream doctor replied, "She should have kept pace with the rest of the world," and laughed in the same frightening way he had in her dream. As he got closer to her bed, she felt a sharp pain in her chest and as the bad dream doctor reached toward her she tried to move away and could not. He leaned down, linked arms with her and began to sing the loud cowboy song he had sung in her dream. She gave in and they began to dance that same fast, whirling dance until she again stumbled and fell. But this time she fell much further. She floated into the soft arms of her Mother Earth and lay nestled there near the fire—waiting for the Creator, waiting for her life to be complete.

Pearl was up early the next morning. She wanted to get some of Ahniwake's things before going to the hospital. She also needed to find out what had happened to the Seminole doctor. She telephoned Billy Harjo's and found out that he had gone to Ahniwake's house while they were at the hospital and finding no one there had returned home. She wanted to take care of all her other errands too so she and Ahniwake would be free just to talk when she arrived at the hospital. She knew her grandmother would be mad because she'd taken her back to the hospital but they would talk about it. Pearl was sure she could convince

Ahniwake that she'd done the only thing she could. They had always enjoyed each other's company. They would talk for hours, more like girlfriends or sisters than grandmother and granddaughter. Because of Ahniwake Pearl had learned the Cherokee language and knew many of the ancient tribal stories.

The past few days had been so extraordinary that when Pearl got to Ahniwake's she paused for a moment to absorb the familiarity of the house. She had always liked this house. Levi had built it when he and Ahniwake were very young. It was lighted by coal oil, heated by wood, and Ahniwake still drew her water from a well out back. Pearl's own father had been raised in the wood frame house and Pearl herself had spent many years there. It was warm with memories and if houses could be friendly, then Ahniwake's house was definitely so.

Pearl got to the hospital in the late morning. When she stopped at the nurse's station to ask for the room number of Ahniwake Buckskin, the nurse said, "You need to talk to the doctor."

Pearl felt a surge of fear. Questions went rapidly through her mind. What was wrong? Was Ahniwake still in a coma? Was she still in the emergency room? What was it? The nurse asked her to sit down but Pearl leaned against the nurse's station and watched the hallway until she saw the doctor. As he came towards her she knew that he had no good news for her. Before he could say anything, Pearl surprised herself by yelling, "What have you done to Grandma? I want to see her now. Where is she?" Pearl knew she was shouting to keep the doctor from talking and to keep herself from thinking.

The doctor put his hands on her shoulders and said, "Pearl, Ahniwake died of a heart attack last night. I can't explain it. We decided to perform an emergency amputation of her left foot. It's really a relatively minor surgical procedure. She was in the recovery room. I was there with her. I thought I saw her move her head slightly so I went over to examine her. She suddenly looked terribly frightened, as if I were some sort of monster. She had a massive heart attack. There was nothing we could do."

Pearl shook his hands off her shoulders, slapped him as hard as she could, and left the hospital.

Pearl went to her uncle's house and asked him to go to the hospital to get Ahniwake and let the rest of her relatives know of Ahniwake's death. Pearl then went to Ahniwake's house to wait for the others to arrive for the wake. She built a fire in the old wood stove and sat and watched the flames. She knew she should put on coffee and stew or beans for the many relatives who would come to see Ahniwake one last time but she did not move from her place in front of the fire.

It was now almost dark and the house was lighted only by the fire. She suddenly felt warm, as she had often felt when she and Ahniwake were together and her eyes were drawn to a certain spot in the fire. She leaned forward and looked more closely. There, in the back of the flames, she saw Ahniwake with old man Charlie Christie on one side and Levi Buckskin on the other. Ahniwake looked very happy but Pearl began to weep. They could not speak to each other across the worlds that separated them but Pearl knew the message Ahniwake was sending. Once again she heard Ahniwake saying, "As long as the Cherokee people honor our ancestors and our Creator, the roots, herbs, and medicine songs will be available to us. These things will be shown to our people again. They are never really lost as long as we are not lost."

There in the warmth of these words, Pearl knew what it was she had to do. She vowed to do all in her power to restore and revitalize the traditional Cherokee way of life as a tribute to Ahniwake and to the lives of other Cherokees who are yet unborn.

Wilma Mankiller was the principal chief of the Cherokee Nation, in Tahlequah, Oklahoma, from 1985 through 1994. Named *Ms.* magazine's Woman of the Year in 1987, her autobiography *Mankiller, A Chief and Her People* was published in 1993 by St. Martin's Press. Her writings have appeared in *Native Peoples* magazine, *Southern Exposure*, the anthology *Reinventing the Enemy's Language* (edited by Joy Harjo) and other native-oriented publications. She is, with five other women, co-editor of *A Reader's Companion to the History of Women in the U.S.*

Ron Rogers

WHAT BECAME OF TRIBAL EUROPE?

1.

THE FLINTSTONES ASIDE, the common image of Stone age man is that of a subhuman gorilla dragging sexy cavewomen home by the hair of the head. We call such ideas preconceptions or stereotypes. We all know, intellectually at least, that preconceptions damage our ability to see the truth. The people of the old Stone age were human as you and I are human. We too often assume that cultures evolve upward from primitive to civilized in a natural, and somehow inevitable way. In most cases, however, civilization comes to so-called primitive people by force of arms.

In recent years, films like *Little Big Man* have helped to break down some of these stereotypes. In that film, old Lodge Skins surveys the destruction of a helpless Indian village by the whites and expresses a sentiment that has lately become a cliche: "They don't seem to know where the center of the world is."

He spoke indignantly, as if such knowledge were self-evident. Long ago, all men knew where the center of the world is—all men everywhere.

Some 40,000 years ago, the world over, tribes of nomadic hunters stalked the longhorned bison, the mastadon, the saber-toothed tiger, and the great sloth. They all used tools and weapons of stone, wood, and bone. Common on a global scale were the bow, the spear, and a great variety of spear-throwers which the Aztecs called *atlatl.*

A cave painting of Stone Age origin was found in France. Archaeologists call him the "Sorcerer". He is a male human with dangling genitals, and he dances. His arms are shortened and bent like animal paws. He has a horse's head and tail, and from his temples sprout the antlers of a stag. Antlered figures are common among tribal people on a global scale. They range from paleolithic China and Europe, to the Iroquois at the coming of the whites, and still persist in Africa and North America as living religion.

"In their roles as hunters," writes Alexander Marshack, "Men had a special relationship to the world of animals and animal images." Marshack's studies leave no doubt as to the intellectual and spiritual sophistication of Stone age men. He examined ancient artifacts under a microscope, or ultraviolet light, to compensate for the wear of ages.

A little rock bore engravings, evocative of Miro, of a woman and a baby joined together by an umbilical cord. Above them is etched, very realistically, the head of a pony in its winter coat. Still another stone bore engravings which archaeologists had long assumed to be random, decorative notches. Marshack's examination showed, clearly, a correct record of the moon's phases over a period of 9 lunar quarters.

Under a microscope, an old stone knife showed no signs of use along the cutting edges, and Marshack concluded that the artifact was ceremonial. One side had carvings of conifer branches, a dying plant, and a bison with a protruding tongue, which is common in the autumn rut. All these are autumn images. The other face was carved with flowers, a doe, and an ibex with notched horns—all images of spring. Because the knife may not have been ceremonial, a distinction should be made. A knife which separates autumn from spring is a complete and true creative statement. If the knife was not ritual, then it must have been art.

Marshack confined his studies to paleolithic man in Europe, but the period shows a striking uniformity of lifestyles on a global scale. The world over, nomadic peoples built shelters of natural material, wooden poles and animal skins, which were easy to carry when following game. Later, the agrarian tribes of northern Europe lived in villages not too unlike the native farmers of North America. At one time, then, all men were tribal. Why? What accounts for this odd human unity?

Freud tried to explore the roots of tribal religions, but applied the wrong concepts. He tried to make universal the psychological repressions of Europe. He related sympathetic magic to a mental and spiritual state which is, essentially, neurotic, and labeled tribal people "pre-religious".

"Taboo," he writes. "Is a Polynesian word, the translation of which provides difficulties for us because we no longer possess the idea which it connotes." Freud's ignorance, then, is self-confessed.

Freud was a product of his age, and at first it seems unfair to expect him to remember tribal roots so distant, and hazed by centuries. No one has a complete answer to the question of why civilizations develop. We only know that for various reasons they sprout up now and then. But, if the evolution of cultures from primitive to civilized is as natural as we often assume, why have we blocked out our ancient origins? For example, the Native American creation stories predate all our archaeological evidence, yet few experts are willing to take the ancient stories as true accounts of the origins of the universe. Why?

Our issue now is blunt: Where's tribal Europe? The answer has long been the domain of scholars of ancient history, unfortunately. The story holds great significance for tribal people today.

2.

A major factor in the spread of Christianity as a world religion was that it replaced strenuous tribal ceremonies with ideas of faith and belief. The focus of the Christian spirit is more conceptual, intellectual, rather than active. A few of the old pagan rites, like the Communion, remain, but on the whole tribal religions and Christianity follow vastly different paths.

A good example of this diversity is in the Christian view of the Tree of Life. The Tree of Life is an important symbol for many tribal people globally. For the ancient Europeans, this tree stood at the center of the universe. For the Iroquois it symbolizes peace among many people. For the Christians, however, a very similar tree was the cause of Adam and Eve's exile from Eden.

In 681 A.D., the Council of Toledo discouraged the "worshippers of idols, those who venerate stones, who celebrate the rites of springs and trees". At about this time, the Archbishop of Canterbury issued the following edit: "If anyone at the kalends of January goes about as a stag or a bull; that is, making himself into a wild animal, and putting on the heads of beasts; those who in such wise transform themselves, penance for three years because it is devilish." He imposed special penance for "making vows at a clump of trees, at certain rocks, or at a place where boundaries meet". The Archbishop thought that the followers of the Old Religion could turn themselves into animals. St. Caesarious of Arles had a similar complaint: "Some dress themselves in the skins of herd animals; swelling and madly exulting, if only they so completely metamorphose themselves . . . that they seem to have completely abandoned the human shape."

A Nordic myth illustrates this point very well. "The Otter's Ransom" is probably a later story. Along with iron weapons, the idea of gold and treasure was probably brought to the northern tribes by the Romans.

* * *

The Otter's Random

Odin and Loki were out walking around one day, and passed by a waterfall. They saw a fat otter sitting on the shore, lazily eating a salmon. Loki threw a rock at the otter, killing it, and then bragged of his double catch. Odin and Loki gathered up their kill and went on to the home of a man named Hreidmar.

Hreidmar, on seeing the dead otter, angrily told them that they had killed his son in animal form. He and his other two sons threatened to kill Odin and Loki unless they paid a ransom. Hreidmar wanted the otter to be stuffed with gold, then laid out on the ground and buried in more gold until it was hidden from sight.

In order to meet the ransom demand, Loki set off to find a dwarf named Andvari who was known to possess such a treasure. He found Andvari hiding in the shape of a fish. The dwarf willingly gave up his treasure, but held back a single gold ring. The ring, he said, would soon make him rich again, but would surely destroy anyone else who held it. Hearing this, Loki took the ring away by force.

When the otter had been stuffed and covered with gold, the end of one whisker was sticking out. Odin used the ring to cover it. With the ransom paid, Odin and Loki went on their way.

The gold ring did eventually destroy Hreidmar, who was murdered by his own greedy sons. One son, Fafnir, turned himself into a dragon and laid down upon the gold.

* * *

During the period of the Roman Empire, the northern European tribes were left virtually unmolested. The Romans could not extend themselves far enough north to cope with their warrior societies, who were ferocious in the extreme. The most feared of these were the Berserkers, who got their name from the peculiar frenzy which possessed them in battle, a rage so complete that they felt neither fear or pain. Another name for the berserkers was the Bear Shirts. Shirts of wolf skin were used in their initiation ceremonies. Wolf skins were sewn into the bare flesh of the initiates and then, when the dancing had reached its peak, were forcibly torn off by the older men. All Bear Shirts had to carry those scars. The hangman's noose originated among these people. All captives taken in battle were hung from trees with a calf's intestine and run through with spears. The Romans had spread themselves too thin to deal with such ferocity. Where the Romans had failed the Church finally succeeded, but the struggle was long, bitter and bloody.

Christianity began in Rome, and when the Roman Empire crumbled a series of Christianized emperors took power there. The power structure of dying empire eventually became the Holy Roman Church. Unfortunately, along with Rome's social structure, the Church also inherited its expansionism. Gradually, Christianity won converts in Europe. The transition of Europe from tribal to civilized is commonly called the Middle Ages. With its conceptual approach to spiritual matters, the early Church was openly hostile to sympathetic magic, to shamanism.

Scholars have pointed vividly to the shamanistic nature of the myths of ancient Europe, and the Nordic stories are a prototype for a wide range of gods worshipped all over the continent. There is a tale of Odin himself being pierced with spears and hung from a tree in order to gain wisdom. Freyr, the god of fertility and plenty, carried in his pouch a "vessel large enough to hold all the gods . . . This ship could travel at will in any direction, since it always got a favorable wind". Freyja, his wife and a goddess of fertility and love, was a seeress. She could put herself in trances and foretell future events. Medicine people went from village to village in Medieval Europe and performed healing acts and told of hidden things.

Christianity was spreading too slowly in Medieval Europe, and the Church used the shaman's magic to justify genocide. It is estimated that some 10,000,000 men, women and children died horribly in the Witch Purges of the Middle Ages, a decimation second *only* to the genocidal policies of the early United States against the tribes of North America. The followers of the Old Religion were hunted down like animals, tortured, and burned alive.

Most witch hunts took place in rural areas. Even then, the fledgling cities of Europe had removed themselves a long way from the rhythms of the seasons, the cycles of earth and sky. But in remote areas – and there were many – the Old Religion survived.

The northern tribes fought hard, mounting swift, ferocious attacks on pockets of Christian power. The Viking raids are still vivid memories in Europe. Other Nordic peoples left Europe altogether for colonies in Iceland, Greenland, and eventually North America, this about A.D. 1000. The decimation of the northern tribes in Europe, like the genocide of the Native American tribes, went on for some 400 years. In both cases, the Christians emerged victorious.

From the Middle Ages onward, the Christians had so repressed the Old Religion that its converts lived in constant dread of witches and warlocks, of werewolves and vampires. The Church took the horned spirits of the tribal religions and turned them into the prototype of the Devil. The persistence of these images shows how deeply they are embedded in our souls. Our modern Hell is rooted in the ancient belief in the god Hel, ruler of the underground world of the dead. Our werewolf is very likely derived from the Bear Shirts.

With their tortures, the Inquisition wrung "confessions" from their victims which are highly questionable as to accuracy. Still, many of the "Black Sabbaths" described are consistent with the rites of Odin and Thor, of Freyr and Freyja.

Why did the followers of the Old Religion resist Christianity for so long? Why did they carry on the ancient rites in the face of such brutal opposition? Likewise, why has the United States government had so much trouble in civilizing the American Indian tribes? Why does America's "Old Religion" persist in spite of the genocidal policies leveled against it? Most importantly, what accounts for that strange uniformity of human life-ways in that time so long ago?

3.

Questions can be answered with questions. Have you ever ridden in a car when the driver was going too fast? And did your foot reach out for an imaginary gas pedal when the inevitable emergency came? Did you ever punch at the air to help a boxer in the ring? Or tap your foot to music? Several anthropologists have suggested that these kinds of sympathetic movements are the root of dance and sympathetic magic. The term "sympathetic magic" is very likely mistaken in some particulars, when compared to actual tribal religions, but it is accurate enough to make a crucial point.

Men are instinctively tribal creatures. Apes, like men, display sympathetic movements, and have even been observed dancing in the wild. In general monkeys travel in groups, as do men. The tribal instinct is irresistible, basic to the beast. How different are we? It has been noted of the tribal instinct in apes that "individuals separated from the group might die, even if given identical food and amenities". Many Indians taken into slavery by the European colonizers refused to eat and died in just this manner.

While this argument is tenuous at best, if it has any validity at all, and it must, then Freud was wrong in applying the concept of repression to tribal religions. He used the same idea more effectively in his study of civilization and its relation to mental illness. "Conscience," he tells us. "Is a result of instinctual renunciation, or; Renunciation (externally imposed) gives rise to conscience, which then demands further renunciations." This is the mechanism of instinct-repression. Freud used similar arguments to define tribal religions, but the above quote is taken from *Civilization and its Discontents.*

Freud did not remember his tribal roots because the Old Religion in Europe had been deliberately obliterated. Many Native American young people remember little of their old ways for just the same reason. The genocide of the North American tribes was not spontaneous greed and viciousness. It was, rather, an established practice hundreds of years old. Instinct-repression is only partially psychological. It is, in a very real sense, political.

Among tribal people, if they have retained their sovereignty, murder within the tribe itself is almost nonexistent, however hostile the group may be to outsiders. On the other hand, we of the civilized 20th Century are witnessing an epidemic of mental illness and mass, ritual murders. An increasing number of these murders are taking on a mythical, or symbolic, nature.

Freud did serve to warn us that strange and terrible displacements can occur when the instinctive powers — yes, powers — of the human spirit are thwarted. Charles Manson and his family had evolved their own mythology. Manson believed himself to be the Fifth Angel of the Apocalypse. The Tate-La Bianca killings, while outwardly senseless, were, in the minds of the Family, symbolic acts which would bring about Armageddon. Manson and his followers planned to wait out the Final War in a bottomless pit somewhere in the desert. When they emerged, Manson was to be proclaimed king of all the earth. San Francisco's Zodiac killer meant the spirits of his victims to serve him in the afterlife. Both Manson and Zodiac worked their havoc against their own society. Both series of murders, significantly, occurred in urban areas.

Native Americans consider themselves the keepers of the earth but, unfortunately, the whites are the keepers of the Native Americans. The civilized people "own" and exploit the earth. In turn, they are plagued by crime, insanity, and environmental problems of various kinds.

Consider this: In the Middle Ages in Europe, and just after the Middle Ages in North America, tribal religions which had developed naturally for tens of thousands of years were forcibly overrun. They were overrun by an alien religion barely a thousand years ago. Do we honestly believe that, in all that time, tribal people had learned nothing? Day by day, the current studies in ESP and telekenisis draw closer and closer to the conclusion that the shaman's powers are real. The medicine people of Freyr really could summon the wind. There are things you can do to make rain. The energies dealt with by the shaman are the energies of life itself.

Now, many non-Indians want to explore Native American religions. Their interest is healthy, but misguided. Europeans have their own tribal roots.

They would do well to find them again, and quickly.

BIBLIOGRAPHY

Breuil and Lantier, *Men of the Old Stone Age*, St. Martin's Press, New York, 1965.

Ceram, C.W., *The First American; A story of North American Archaeology*, Signet Mentor Books, New York, 1971.

Davidson, H.R. Ellis, *Gods and Myths of Northern Europe*, Penguin Books, Baltimore, 1964.

Eliade, Mircea, *Rite and Symbols of Initiation*, Harper Torchbooks, New York, 1958.

Farb, Peter, *Man's Rise to Civilization as Shown by the Indians of North America*, Dutton, New York, 1968.

Freud, Sigmund, *Civilization and its Discontents*, Doubleday Anchor

Books, Garden City, 1958, and *Totem and Taboo*, from *The Basic Writings of Sigmund Freud*, Brill, A.., editor, Modern Library, New York, 1965.

Hughes, Pennethorn, *Witchcraft*, Penguin Books, Baltimore, 1965.

Marshack, Alexander, "Exploring the Mind of Ice Age Man", *National Geographic*, Vol. 147, no. 1, January, 1975.

Wilson, Colin, *Order of Assassins; the psychology of murder*, Panther Books, London, 1975.

Of himself, Ronald Rogers has said, "Born Claremore, Oklahoma, 20 november 1948. Cherokee/German/English. Christianpagan. (We all are.) Educated at the Institute of American Indians Arts in Santa Fe, New Mexico and the University of California at Los Angeles. Graduated University of California, Santa Cruz, in 1973."

Co-author of *Man Spirit*, a collection of poems, essays, and stories (with illustrations by Ted Palmanteer), he was a 1977 Fellow with the Newberry Library's Center for the History of the American Indian researching a book on the Indian side of the American Revolution. Currently living in Albuquerque, he has taught English, Creative writing, and Journalism at Pikuni Community School on the Blackfeet Indian Reservation in Browning, Montana and been an instructor in Title IV Indian Education Programs in Albuquerque. From 1973–76 he was an Instructor in Literal Arts at the Institute of American Indian Arts. Winner of two First Awards, Short Story Division, in the Scottsdale National Indian Arts Competition, his poems and stories have been anthologized in *The Whispering Wind* (Doubleday), *The American Indian Speaks* (South Dakota Review Press), *Literature Skills for Indian Adults* (American Indian Curriculum Development Project), *Nova* (Scott-Foresman), and *The Remembered Earth* (University of New Mexico Press).

Ralph Salisbury

THE SOLDIER WHO
WOULD ASK

BEFORE THE WHITES conquered us, our tribe, like many others, was centuries building a spirit bridge to the Land of the Dead, and before conquest was complete, most of our people were no longer dreamers but dream.

The Bridge of Prayer may be the only one not destroyed, rebuilt and destroyed again in this present long war. I no longer remember how often I have slipped away as silent as a dream through miles of enemy terrain before the bridge launched up like a rocket for brief flight.

With Mother's and with Father's death, I felt my body lifted in darkness as if explosives were hurling a bridge girder high, but the force was silent, the silent chanting bearing me above earth not friendly, not gentle, but not hostile either, only very serious and intense.

This time when I was lifted I sensed animosity.

Two days back from a Personnel-Destruct mission. And again the landmarks of that mission were drifting by, as if – a few feet above my barracks bed, with the earth spinning beneath – I was held, unaffected by gravity, fixed.

The huge enemy training center – again as if it had been before my rockets turned it into flames – slid past, the boys who had been sleeping there calling out, at first in the voices of the children they had been, then silent, as the rivers and oceans of my blood surged on, my flesh like Earth's robe of air, weighing no more than air.

The air of the enemies' cries entered my lungs, a tidal-wave curled over, an impulse of ocean thrown back onto itself, and I was gliding over the graves of every person I had killed, the graves open, the opened throats of children grown to be sentries exposed, the pieces of bodies bulldozed into the same pit after rocket explosions forming again.

I feared now – as I had never feared in a dream or in life – some destruction beyond destruction, some death beyond death – the vengeful spirits of an enemy people bearing me relentlessly, no way my spirit could flight, my own spirit people safe beyond our centuries – built bridge and no way they could reach me to help though I had prayed for them every day of my life – and prayed for them now – prayed that nothing should ever wrench them as I had been wrenched, out of deep rest and into this surge toward something so fearful I could not envision it, only felt that I was growing younger, younger than forty, younger than thirty, hurtling into the scene of a vast battle, past explosions, into a calm – soldiers, their weapons stacked, moving slowly between houses – houses I had entered with my buddies and stared down at their cast off uniforms, dazed, unprotesting, or, desperate with loneliness, despair, lust, did what they did, my own wife, many years faded from my only photograph, in one of the houses the enemy lined up before, my own children pressed back against the wall of that house, their hands pressed over their eyes, the house become a wigwam, the uniforms on the floor beside the bed, on the ground beside the buffalo-skin pallet, changing, the uniforms changing, the buffalo rising from its blood, a calf scampering through tall and taller grass, into bloody placenta, tightening to fluid-filled womb.

I was back on my cot, back in a barracks safe miles behind the front lines, just back from successfully rocketing a barracks miles behind enemy lines. Three weeks before the next mission. But each enemy waiting to be killed three weeks from now had already had his revenge.

"What's next for you?" a buddy would ask, to be polite.

"Suicide." However my orders might read.

But like the soldier who would ask — like all soldiers — I would keep the Top Priority Military Secret — kept through all the centuries of Man — I would say what the orders said, nothing more.

ONE INDIAN AND TWO CHIEFS

AN INDIAN come chasing after a White girl he'd met in college—
The Three White Sharks set out to cut that Indian's braids and
leave them glistening like black-snakes in the dust of the Allport
High School parking-lot. And they planned to let their fists go
hard the full length of work-and-football-toughened arms to
slam into something softer than knuckles.

They felt like letting out some of the meanness that had
tensed up through the years of wishing to hell their goddamed
dads had stayed off the bottle long enough to get seniority in a
factory job in Portland—whose beautiful chicks were, older
brothers smirked, more willing than Allport's ugliest hungriest
whores, and accustomed to paying for their share of an evening,
as well.

The Three White Sharks—the toughest kids in Allport High
School. And about to graduate.

Their hatred included, vaguely, shame at television images
of Black people chasing White police in California and shame at
images of frightened Americans fleeing from Vietnam.

They told each other that pretty-boy Indian would be damned lucky if they only cut off his hair.

An hour later, with the help of a burglar-prevention spotlight, the three stole a first-aid kit from an unlocked sailboat and bandaged the wounds inflicted by their own shears.

"You shoulda rammed them scissors into his goddamned throat instead of letting him pry them out of your goddamned hands to use on us." Big's knife stabbed into the rotting dockpost Vince leaned against.

"He wouldn't have got the scissors if you'd kept his arms pinned." Vince told Big.

The post quivered against his shoulder again, but Vince held steady. Big was still leader, he knew and would have known even if Big hadn't started flourishing the goddamned knife. Big was still leader, but after the Indian had shot an elbow back into Big's solar plexus, Big had sat down on his huge ass, wheezing like a bull sea lion. Big was strong, but he was also slow and stupid. He was leader. But only for awhile. And only within limits. And that goddamned nickname "Vince the Wince" Big had started three years ago—it was as out of date as crap in diapers.

"Vince is right, Big." Jerry's band-aided fingers put cigarette-lighter to roach. And didn't offer.

"What a ya mean he's right?" Before getting cut, Big would have squeezed that roach out of Jerry's long thin fingers.

Jerry held the toke while Big muttered "Right about what?"

"About going to the Boys Club just to waste one Indian," Jerry said at last, through a pale exhalation of smoke.

Big sheathed his knife, looked down on Jerry's thin crew-cut glowing orange in the dock-light, then sent a last scornful look, which fell someplace between Vince's long, blond hair and the rotten post's new blond gashes. "Chicken Shits," Big said and strode off down the creaking planks.

"Vince." Jerry was passing the pot.

Rough weed, local-grown cut-rate, but it would help, calm things down a little.

"I'll take some of this and a few beers around to Big's place in an hour or so," Jerry said, his orange fuzzed eyes, nostrils and mouth all tight. "I've got a plan for us to waste that Indian tomorrow morning without anyone knowing we did it. Only thing is we can't let Big mess everything up like he did tonight."

Vince took a second toke, a long one, before passing the reefer back.

Nobody had messed up. Big had started to get the Indian's arms from behind okay just like he'd said he would, and the rest ought to have been easy – scissors at throat until the Indian held still and they could hack off his braids and leave him looking so damned odd no chick white or brown could look without laughing. A little of the old punching bag routine then. And dump the Indian into his Volkswagen camper buss – telling him to keep on driving down to California to stay with the niggers and Mexicans.

"Stick that Indian, Wince. Cut his goddamned throat," Jerry had yelled as Big went down from an elbow into the lungs. But there hadn't been time to think about Jerry's order. The scissors, twisted loose, had slashed his hand, which had been clutching the Indian's leather jacket lapel. Jerry got his arm gashed when he tried.

Right then one of them should have thought to run get the knives they'd hidden in Big's pickup truck just in case a patrol car came along, but, full of fright, they'd all three run after the Indian, and Big, stumbling ahead of all of them, had stopped, his knuckles cut so bad he couldn't have punched a baby, and, then, they'd all quit.

No no, Big hadn't messed up. The Indian was quick and tough. He might be a spoiled, rich college boy now – that shiny Volkswagen camper van – but he could fight. And no point in telling him to forget the new plan, which could fuck up just as likely as last night's and get them all in prison. Instead of trying to argue, Vince muttered "The Indian won't be around tomorrow. He knows he's already used up all his luck."

Jerry passed the roach.

"He'll be around."

Vince sucked deep, couldn't get enough into his lungs and into his head. "No job to hold that Indian here," he told Jerry. "Sleeping in a camper van in parking lots. A college guy with just a summer of fun to spend, as good someplace else as here. That Indian's half way to Seattle by now."

"There's one thing that ain't in Seattle."

"You mean Angel Twot? There are White girls everywhere."

"I mean Angela Woodlawn – Vince. After I've found out for sure which of his camping spots the Indian has gone to for the rest of the night, I'll take that six-pack around and talk to Big. We'll pick you up outside your house at four tomorrow morning. Bring perch-fishing gear and your pocket knife but not your sheath knife."

No knives – big clubs they could throw away afterward. Like they'd done before. But this time not just for a little blood. This time, murder.

The Indian would wake up when they broke his van windows, and there'd be the scissors flashing in dimness for sure, a tire tool maybe, or maybe even a gun.

Jesus, Vince thought, if that dinge had just let us cut his goddamned hair and slam him around a little, he'd be out of it, we'd be out of it. Jesus.

That damned Angela Woodlawn – that damned Angel Twot. She'd turned Jerry down. Naturally. Her a year older. And in college. Jerry was smart enough, a brain, even when he wanted to be, and when it wasn't football season, but he was a mill worker's kid, and Angel Twot's old man was a snotty University Marine Museum fish-scientist. Jerry had probably talked Big into going after the smoothie, good-looking Indian, and Jerry had tricked Big into thinking the braid-cutting was his own idea. And sure as hell he'd get big drunk and talked into going after the Indian again tomorrow – no way out of it – Jesus, Jesus, Jesus.

"Well, look now – Pokyhontas, it sounds like these high school kids were just out for a little fun and you maybe hurt them bad with that scissors there."

"No, Sergeant," Jim Redwolf said, "they weren't badly hurt." He realized he'd better shift ground fast. "You're probably right, Sergeant, they were just horsing around, and I should be moving on down the road so there's no more trouble."

"First, I'll check your I.D. Maybe you dodged your time in Vietnam before the fighting ended."

Before the Communists whipped hell out of us, Jim Redwolf thought, but only got his Honorable Discharge copy.

The cop glanced at it then handed it back, blue eyes aimed at some red neon and shadows twisting across a small gray filing cabinet by the window. "I was a rifleman myself," he said. "Korea." Then, "You'd better haul ass out of town before those three catch up with you. The Three White Sharks Club is probably what you tangled with, and what they lack in smarts they make up for with being mean — pure mean."

The neon-reddened street was crowded. Friday night — high school kids free to hell around, the three who had jumped him now part of the crowd maybe and watching for their next change.

He unlocked the camper-van, got in, and locked the door again, starting the engine before bending down to the dark floor and bringing his sheath knife up onto the seat beside him.

When traffic had cleared for a long way up the dim street, he pulled out. Headlights went on and pulled out half a block behind him, then followed him up to the highway. At the stop sign, he did a quick turn right, causing a driver to brake like hell and angrily blink lights.

After a few blocks he could see a car weaving in and out of traffic a long way behind him, but traffic was heavy and when the Old Harbor turn came, he decided to risk it.

All the way to the crest of the first hill, he watched the black door-mirror silhouetted against his headlights. No one had turned onto the road after him.

He drove beyond the abandoned Coastguard wharf, where he usually parked to fish, turned behind a screen of willows and switched off the lights.

When he stepped out into the warm, damp darkness, he thought of home — his kid brother and some others maybe crouched in somebody's pick-up truck right now, parked behind a mesquite thicket, a White gang mad about something they thought had happened at the dance hall, or just drunk and feel sadistic.

He thought of Vietnam, the rifle, that could make you the equal of a dozen enemies, clutched. With mortars slamming big rubber trees down like dry grass, the rifle seemed puny maybe, but it was a comfort. You cleaned it, made it yours, and you felt secure — felt you were doing all you could, and if you were killed, it wouldn't be your fault — not as if you'd done it to yourself.

The driver's seat was still warm as his hand moved across it, finding the sheath knife, to take with him into his bed in the back of the van.

At daybreak he would fish and try to catch enough for all day. He'd cook on his butane stove so there would be no smoke.

The next day, he'd park outside the Marine Biology Museum, a place public enough so he'd be safe, and once he'd seen Angela's father drive up for work, he'd call Angela from a pay-phone.

Her mother and father would be delighted that he had to flee town, but he wasn't sure he could convince them or Angela that she would be safer going back to California. And maybe, with him, she wouldn't be any safer in California. Or anyplace.

Grasping a braid in the moonlight, he made up his mind to one thing. Tomorrow, in the long time he'd have hiding out, he'd cut his hair, using his safety-razor and the rear-view mirror. It was too bad he had taken the shears to the police-station. But at least he'd found out what to expect from the law. Tomorrow, he'd get himself to looking as much like a Chicano as possible. And hope that was the lesser of two evils.

"Son of a bitch has scalped himself, but it's him all right," Jerry said. "Knew he'd be there as soon as I saw him turn onto this road last night." If he'd know what was good for him, he'd a kept right on till the only hitch hikers was penguins."

"He's going to get more than hair cut off him today," Big said. "Teach that fucking Indian to slice my hand. I'll cut his goddamned family jewels off him and drop them into Angel Twot's mailbox for her to find when she comes back from that sister's wedding in Portland."

"You shouldn't have brought that sheath knife, you dumb son of a bitch," Jerry told Big.

"Huh — Who you callin — ?"

Jerry whirled away from Big, strode to a ditch lined with saw-grass and raised up with an eight foot willow sapling about as thick as an arm and with a canvas pad wired like a boxing glove on one end. "Won't be a mark on him," he said. "Here. He held the pole like a rifle across his chest and threw it to Big, like a drill-sergeant throwing a recruit a rifle in a movie. "Vince."

He put his hands up, but Jerry only handed him his pole.

The Indian had probably started reeling in his fishing line as soon as he'd heard the two trucks, and even though he'd been way out at the end of the old wharf, he was almost back to shore, a white fiberglass spin-rod in his left hand, a string of four perch silver in his right, and a knife in that hand also.

Jerry charged out onto the wharf, the pole out like a lance.

The Indian tried to duck under it, but Jerry just slanted the padded prod lower, and toppled the Indian into the water.

It was a six foot drop. The Indian sank deep and didn't surface until he'd swum out of reach of the pole. His bare arms glistened like metal as they cut the murky tide.

Vince thought of the Indian's strength, wrenching the scissors from his hand last night, and he thought all right, let Jerry do it all. But when Big started running down the shore to keep the Indian from landing, he started to follow Big, as he'd always done.

"Vince, you stay put," Jerry yelled.

It was like getting a deer – quiet and sneaky in the gray dawn, then all hell cutting loose, Jerry and Big shouted "Run here" or "Climb that – cut him off".

The Indian had stayed well out from the reach of Big's pole, and when the tide caught him, he was spun thirty yards into mid channel.

"Not a mark on him," Jerry laughed. "He's swimming for the other shore, but the tide should take care of that. I'll drive on over just in case. There's nobody on the fishing docks this early, not on Saturday. I'll pick up Big and drive on over there. Just to make sure the Indian doesn't grab onto something to float him on over. You patrol this side."

Jerry was unhurried now. He put his pole diagonally onto the bed of his dad's pickup. He'd cut the pole as long as he could and still get it out of sight on the pickup bed.

"Pull the pad off and throw your pole back into the ditch," Jerry said. "Then get to catching some perch. They're our alibi. Too bad the Indian didn't leave his string tied to the dock. But now you'll have to catch enough for all of us. Once the Indian's gone down for sure, Big and I will drive up-river a few miles on the other side. When you see us drive off, you drive Big's truck on after us. You'll see where we've parked. And we'll spend the rest of the day fishing. A perfect alibi."

Jerry drove off as leisurely as any fisherman, picked up Big and continued slowly driving toward the bridge. He'd planned it all, and he'd damned near done it all himself.

The Indian's naked leg flashed up like a fish into sun as the tide twisted him.

It was weird seeing his body so tiny far out where only motor boats could make headway against the outgoing tide. The Indian had gotten his pants off and knotted to hold air in the legs and work like a life preserver. He might make it to the other shore. But it was slow going crosswise to the tide.

Vince saw Jerry's blue pick up truck park where the commercial fishermen parked when the fishing was good.

The Indian stopped swimming and sort of straightened up, treading water, when he saw chrome flash in sun rise up on the docks, and when he saw Big and Jerry coming down to a rowboat tied against the dock, the Indian turned and went with the tide.

The air filled pant legs keeping his head up, he was still swimming with his legs even though he was headed for no place this side of Japan.

Son of a bitch, Vince thought, that red dude has got something going for him all right.

Makes jack-shit to me, he told himself. Serve Gee-ron-i-mo right for sticking it to Angel Twot.

He had got his fishing pole out, but he kept on watching the Indian growing smaller and smaller, his legs like dark bug feelers frantically twitching.

He saw a boat, and for an instant thought it was someone coming to the rescue, but then he recognized Big's huge red-shirted back bent to the oars.

The blue pick up truck was whirling out of the lot.

Something had sure as hell gone wrong, Vince realized. He saw Jerry pull up at the westmost pier and saw Jerry waving to Big, who was rowing to beat hell but hadn't yet got that far.

Beyond, there was nothing but steep rock for a mile and then the new Coast Guard Station, cyclone fence glittering in the sun, the big red white and blue cutter tied at its dock.

The Indian had abandoned his air filled blue jeans to try to outrace Big, and it was hard to tell the strokes of his distant arms from the shadowy chop of waves.

I hope it makes it, Vince thought. By God, I hope that guy makes it.

He threw his fishing pole into the back of Big's pick up truck, started the clunky old engine and took off, gravel shooting like machine bullets against the Indian's camper van.

By now, white uniformed Coast Guardsmen were clustered on the dock beside their cutter, the Indian's glistening, naked figure among them.

The first blue puff of the cutter's engine smoke glided like a manta ray over the water as Big's rowboat drifted past the dock, Big no longer rowing, nothing but Japan ahead of him, only hope the Coast Guard cutter and prison.

Vince knew it couldn't be Portland. The sheriff would remember that his brother was there. But it had to be a city, where a parked pick up truck wouldn't be noticed. He chose Salem, and the memory of its gold capital dome reminded him of his long blond hair. On a logging road, a mile from the freeway, he parked, got out his little pocket knife and, using the outside door mirror, hacked off enough hair so he could get the rest of it under his knit cap.

In the parking lot of a factory too small to hire a guard, he changed license plates with a painter's van, figuring the guy would never check the plates, which looked about the same as the ones he had.

With a section cut off somebody's garden hose, he siphoned gas from a car big enough to have plenty.

The rest of the night he slept in the cab of the pick up parked amid others outside a lumber mill, got in line with the vehicles of the graveyard shift, mingled with heavy morning traffic getting onto the freeway, and headed south.

In San Francisco, he got a short haircut and sold the truck cheap to a guy who didn't know the difference between an Oregon Registration Form and a certificate of title.

After an all night bus ride to Houston, Texas, he felt safe.

He got a job as a dishwasher. With what was left from his sale of Big's uncle's pick up truck, he bought an old red Ford sedan, which was mechanically o.k. but beat up and rusty from Gulf of Mexico salt spray—just like it would have been with Pacific spray in Allport.

He drove to a plastics plant on his morning off from dishwashing, and he got a union-scale job.

The day he would have graduated from high school, he drank half a case of beer and slept with a whore and, for the first time in his life, was able to pay for an all-nighter. The whore was black. But much prettier than the two white whores working the same bar.

"I'm from California, and I'm part Indian and I'm not prejudiced," he drunkenly, lovingly told her.

"Ahm from Houston and Ahm not pretchutiss eithuh."

His billfold was empty the next morning, but he only chuckled. That chick knows how to look out for herself.

So do I, he added, blurrily, wishing she'd have at least left him a cigarette, then thinking what the hell, I can eat at the plant cafeteria and they'll take it out of my pay. I'll get along.

He wondered how Big and Jerry had celebrated the graduation they weren't going to have.

In prison, they could work it out who was going to lead who, who was going to push who around, and how far.

As he pulled on his pants, he noticed a throb in his dong—hard use, he hoped—but if it was the clap, he could get himself fixed up at the factory clinic—and, as he realized that at least he wasn't going to have a hangover, he thought of the Indian and Angel Twot—Big's name for Angela—Angela Woodlawn.

He thought of the Indian swimming out of reach of the poles, then shoes off, pants off knotting the legs and catching air in the them while treading water, thinking quick and not wasting one second of his luck.

Indian, I have a hell of a lot more to thank you for than just Manhattan Island, he said, and raised gratefully to his bruised lips a quarter of a bottle of stale beer he'd overlooked last night in his hurry to get into the saddle.

Number one, was how he put it, summing it up for himself for the first time since hitting the road. Nobody wants to lead you for just no reason, he thought. Number One is who you live and die as. And you'd better, by God, hadn't let yourself to go off to sleep at the wheel.

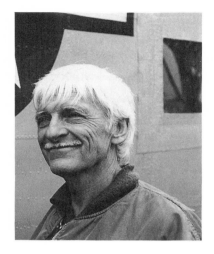

Ralph Salisbury has published five books of poems. Poems, stories and chapters from his nearly completed novel *The Raven Mocker Wars* have appeared in journals, anthologies and over the National Public Ratio program *New Letters on the Air*, with an interview by Joseph Bruchac. Son of a traditional Cherokee story-teller, he has presented his work before audiences and over radio and tv in the U.S., Canada, India, Great Britain, Germany, Denmark, Finland and the Soviet Union. His book of short stories *One Indian and Two Chiefs* will be published by Navajo Community College Press in 1995.

Jean Starr

DREAM IN THE HOUSE
OF STRANGERS

I DREAMED I was standing barefoot in the middle of a wide
prairie. I was completely alone. The waist-high grass stretched
out in front of me, on and on, a light green gently curving
dome. At the edge of everything, it met a blue dome sweeping
high overhead with a clarity of color that seemed to pierce my
heart. I stood watching wind-shadows ripple across miles and
miles of grass. I stood watching with mindless acceptance as
the butterflies lifted and fell, first one by one, then together in
a cloud, floating in the brilliant light. I began to turn slowly,
scanning the horizon, until, having turned almost full-circle, I
saw dust, then movement, and by some mysterious process
identified horse and rider, coming toward me, coming very fast
indeed.

That same strange internal awareness that said "horseman"
now said "dangerous: run, get away." Still, I stood there,
watching butterflies and ripples in the grass, smelling hot
dust, dried grass, and a green-and-growing scent on the breeze

with increasing pleasure, feeling better all the time. This consciousness I had was anxious, fearing, terrified, yet I was
warm, happy, really pleased with life. As the horseman drew
closer and closer, finally the terror-thoughts became resigned
despair: "At least stand still and get raped/killed/mutilated
with some dignity, not like a rabbit trying to burrow under the
roots of the grass."

And he rode on and on, nearer and nearer. Suddenly I knew
him, and I was incoherent with joy and the shock of that recognition, screaming "Oh, Frank! Oh, my husband!"

And as he came nearer, I saw that he was wild with it, triumphant, transcendent with joy, yelling wordlessly above the
pound of the horse's hooves on the hard ground. He rode
straight for me, slowing, swerving, never quite stopping, and he
swung me up behind him with a hard-gripping hand.

"I got away! I got away!" he screamed in the wind of our
passage; I clung to him, sliding precariously on the saddle blanket as we flew across the prairie faster and faster. I tried to ask
him where we were going, but to tell the truth, I was so happy I
didn't much care.

On and on we went at breakneck speed. Just at dusk, we
began to climb. I recall tall trees outlined against the sky, pine-
smell, water-smell, coolness; we went higher and higher in darkness. Finally the horse stopped moving. Frank said, "We're
here," slid from the saddle, and lifted me down.

I was standing. I saw, before a tiny lean-to cabin built of
peeled logs, with a roof of fresh-cut cedar branches. We were in a
little valley, a sort of cup, on the side of a great mountain, very
high up. I could hear water falling from a height somewhere out
of sight, a thin and silver sound. I was looking up at stars so big
they were like the starflowers blooming in the prairie grass:
flowers of light, I was thinking, and all at the same time, Frank
was walking me, his arm wrapped tight around me, half-
carrying me, to a pile of those soft cedar boughs covered with a
blanket. He wrapped another blanket around my shoulders and
I watched him light a fire at the stone hearth at my feet and
swing an iron kettle over the fire to heat. Soon he was pouring
hot liquid into a cup. Carrying it carefully, he came and sat down
beside me, putting his arm around my shoulders, and he held the
cup to my lips. It tasted like all the prairie grasses and flowers

distilled together; It warmed my mouth, my throat, and my belly; it healed and soothed old injuries, old pain, and nothing bad mattered any more.

"Ah, poor old Liz, poor girl," Frank said. "I've rode you a hard ride today, though you never whimpered about it, but I've got you away, safe away, you see, just the way I told myself I'd do."

I leaned against him, burrowing my head further into the hollow of his shoulder, turning the side of my face against his chest. I was thinking how good he always smelled, even with the added aroma of horse and the expensive-men's-cologne smell of cedar and woodsmoke and sage. I was thinking how happy, how happy I now was. And we began to talk drowsily there in the firelight, and, as the coals burned down, I suddenly knew we were not talking same-old-everyday English, but some other tongue, some language so acute that we could say our very thoughts. We lay back on the cedar boughs in each other's arms and talked on and on, each one exclaiming, "Oh, you, too? You, too? I never knew you thought that . . ." and never, never had I loved Frank as I loved him then, nor known as clearly his love for me than at that moment.

It was then that I woke up, and the tears of loss and sorrow ran down my face. Frank lay there beside me, sprawled out, dead asleep. I sat up, moving very carefully so that he would not wake up, and watched his unconscious face in the light of the streetlight pouring in the window. I looked at the beautiful shape of his mouth softened in sleep, the way it never was when he was awake. With coming consciousness, his mouth would harden, his lips would set, jaw tighten, in readiness for that world of people outside our battered door. My throat prickled with tears. I carefully got up and went to the kitchen, trying not to break into uncontrollable weeping before I shut the door. It was hopeless; I could never tell Frank of my dream.

Who is to say how much a man can take? I could imagine myself talking to him as he sat in the overstuffed chair from the Good-Will with the corded brown bedspread thrown over it to (kind of) disguise that the upholstery was leaking, sitting there gray in the face and shaking with exhaustion, from working all day lifting and hauling, unloading trucks, washing down long-haul rigs, or any of the back-breaking spirit-killing jobs he was struggling to get and keep, for the money, the money to pay the rent, the money to eat, the money to send back home, the money to get things for me which he would hand me wordlessly to say the things that choked in his mouth.

In the face of all that, I could say, "Well, Frank, it's like this: I dreamed this wonderful dream, and I was happy. I can't tell you how happy I was, because you've never in your whole life seen anybody as happy as I was in this dream. Well, what I was so overjoyed about was this: you came up on this horse and you rescued me, taking me to this perfect little paradise in the wilderness, and, get this, Frank: we could speak our every thought to each other. I mean, I understood you, and you understood me, and I never loved you so much nor you me! Well, it was really great, and then I woke up, right back here on good old 14th Avenue, in the same old crummy walk-up, which is all that we can afford." I could do this about as much as I could kick him in the face, and, I thought, the kick would probably hurt less.

I never did get back to sleep.

By the time Frank woke up, I had coffee made, eggs frying, hot cereal started. As usual, I showered while he ate. Not as usual, I was still in the shower when he was ready to leave. He stuck his head around the shower curtain for a soggy goodbye kiss, and was off to catch his bus. I wandered around, wrapped in a damp towel, sunk in misery, brooding over what I wanted to wear, trying to think what I wanted to take to work, what I wanted to eat for lunch. I knew that in fact I did NOT want to get my clothes on, get on the bus, did NOT want to go to work, eat lunch, be normal and ordinary.

When I got to work, I walked past the pushing, screaming crowd of children into the front door of good old P.S. 109, and I walked down the corridor to the staff lounge, still on auto-pilot. As I opened the refrigerator door to put away my bag-lunch, I had an instant vision of myself sitting in one of the lounge's beat-up red plastic imitation-leather armchairs, leaning forward and telling my dream to somebody, but I couldn't imagine who it would be. Not the principal, nor the school nurse, nor even the teachers I worked for. My tongue seemed to stick to the roof of my mouth. I thought of a poem I hadn't remembered for years, written by Dylan Thomas: "The Force That Through The Green Fuse Drives the Flower." When I was little and literal-minded, in fact, when I first heard the poem, I thought the part that goes "And I am dumb to tell" meant "I am *stupid* to tell" instead of speechless. Now "dumb to tell, DUMB to tell" was resonating in my head.

Well, all day, through pinning up the children's art work and marking their papers and running off dittos and taking a line of boys from Mrs. Robertson's fourth grade to the bathroom, through play-yard supervision and library check-out and lining them up for lunch, all of it was accompanied by phantom hoof-beats and aching loss, by the memory of feeling that awareness and acuteness. There in the dream I could almost hear grass grow. And here I was, out on the play-yard with Mrs. Johnson's Late-Bird third-graders, shepherding dodge-ball players, the same old dull-normal me.

I never did remember to eat lunch, which was just as well. As I helped Mrs. Johnson bring the third-graders in from the yard, one of them threw up: it was Sonya. (In fact most things of note in that class involved Sonya.) Since vomiting is usually epidemic with kids that age, she didn't get a great deal of attention; four more children began to heave, and Brian, who was standing next to me, threw up on my shoes.

After a few hectic minutes which would probably have looked like total chaos to an outsider, we two adults got all of them headed in the proper directions; the five who were sick I gathered up and took to the nurse's office, while Mrs. Johnson organized the rest.

Finally I got the chance to clean up. Standing barefoot in the staff women's restroom, trying to breathe through my mouth to avoid the stomach-wrenching smell, I was scrubbing my sneakers in the stream of water from the faucet, and muttering through my clenched teeth "I WANT this job; I LIKE this job; I NEED this job" when Mrs. Johnson opened the door behind me. "Well, I'm sure glad to see you're mad, Liz," she said. "When you looked at Brian with that angelic smile and told him your shoes were washable, I was struck speechless. Never in a million years could I come up with a reaction like that!"

We both laughed, she, I think, because she thought it was genuinely comic and because she's like that, bubbling with high spirits and humor, and me because I suddenly realized she like me, cared about me, in the middle of all that commotion, and getting the kids calmed down and back in the classroom, she thought about me and took a minute to see if I was all right. "Hey, I guess I'll break the rules and go barefoot," I said.

"Well, I doubt if the P.T.A. Clothes Closet has your size," she said, grinning, and we walked back together in harmony, really the best moment we'd had.

On the bus going home, it was jam-packed as usual, full of high school students and late afternoon shoppers and old gray men and women and a few of the usual weirdos. I got on and slid into a seat just ahead of a very fat lady with six or seven parcels in the hope she would ride most of the way with me, and stay between me and a couple of drunks I saw toward the back. I sat thinking all the way home about that wall of glass that seemed to stand between me and everyone. It was there from the time we came to the city; the dream just made me think about it.

Well, sure, it says in the magazines you are supposed to practice honest communications. (I can't afford to buy them, but I read a lot of magazines in long supermarket check-out lines.) O.K., I sit down with Mrs. Johnson and I say, "You know, when I was in school, they gave the kids lessons in turning on the faucet. Also toilet-paper and flushing."

Try again: "They came and got my mother and took her away to school by force when she was six. She never saw her mother again; she died while Mama was in boarding school 500 miles away. They used to beat them up for talking Indian. I only got slapped in the face."

Well, there's two reactions to that kind of thing. People either get really sympathetic and treat you like "poor thing" from then on, or they make a few polite noises and have as little to do with you as possible: you're in another category, either way. Me, I'd rather be "the girl" or just another pair of hands than a living example of a Christmas Basket's results.

As the bus lurched on, I envisioned introducing Mrs. Johnson to my Grandfather, the way he was at the last, old and bent, hair in two pencil-thin white braids, wearing the old shirt with the mismatched buttons we couldn't persuade him to give up, refusing crankily to speak English at all.

"Oh, Grampa, what do I do now?" I thought. In school, so much of what we learned was garbage, just junk: the boarding school kids were all taught to be house-painters or cooks, but they don't paint houses that way in Los Angeles or Reno or Santa Fe or anywhere except at boarding school. They use modern things like sprayers and rollers. And cooking was the same; all the girls learned was institutional cooking, the kind you only eat if you're locked up. It was all like that, what we tried so hard to learn so that we could compete off-reservation: typing on 30-year-old machines, and learning the antique switchboard and sweeping the principal's office so that we could be secretaries.

But the old things, the Indian things, they don't work, they taught us, that's ignorant. And what else did we have, Grampa? I mean, you couldn't help it, but you know, a frail wizened-up old man whose greatest secret weapon when he's backed into a corner by his tormentors is to refuse to understand their language isn't exactly someone to inspire a lot of confidence. And all they'd do was to roll their eyes and make remarks about what a dummy you were and go get an interpreter. No, you couldn't make a getaway, could you, Grampa? Daddy did; fine getaway that was, dead of alcohol at 37. But I wanted you to win, I wanted Daddy to beat them all somehow, and you never did, never once. Well, sweet suffering Jesus, you couldn't even manage to get to town by yourself, not even on the bus, so we're supposed to believe you had some answers that would help us deal with what we're doing now. I say "Native American" if it ever comes up, I tell myself that this is my country, even 14th Avenue and P.S. 109, but in my heart I know I'm living in a House of Strangers, and I'm scared to death.

I AM ALL ALONE, GRAMPA. ALONE IN THE HOUSE OF STRANGERS, and there is no one at all that I can tell the truth to. There is a silence like a wall of glass between me and my husband, my darling, my man. I am ALONE, Grandfather, and what do your medicine and your bird-bone whistles and your sacred smoke have for me today in the way of answers?

I saw with my eyes tight-shut, as if the Voices on the Wind might just penetrate the smog today, and I almost had a heart-attack when a little old lady tapped me on the arm and asked me if I was all right. I mumbled something and got off, embarrassed to death and ten blocks past my stop. As I walked, over and over again I saw the words DREAM, and GLASS and

WALL and ALONE. It was as if the city streets and I were having a idiot conversation, and one of us couldn't speak the language too well.

I climbed the stairs; the phone was ringing; it was Frank, working overtime, he said. "O.K." I replied, "See you then."

Well, that's the problem. How can I give a big encouraging cheer for Frank's getting a chance to work until he drops? But how can I say, "Oh, that's terrible, honey" when he's thankful he's bringing home more money? And he probably wouldn't get himself something to eat, either.

I began to scrub the kitchen floor, Mama's old version of psychotherapy. Right about the middle, beside the stove, I began to remember Grampa talking to me. It was so clear, so clear, like a tape recording. He was just rambling on, the way he used to do the last year of his life, when I was in fifth grade. I used to sit beside him on the porch and say, "Yeah, Grampa, yeah, I'm listening," whenever he stopped, hours and hours of it.

". . . all alone. You got to be all alone, you see. They don't let nobody go with you, not your nearest nor your dearest, 'cause that's when They speak to you. Sometimes They speak and sometimes They come. They can look like anyone, you know, like animals or friends or strangers. You fast and you pray, fast and pray, and you sit in the sweat-house to purify yourself, and out there on the hill-side alone They come with the wind and the night, come with the dawn. And what They have to say, you won't know what it means, not then, but it means *something*. You know to tell, and you know NOT to tell. And some day, what you're supposed to know comes to you. And the rest of your life, They speak to you in the day and the night, in voices and in dreams, and you know it's Them talking to you, 'cause it's a dream that stays with you and won't let go."

I thought about it.

I made some thick sandwiches and cut up onions and bacon into a can of baked beans and put it into a pan to cook slowly. I didn't intend it that way, but when Frank finally got home, I was asleep, and when I woke up, it was the alarm clock that woke me. He was up and gone again, leaving a note: "Gone to wk. early shift."

All day I felt kind of shaky, like I was learning everything all over again, how to do each little thing with the kids, and the way they looked and sounded and smelled when I sat down next to them to tutor them. At the end of the day, I was putting away the crayons and the paints in Mrs. Johnson's third grade room, and I decided to stay a little after school and make a really good job of it. I was tackling a spill in the supply closet, and I had everything out on the table when idly I began to mess with the dry tempera. Wet brush, touch the powder; touch, touch the paper. Delicate little touches; I hadn't forgotten how. How much we forget in time.

It hit me: one day the dream would fade, the whole thing gone. I had an awful feeling, a depression of spirit as actual as a rain-cloud. I picked up a fresh piece of paper and I began to paint, faster and faster, the camp-site in the little mountain valley, in the deep dark, and me, and Frank, and even the steel-dust horse and the stars that bloomed overhead. Tiny little strokes in the old Kiowa Five style, the way my teacher taught me, my teacher who knew all those old-time painters.

Finally it was done. I laid it down to dry, and slowly cleaned up, kind of afraid to look at it again. But it was all right, it was fine. I put it between two pieces of cardboard and walked slowly through the deserted building, surprised to find it was almost dark. I caught the bus, and rode home, and climbed the stairs. I was only halfway up when Frank threw open the door of our apartment. He ran down the stairs and gripped me by the elbows; shaking me for emphasis, he said, spacing the words out, "Where—have—you—BEEN?"

It was too much—I started to cry. He grabbed me, mashing my face against his shirt-pocket, patting the back of my head as if I were a horse, and pressing his face against the top of my head. He hauled me up the stairs, talking and talking; he was just about to call the hospitals and the police when I showed up; and he was pushing me into the armchair and shutting the door and wiping my face with a paper towel, and saying, "But what happened? Why were you so late?" and stopped.

I couldn't talk. I gave a couple of dry sobs and handed him my dream painting.

He froze. "How could you paint this, Liz?" he said slowly, reaching out his hand to me, "It's my dream, honey, you've painted a dream I had."

And I could understand him, and he could understand me;

we could say our very thoughts, and all that night, we lay there in each other's arms, and talked on and on; never, never had I loved Frank as I loved him then, nor known so well his love for me.

Jean Starr, who passed away in 1994, taught English and ethnic studies at American High School in Sacramento, an inner-city alternative school. A teacher for more than a quarter century, she was the first director of the American Indian Education Program for her school district and a former officer for the National Education Association's American Indian/Alaskan Native Caucus.

Of her family she wrote, "I come from one of those families with very few records or documents; neither of my parents nor their 24 siblings, nor my grandparents and their 26 siblings had any birth certificates. My father was 19th in his family, my mother also a younger child, and both sets of grandparents were youngest—if there ever was a family Bible, it certainly went elsewhere. My mother was a Gaines; her father is said to have been a full-blood Cherokee from the hills above Bristol, Tennessee. My maternal grandmother was a Marks; her family is said to have been one of those Blue Ridge Mountain families displaced because they were north of the treaty-line. My Marks grandmother was a Deaver, and her mother was a Tuya or Bean, said to have been a Going-back, escaped from Oklahoma. (I have located some possible cousins in Tahlequah, descendents of my Tuya great-grandmother's brothers, we think.)

"My family were, for the most part, poor uneducated subsistence farmers who spent their lives having a yard full of kids and trying to raise enough corn and chickens to feed them. Most of them were too poor to have a tombstone in a cemetery, so that the only record of their having been on earth is their descendants.''

The author of *Tales From The Cherokee Hills*, her poems and stories appeared in numerous magazines and anthologies, including *Nimrod*, *Tamaqua*, *Poetry East* and *Returning The Gift*.

Winn Starr

DEATH IN THE OIL PATCH

CHAPTER ONE: SPUDDING IN

I LEFT MY BIKE in front of the Derricktown Post Office, looking up to see if one of the gushing Oklahoma spring rains was imminent. Not quite. At the General Delivery window, the Postmaster, Lloyd Owens, was standing, dressed up as usual, with a big gold and diamond Shrine pin in his tie. He loved to wear the Shriner stuff. Since the O'Connor brothers had got back from working on the big Middle East Pipeline they kidded Mr. Owens a lot, saying if he had lived around people who wore fezzes and such he wouldn't think it was so glamorous, and all the Syrians and Lebanese around town said the only reason the Arabs weren't insulted was that the Shrine costumes were so hokey the Arabs didn't know who was being satirized. That's Mamma's word for it. But, anyway, I asked Mr. Owens if there was a package for Samuel Houston Douglas. He whipped it right out from a shelf, commenting, "Must be important — comes from the 'Investigative Resources Agency of New York'," so smooth he had obviously studied the package until he memorized it. Old Jake Bower, the town handyman, was hanging around close. Mamma said he knew more about everybody's dirty linen than the doctors and lawyers. He made some remark about letting kids waste money, proving he not only knew everything, but gave his opinion on it. This particular secret was my detective kit advertised in the back of the Phantom Detective magazine. If they hadn't sent the kit this week, they would have lost my business. Tenny and I had been waiting a month to get started on our detective careers. (more later.)

I put the package in the handlebar basket and rode down Skelly Street. The usual Saturday bunch of country and oil camp people had started to wander around. They caught up on the gossip, looked in all the stores, had a sort of picnic lunch on cheese and crackers, canned peaches and bottles of Nehi; and finally drifted off to the country again with what staples, like flour and molasses, they could afford. It made the town look pretty crowded for a while.

I sighted Auntie Horse in the midst of the Saturday shoppers, kicking her bright skirts out before her with every step, as she searched for Evil. People were giving her uneasy looks, but I didn't see her swooping on any victim.

It was just starting to rain a little as I went past the Passtime Theater and looked to see what was on. It was Hoot Gibson with a Flash Gordon serial. I filed it away as a possibility.

If I seem to have covered a lot of subjects, it may be because of what Judge Ellsworth calls my 'proclivity for *obiter dicta*'. That's not exactly a criticism, because the judge says the little side remarks in legal decisions are the only sensible part.

By this time, I was out of what you might call 'downtown' and was going past the Park, with the picnic tables and amphitheater the WPA had built. That's besides the library and the high school gym, etc. Mamma says it just proves what you can do by leaning on shovels long enough. 'Satiric', again. Mamma likes to meet Mrs. Sidebotham, the big Republican, at the weekly variety shows at the amphi, and go on about how it's too bad the WPA never did anything useful. The Sidebothams went to the free shows, too, even if they had money. He even represented the Chamber of Commerce on the Park Program Committee, now and then, kind of seething that he couldn't call it

Communism because they all figured it was good for business. It was pretty cheap, too, because there were so many groups that would perform for gas money and the publicity. The shows didn't start until May, (I mentioned the spring rains) but they already had a shrine band from Tulsa, a Guthrie dance school and a Little Theatre from somewhere lined up. Roosevelt was starting his second term, after wiping out Alf Landon, but Mr. Roundtree said times were still bad enough to make people appreciate anything free.

On one of the park benches, poor Old Robert was dozing off his latest swig of quasilegal paregoric. (Some people could get it legally, but Old Robert didn't.)

Mr. Roundtree had taught me a couple of lines from a German poem when asked what was wrong with Old Robert. It went (Mr. Roundtree was funny about the spelling.): "*Es liesz ein jeder Frontsoldat/Win Stückchen Herz im Stacheldraht.*" "Each frontline soldier left a piece of heart in the barbed wire." Old Robert had used up too much heart.

We lived sort of at the edge of town so it was a while before I rode up the driveway and parked my bike *beside*, not in *front* of, the garage. Daddy-Doc needed to get his car out or in *right now* so often that I had quit leaving a *ragdoll* in the drive by the time I was three. Daddy-Doc (I called him that only to old family friends, or him when he was feeling good) was about as nice as any father in town, but doctoring came *first*. Once you understood that, you could sort of work around it and get along.

Mamma's car was gone. That meant she was out doing good, or having one of their many thick cups of spicy coffee with Mrs. Habib at Habib's Dresses for Less, or gone to Tulsa after one of the bargains advertised on the early shopping show from radio station KVOO. They were often worth a couple of gallons of gas. I went to the back door with my new package. Surprisingly, Arnold Fetz, who was raised back East, in Pennsylvania or somewhere, had to learn to use the back door all the time, like we did. The front door was for formal occasions. One of the town constables often said that it wasn't true that people around here never locked their doors; they locked the front; it was harder for a stranger to explain what he was doing in your back yard than on your front porch. One of my personal "Items for a Detective to Know" was that most back yards are visible from at least five back-doors. I yelled for Tenny as I stepped in, holding the package up like a trophy. She was in the kitchen, probably finishing the clean-up from breakfast. In Daddy-Doc's house they cooked three meals. The swish-thump of Tenny's walk got to the utility room, where I was holding up our prize, and she drawled, "Well, we're in business. Let's spud in."

(A "spud" is a long, narrow-bladed space you dig post-holes with. "Spudding in" was digging a hole to guide the drill bit straight into the ground when you started a well.)

Practical, as usual, Tenny had me put the package on the breakfast table, so we could spread out the contents as we unwrapped them. It was a real treasure, with a book on how to be a detective, a fingerprint kit, make-up for disguises, and lots more. Not knowing where else to start, I opened the book to the first page, and realized that it was going to be lot of help. The heading was "How To Find A Crime To Solve". You can't get much more practical than that!

Tenny and I sat right down and started going over the local news. As far as crime was concerned, we couldn't think of anything but the usual run of bootleg liquor highjackings. Prohibition had been over for four years in the rest of the country, but as Will Rogers said, Oklahomans would vote dry as long as they could stagger to the polls. They weren't the sort of crimes anyone got a regular detective for, since it was a matter of rival gangs, who didn't want the police any more involved than they were, which was plenty. As Mr. Roundtree said, if they weren't partners of the bootleggers, the taxpayers might have to pay them. What we needed was some local, individual crime. Tenny suggested, kind of joking, that we might just poke into anything that had gone wrong lately, for practice, and if it turned out to be criminal, we would have a head start on solving it.

If I'd been one of those lady writers Mamma was so fond of, that kept saying, "If only I had known!", this would have been a good place to use it. But I've refrained.

STORIES THAT MIGHT EVEN BE TRUE

BELLE STARR AND THE RANCHER'S DAUGHTER

PEOPLE THAT TELL you how to write stories tell you everyone needs a name. Personally, Cop A and B or Robber 1 and 2 would be o.k. But here we go: Douglas? Cameron? Buchanan!

Lem Buchanan was a half-breed Cherokee rancher, with lots of beef, and a 15-year-old daughter, Betty, who one day was sitting on the shady side of the ranch-house veranda, shelling peas and wishing she wasn't.

Pretty soon a welcome interruption came up to the house: a woman riding a roan mustang. She was riding sidesaddle, so she must have been female, though you couldn't tell from her face.

Betty didn't know her, but a couple of the older and rougher hands, Tux and Teece, did, so they drifted over to keep an eye on her.

"I'm Belle Starr," she announced in a whiskey baritone. Betty asked her to light and have some coffee, playing hostess.

Well, they commenced to talk, and by the time Lem came by and saw them (Betty's mother having lost a bout with typhoid) the ladies were thick as thieves.

Belle being in one of her spells of good behavior, or at least not having any outstanding warrants on her, Lem couldn't think of any good reason to run her off without a family fight.

He went over to talk with Tux, Teece having figured two hands watching the veranda was too many, and Belle went back to telling some of her lies that found such favor with young folks and lady authors, like "Belle Starr, Teenage Scout for Quantrell", or "Belle Starr at the St. Louis Grand Cotillion".

After a while of this, Belle graciously agreed to go out for a ride with Betty, and again Lem wasn't able to say no.

Tux threw a sidesaddle on a little gray mare while Betty changed, and soon the ladies cantered out east on the prairie.

Suppertime came, and no Belle and Betty. It started getting dark, and everyone was standing around outside, but Tux and Teece had saddled up, and were bringing Lem's saddle out when he finally said, "Let's go!" They were used to roundups and had men assigned to a search pattern in a few minutes. Just in case they didn't find her, they agreed to come back at midnight. They told the cook to have a big pot of beans and lots of coffee waiting, and scattered.

The first bunch back smelled burning beans on the west wind even before they noticed the quiet. The quiet only lasted 'til they finally saw the open corral gates in the light of the new moon, and it got downright noisy when they found old Loony Squirrell lying hogtied by the smoking beans and boiled away coffee on the stove.

Belle and Betty came riding in an hour after dawn, smiling and explaining how they had got lost and wound up at a ranch a long way off, and spent the night.

Lem and Tux and Teece agreed sending someone for the Sheriff would be a waste of time, when they could be looking for any fresh horses the rustlers had missed.

They were gentlemen. They even gave Belle breakfast before they escorted her off the ranch.

Betty waved goodbye.

THE HAWK

Blueford West Starr, son of Blueford West Starr, was riding along with a bunch of other cowhands one day, back in the 'Eighties (*Eighteen* Eighties, that was).

Nothing much was happening, and when a hawk flew over a ways off, Blue drew his pistol and shot it out of the air, one shot.

He immediately started to reload, as anyone with sense would do. The other hands were just looking at him as they rode.

At last, one of them asked, "Can you do that again?"

He didn't even look up. "I," he explained, "don't have to." Inside of a week, the whole Nation knew about the hawk and Blue's answer.

As far as anyone knows, Blue never had to shoot a man, either.

THE DECEIVERS

A buddy of mine was a rifleman in the 411th. I think it was Ralph Quigley. It's been a long time.

Ralph swore it really happened, and I've seen stranger things myself.

"It" took the form of a German officer in full regalia, including the Iron Crosses. He came striding up to Ralph and his friend Mike Kovacs, ceremoniously dropped his Stahlhelm and his pistol belt, and said in flawless English (it's *always* "flawless"), "I give up! You Americans are so tactically screwed up you're driving us crazy. We know what you *plan*. Your battalion staff *plans* to attack at 5:00 a.m. At 4:30 some G.I. drops his rifle. It goes off; someone yells, "The attack's started!" And here you come shooting and yelling, and we aren't in position. Or you plan to attack from the South, get lost in the woods, and hit our flank from the West.

"It's hopeless. Please—let me sit out the rest of the war in a nice, quiet P.W. camp!"

They obliged him.

INHERITANCE

Mick Smith was looking for clay. He was an Industrial Arts type, but he had gotten trapped by some artsy-craftsy do-gooders with money. They were clever – they gave him some of it.

These people knew that Indians were "good with their hands" and were at least willing to put up some front-money, so Mick had already built looms and had a stable of Cherokee women producing native cloth for the organization to market them. (The Cameron and McLachlan ties they made from the cloth were bestsellers.)

He was even getting some halfway decent peace-pipes and horses from some old guys back in the woods who spent most of their time whittling anyway.

The trouble was, he had some books from the Bureau of American Ethnography with pictures of Cherokee pottery someone dug up, and the sponsors were pushing for some traditional family pots.

Mike had a little shop set up in an outdoor arbor, including foot-powered wheels. (He figured "coils" were too advanced for his people at this stage.) Now he needed clay.

I guess he could have sent off, but the budget wasn't that good. So he and Sam Squirrel, his assistant, started talking clay, Cherokee style. That means, not so much in Tsalagi (although they spoke it) as in hinting, beating around the bush, maybe if you know someone who knows talk.

It wasn't long til Sam came up to the arbor one morning, grabbed a big bucket and a shovel and threw them in the back of Mick's pick-up (the "Indian suitcase"). That's another dialect Mick and I understood, so we jumped in and took off.

We went down a highway, a couple of country roads, and a trail that ended at a barb-wire fence in the woods. Sam carried the shovel, and led the way; pretty soon we saw a little shallow creek, which Sam scouted up and down. Then he looked close, waded the stream, and gestured for the bucket.

I wasn't shod for wading, but as well as I could see, the place on the bank where Sam dug hadn't been disturbed for a hundred years. He went right through layers of hard-packed dirt, cleared it out some, and there was a vein of smooth whitish-gray clay.

Sam filled the big bucket, "heaped up and packed down," like it says in the Bible.

Mick showed me how to use the wheel. The clay worked. The last I saw of him that time (I went away to school) he was copying ancient, traditional Cherokee designs on the pots and firing them like crazy.

Sam never said who told him. If you live around people who've been picking the same patches of huckleberries for a hundred and thirty or forty years without anyone outside the family knowing where they are, you can keep a tight lip.

METROPOLIS

Blue Starr was riding along in the high grass. I don't know where-from, except it was on one side of the Arkansas River, and where-to was on the other. That time of year it was too deep to ford, but he was ready.

When he got to the water he took off his pants and gun belt, and put them over his shoulders, and swam his horse across.

As he was wringing out and dressing on the other side, he noticed some tents a little way off. When he was ready, he rode over and asked some men what the place was called. They said, "Tulsy Town".

Nobody criticized Blue for riding without pants. Oral Roberts wouldn't arrive for a couple of generations.

FORWARD

A naïve, hopeful Philadelphian decided to risk 3¢ to satisfy his curiosity, back in June, 1931. He licked the stamp and stuck in on an envelope addressed to "The Cherokee Medicine Man," then dropped it in the nearest street-box, laughing at himself.

A postal clerk in St. Louis turned to a fellow worker. "What town is Will Rogers from?" He wrote the answer, "Claremore, Oklahoma" on the envelope before him.

In the Tulsa Post Office, a woman sorting mail followed the unofficial, word-of-mouth rule — "if it's for a Cherokee, or Cherokees, route it to Claremore."

The Claremore Postmaster told his wife, "We got two more of those letters to your cousin today." They both laughed.

Oswald, the letter carrier, trudged up the steep Main Street of Drumright, eventually reaching the even steeper stairs to the doctor's office.

The nurse-receptionist-bookkeeper, Brenda, received the packet of letters and medical journals from Oswald, telling him to take the weight off his feet while she checked to see if all those letters were really here. He would be happy to.

The letters ran about the same as usual — some "O.W. Starr, M.D.", some "Dr. O.W. Starr", some "Starr", an "Indian Doctor", two "Cherokee Medicine Man's", and one "To the doctor who cured my typhoid."

Brenda looked at the name of the sender on the last for some time, then she stared musing at the ceiling and added, "Dr. Reynolds" to the "address". "Here you are, Oswald. You guessed wrong on this one."

She handed it back with several other letters in her 'out' basket, including the one from the sweeping-cleaning-and-errand girl, Ursula. It was addressed, "To the Funniest Man in the World".

It eventually got to Will in Santa Monica.

I am Oliver Winn Starr, grandson of Oliver Ellsworth Winn, the toughest schoolmaster in Southern Indiana; Charity Evelyn Rector; Blueford West Starr, orphan, cowboy, rancher, tribal councilman; and Jesse Marion Hutchins, whose mother was a D.A.R. at Mt. Holyoke. My father, Orange Starr, was a cowboy who taught rope tricks to Will Rogers and got his M.D. at St. Louis University. My mother was a suffragette and the best teacher who ever chewed out a superintendent for not asking permission to enter *her* classroom.

I was born within earshot of the discovery well of the vast Cushing oilfield, grew up middle-class, semi-rural and bright. I was saved from nerdship by eighty mile-per-hour "bootlegger turns" and shooting quail with a .22.

After a tour of Alsace and the Rhineland with a 105 mm howitzer, and sometime in total immersion in German, I returned to Oklahoma University with an A.B. in Spanish and an M.Ed. in Secondary Teaching. I taught three years, here and there, and wound up working thirty years for the California teacher certification agency, the latter part as a "de facto" expert on education in the rest of the world.

First marriage, one son, one daughter. After a few years to heal, Jean and I met, fell in love, and had a twenty-year honeymoon, more than I deserved. We shared poetry, the National Education Association, and lots of Indians.

Glenn J. Twist

THE DISPOSSESSION

THE UGLY BRUTE of a man squinted down at me with uncaring eyes. "Woman," he said, "have you see'd Werfford about?"

I knew the sheriff and a number of ne'er-do-wells he had deputized to back him as he undertook the day's meanness. The calvary-men, a sergeant, a lance corporal, and a private first class, who rode up with the sheriff appeared to regard the law-men as strangers. Because they were careful to keep several yards between them and the sheriff's bunch, I gathered the soldiers didn't want to be considered a part of the sheriff's business.

I knew why the sheriff was in our yard this morning. At a considerable personal risk for his own safety, the Reverend Colerain had brought word last week that our homeplace was to be put in the next lottery, which meant the sheriff would be out in a few days to dispossess us, and give everything we owned to the white man who drew our name. I didn't know the reason for the military's presence.

If the lawman knew the reverend had brought us warning,

the good pastor of the mission at New Echota would likely be put in chains and hauled off to jail. So as not to make the "only half-bright" sheriff suspicious, I acted like he and his deputies had stopped for nothing more serious than water for their mounts. "What you doin' out our way so early?" I asked.

"Got business with your husband and Werfford," the sheriff said.

The shivers crossing my shoulders and slithering down my back were from the cold of the misfortune to be visited on us, rather than the chill of the raw autumn morning. Pulling my shawl closer didn't help. Besides, I was angry. It always makes me mad when someone, particularly the likes of the sheriff, treats me like I was no better than a piss-ant. This ol' buzzard was here to pick my family clean, to disposses us of everything we owned. It wouldn't have hurt him none to say hello when he rode up.

"You ought-a be off catching them fellows that done what they did to pore little Susie Squirrel," I said. "When you gonna 'rest 'em?"

"Them boys didn't mean the girl no harm. They wuz out to have a little fun and had a little too much to drink, that's all."

"Sheriff, you're as rotten as they are. You ought-a be horse whipped for talkin' like that. Little Susie was almost killed . . ."

"That's enough of your mouth, woman. Besides, the way I hear'd it, that ol' sot Squirrel traded 'em his girl for a demijohn of moonshine."

"That warn't no trade at all! If Susie'd been a white girl, and the rapists Indians, you'd already had the bastards strung up. Now get on out there and bring them fellers in like you ought-a."

"You kno'w well as I do. It wan't do no good for me to put them young bucks in jail. Ain't no white man gonna testify against 'em, and Susie can't be a witness, 'cause she's part Indian. Everybody knows the law won't let Indians testify against white people."

"I'll testify against them fiends."

"There you go again. The judge ain't gonna let you do no such a thing. 'Cause you're an Indian's woman, the law allows you're the same as them. Now shut your runny-mouth. If'n you keep on a-clackin', I'm gonna turn you up and put some blisters on your bottom."

"You wouldn't dare lay a hand on me, and I ain't a-gonna shut up, at least not as long as you treat my husband's people like they ain't human."

"Confound it woman, you know Georgia don't see Indians the same as people. Around here, the folks that count says Indians are savage heathens, wild animals that belong in the forest. The sooner we gets shet of 'em, the better off we'll all be."

"You only say that 'cause it eases your guilty conscience. You and your pack of thelves spend the week a-stealin' the Indian's possessions, and driving them into the woods to starve. Then on Sunday, you'ens sits stiff-backed in church, a-singin' praises to the Lord."

"You stop that slop-mouthing right now, woman."

"I ain't a-gonna do no such thing. You're here to take our home and goods and turn them over to that fellow you're waiting fer. You ain't a-gonna shut me up too, 'cause I know what you are."

"I don't want to hear it."

"But you're a-gonna. You and that bunch of Sunday Psalm-singers in your church ain't no more'n a pack of greedy hypocrities."

"Here's Werfford now," the sheriff said, sighing.

I guess the man was relieved because he no longer had to talk with me. After talking briefly with old man Werfford, the sheriff turned back to me and said. "Now we can get on with our business. Woman, the judge gave me these papers to serve on Ga. . .ganu. . .ganuteyo. . .teyohi."

"You mean my husband, Ganu'teyo'hi?"

The sheriff shifted uneasily in his saddle. Because he couldn't read English, and he knew I could, he was ashamed. He was about to lose face among the greasy deputies he had along, and this caused his whiskey-pink face to flush a brighter shade of red. "He's the one. Is he here?" the sheriff asked.

"He's gone to the Agency," I replied. "Let me fetch N'Cl'e and my baby outside, then you and Ol' Werfford can get on with your stealin'. "Granny," I called out to Ganu'teyo'hi's mother. "Will you fetch John and leave the cabin to the sheriff?"

"Silas," the sheriff said, turning to Ol' Werfford, "yout better look around the place afore I serve these papers. If you take it, you can't put your name back in the lottery."

"Don't you fet none." Werfford replied. "I know the law."

About that time, the Reverend Colerain rode up. "I'm sure glad to see you parson," the sheriff said. "Fine mornin' ain't it?"

"Little sharp for my taste, sheriff," the parson said. "With you I guess any day's a good day for stealing from the Indians. Good morning, Silas" that being Werfford's first name.

"We're here for business, parson," Silas said. "It ain't no concern of the Lord's. Why don't you go on about your work and leave us to get on with ours."

"Do what Silas says, parson," the sheriff said. "And you can stop that stealin'talk right now. That sharp-tongued ol' witch what lived here has been nippin' at my butt ever since I rode up. Don't you start on me."

"I don't know how you do it, sheriff."

"Do what?"

"Live with yourself after taking everything these poor people own."

"Parson, they ain't people! It's you meddlesome missionaries from up North that makes them think they's human. I've sworn to carry out Georgia law, and I'm doing my duty."

"It isn't your duty that's bothersome. You act like you enjoy driving these people out of their homes, into the forest to starve. That what makes me uneasy. I'm fearful you might end up having to spend your eternity with the devil."

"The law says they gotta get out of Georgia," the sheriff said. "They don't belong among God-fearing folk like me and you. They belong with the other forest animals."

"They're not animals, sheriff, and you know it. They're a conquered people. We owe them a helping hand, not starvation in the woods."

"I know what's eatin' you, parson. You're still sore 'cause I jailed you last month."

"I've forgiven you for that, man. Still, you had no cause. All I was doing was carrying some victuals to those poor devils you already put off their places."

"Dan-burn it, parson! You knew good and well what you was a'doin' was against the law. The prosecutor swore out a warrant. I had to fetch you to trial."

"You didn't have to put me in Irons. I've still got the scabs on my wrists and ankles from the gall of your shackles."

"You tell me how'm I gonna keep prisoners in that tent-jail I got, if'n I don't put Irons on 'em? Besides, you were lucky. The army got you released quick. Some of the Indians in there with you have been in jail for more'n a year. Ain't nobody doin' nothin' for them."

"I saw the cruelty you inflict on them, and I've been trying to get them away from you ever since I was released. Just bein' in your jail is enough punishment, but you keep torturing the defenseless creatures, going out of your way to make your jail a little corner of hell. You do that because you enjoy watching them suffer."

"Parson or no parson, you broke the law and warn't treated no different from everybody else. You'd be helpful if'n you'd go over and keep the women company, and leave me to my business with Werfford?"

"How are you today, Na'Cl'e?" the preacher asked, as he sidled up to the two of us.

Na'Cl'e, "grunted."

"Good Morning, Rachel," the parson went on. "How are you today?"

"As good as can be expected, Reverend," I replied.

The good preacher had knowed my mother-in-law long enough not to expect more than the grunt she gave him, which is probably why he turned to me for a better answer. "How do you suppose she really feels about all this?" he asked.

"It's hard to say," I said.

Ganu'teyo'hi's mother wore a mask, behind which few people had been allowed to peek. Her husband had been killed at Tohopeka, and her oldest son hadn't come home from the Creek War either. Instead, he had taken a Tsikama'gl wife, and they decided to make home amongst her people on the lower Tennessee River. While her husband and oldest son were away, fighting in a white man's war, Federal soldiers raided her village and burned her home. In spite of these adversities, she carried her sadness as easy as she would tote a bag of feathers, probably why her coal-black eyes still shined with a child-like brightness.

"There's a special place in heaven for people like Na'Cl'e," the parson said. "Did Gantu'teyo'hi and Smokehouse get off all right?"

"They left the night you brung us the news. Little Flower and Da'yu-us-dl went with them."

"Think they'll be all right travelling at night?"

"Orter be. The militia ain't out at night. Ganu'teyo'hi's been to councils at Red Clay a number of times. He knows the trail good."

"What'll they do during daylight?"

"There's plenty Cherokee who'll hide 'em from the Georgia guard. The guard's afraid to get off the road. They're fearful of being bushwhacked. The two men will be safe out of sight from the road."

"How come you and Na'Cl'e stayed behind?"

"To make sure the militia didn't notice our menfolk were gone until it was too late for them to catch 'em and seize the wagons and goods."

"Looks like it worked. Have you heard anything?"

"No. Haven't heard a thing. They're all right though. If'n they'd been caught, someone would have brung us word. They'll be waitin' at Red Clay, just like we planned."

"Where's Little Flower?"

"She left with the men, but she ain't goin' all the way with them. She'll be waitin' for us up at the head of Long Hollow."

"How come?"

"She's got the extra mules. If she hadn't took 'em, ol' man Werfford would-a got 'em. When we catch up with her, they'll be animals for Na'Cl'e and for Little Flower to ride on the trip to the West. The mules don't jolt as bad as the wagons."

"What're you gonna ride?"

"Most of the time I'll be drivin' the ox team pulling our wagon. We ain't got enough stock for all of us to ride. When I ain't driving ox, I'll walk. Red Clay, ain't more'n forty or fifty mile. Ganu'teyo'hl will spell me driving ox when he feels like it. I imagine I'll be ready to walk a spell after being jolted by the wagon for an hour or so. Goin' west, we'll do what we have to do. The rest I'll leave in the hands of God."

"I thought the driver walked alongside the oxen?" the parson said.

"Most of the time that'd be right. But Ganu'teyo'hl's got our teams rigged with horse harnesses which lets us drive sitting on the wagon."

"Rachel, we'll miss you very much at the mission. The girls you were teaching weaving all wish you a safe trip. Do you know when the wagon train will head out?"

"I'll also miss the mission, 'n the girls, and all the people. We don't know when it's leaving right now. When he was through, Major Ridge said they were a making up wagons to leave in the fall. We ought-a get to Red Clay in time."

"You know where'll you'll light?"

"No. But, Ganu'tayo'hl says he wants to stay where ther's mountains. He may have friends there somewhere. . . and maybe a brother."

"That's news to me," the preacher said.

"He had a brother that stayed with the Tsikama'gl after the massacre at Tohopeka," I said. "Don't know what he calls himself but we can still run into him."

"I think I heard something about most of the Tsikama'gl going west," Reverend Colerain said. "Did Ganu'teyo'hl ever say how he felt about all this?"

"You know Ganu'teyo'hl, he never says much about anything. But he can't understand why the government doesn't honor our treaty like it promised. He's against ceding more land. He was real mad at The Major and them others for signing the removal treaty."

"I don't know what's right on that issue, Rachel," the parson said. "I do know I'll miss you 'n your family . . . there's just too many white people coming in. Maybe you and Ganu'teyo'hl can find peace in the West."

"That's how we thought. The game's all gone here. Besides, the Georgia militia puts Indians in jail if they catch 'em with wild game. If we stayed, we'd starve, like them others that's already in the woods."

"Sheriff," Ol' Werfford shouted from the front porch of his new cabin. It ain't all here. The law says I gits it all. Make that white-squaw bitch tell where she's a-hidin' the other things."

"Shut up, Werfford, you greedy ol' buzzard," the sheriff said. "I know what's the law."

"Looks like Silas is through with his inspection" the parson said.

"Rachel," said the sheriff turning to me, "we're doin' everthin' fair and square accordin' to Georgia law. You gotta give up your stuff to me, so's I can give it to Werfford. Now where's the rest of your thin's?"

"Fair and square my butt! For the devil, you mean" I snapped back at him. You know Georgia law is the white man's law and its the white man that's bein' the devil here this day."

"I can't help whose law you think it is. Silas Werrford here drew Gan. . .ganu. . .ganuteyo..hl's property. It ain't yours no longer. The law gives you a half-hour to get off the place. I'll see that you get it."

"Talkin' law won't do you and that Werfford fellow no good" I replied. "The law don't say Ganu'teyo'hl can't give away what's his'n. My husband gave some of our things to the mission, some to our starvin' friends a-hidin' in the woods, and some he took with him to the Agency. If'n the Georgia militia ain't already got him, he's at Red Clay by now, safe from the clutches of the likes of you."

"He hadn't oughta done that Rachel. If Werfford here says so, I'll just have to put you in jail."

"You ain't goin' to do no such thing, sheriff, and you know it! I'm a woman and I'm white."

"You ain't white," Werfford screamed. "The law says you're an Indian's white-bitch and that makes you Indian."

"Werfford's right" agreed the sheriff. "The law does say that being married to an Indian makes you an Indian. You're an Indian all right. Now quit hiding behind petticoats and give me Werfford's goods."

"You ol' billy-goat" I said. The slow-witted sheriff didn't understand that I was spurring him a dab and enjoying every minute of his discomfort. Least-wise, there wasn't much he could do. "I'd hide behind the water bucket if'n I thought it'd do any good. You men have everything else. Petticoats is all women got left to hide behind. The Cherokee men treat their women a lot better than white men treat theirs."

"You've been mouthin' ever since I got here" the sheriff said. "Now shut up so's I can think. . ."

"You ain't got nothin' to think with sheriff. Before you put me in jail, you'd have to charge me with a crime. You can't do that 'cause I ain't done nothin'."

Werfford was getting impatient because all the possessions

he'd expected wasn't in sight. "Ain't you goin' to make her tell where's my property?"

"He ain't goin' to make me do nothin' " I said to ol' Werfford, ignoring the sheriff. Then to the law man, " 'Cause I'm married to a Cherokee, the people in your church wouldn't have me. Still, most of the folks there would be against throwing a white woman in jail for something her husband done."

"Rachel, shut your mouth" the sheriff commanded. "I can't get a word in edgeways."

"I'll shut up when I please sheriff" I retorted. "This property Werfford is missin', wasn't mine. It belonged to my husband. I didn't take it anywhere." I knew I had the slow thinking sheriff bested. "Where's my crime?" I taunted.

"Damnit sheriff. You know what to do. Arrest that woman" Silas demanded. "I want my . . ."

"If you throwed me in jail sheriff, you'd just have to feed two, me and my baby. That wouldn't be very smart because we're leavin' just as soon as you buzzards get through with this business."

"Rachel," interrupted the sheriff, "have you got anything that can't be seen? Every bit of what you got is Werfford's. You got to give what's his'n."

"I ain't got nothing more but a pouch of ga'hawi'sitl', and the quilts we'll sleep with. If'n he likes parched homlny, he can take the pouch."

"Get out of my way, sheriff" Werfford broke in. "That white-squaw bitch will talk for me, or else." His 'or else' was a bullwhip he'd lifted from the seat of his wagon. He snapped it real close to my face. The loud pop it made told me plenty about the bite I might feel on my backside.

This Werfford fellow was a rich merchant, accustomed to having his way. Right now he was so upset his face was beet red. An influential man, he was not the sort of person likely to be held in check by the sheriff.

In fact, all the sheriff's men appeared certain that Werfford was goin' to lay his whip to my behind, and they seemed set to enjoy the show. The sergeant and his men took Werfford at his word and spurred their mounts in close. As they did they also loosened the flaps on their holster and checked their sidearms. Much of the time I wouldn't regard the Federal army as friends, but this morning was different. Because they probably saved me from a beating, I was thankful for the army's presence.

"Sheriff," the sergeant said, "the army regards what you're doing here as cruel and uncivilized. But my orders are not to interfere. However, the orders direct me to keep the people safe from bodily harm, and by God, that's what we're going to do. Tell that man Werfford to put his whip back in his wagon."

"This ain't Federal business, sergeant" retorted the sheriff as his deputies began to nervously move their mounts apart. "This is Georgia business. There's no call for you buttin' in."

"I know it's Georgia business. But civil business don't include using a bullwhip on people, especially women. If that man Werfford moves to carry out his threat, he's dead."

"Sergeant" the sheriff snarled, "there's ten of us and only three of you Federals. You gonna risk getting killed just to keep an Indian woman from gettin' what she orter have—a good whippin. This one is plain too sassy for 'er own good." Seeing as how it was hard for him to back down in front of his posse, I guess the sheriff had to bluster some.

"I'm a good soldier, sir. I risk whatever I'm ordered to risk. Should any of your yahoos get ideas about rushin' us," the sergeant countered, "we'll take three of you, maybe more, before you'ens can get to us." Then loud enough for all the sheriff's deputies to hear he continued "You best think about which three won't be eatin' supper at home tonight. Them's the only three that really counts. You might also keep in mind that the first to go down will likely be you."

"Now hold on here" the sheriff bellowed loud enough to be heard as far away as Red Clay. I took it he wasn't interested in taking the sergeant's bullet on account-a one of his men got an itchy trigger finger. "Everybody calm down and put your weapons away. Ain't no call for shootin'. Werfford, you ol' fool, put that damn whip back in your wagon afore you gets some of us kill't."

"Good thinkin' sheriff," the sergeant commented. The slash-bars on his sleeve told he was a veteran of the frontier, a man accustomed to enforcing his authority with fists, and reluctant to back away from a fight. "I was kinda' hoping one of your deputies would make a move," the sergeant went on sorta rubbin' the sheriff's nose in a little manure. "For what's goin' on here, you'ens deserve killin'. Now get on with your business."

"Rachel," the sergeant continued, his voice now had the bite of man eager to get on to other things. "You and the old woman better take your baby and git on the trail. There's rough ground 'tween here and the head of Long Hollow. You folks'll wanta git as far as you can today."

"You'r right sergeant" I replied. "We're both much obliged to you for watchin' out for us. If'n you hadn' been aroun', I think that Werfford would have beat me for sure."

"Prob'ly would have," agreed the sergeant, his voice now softer. "You'ens orter be gittin along."

"Na'Cl'e," I said. "It looks like the time has come. Best we be leavin'."

She grunted and looked at me. She hadn't been crying. I had never seen Na'Cl'e cry. Nevertheless, her big mournful eyes glistened with an unusual dampness. Being a white woman, I didn't have the Cherokee's ability to appear indifferent in circumstances that were distressful or painful, with each passing minute, it was becoming more difficult for me to fight back my tears. Still, I was determined not to cry where I could be seen by the scavengers in our yard. I wasn't going to let them find pleasure in my unhappiness.

"They've stolen our home, Na'Cl'e. But they can't rob us of our spirit if we don't let them. When we walk past those scoundrels, let's look 'em straight in their eyes. Are you ready? You take the ga'hawl'satl'. I'll carry John in a quilt. It'll keep him warm. Head high, da'nagu'sta'. Let's go." I thought I saw a faint smile when I called her by the title, brave warrior.

There was a little knoll about a quarter mile up the trail from our place. Just over the brow, Na'Cl'e and I both turned around for one last look at the home we'd never see again. Our apple trees, heavy laden and ready for pickin', sparkled red in the sunlight. It would soon be cold enough for Werfford to butcher our hogs. The corn stalks, dyed brown by age, were dry in the field and ready to be cut and shucked. Werfford's kids were playing in our yard. He and his ol' woman were already moving their goods into our cabin. The sight of others taking over our homeplace was more than I could bear.

A few yards down the trail I sat on the trunk of a fallen tree.

Then, like a freshet stream pouring down the mountainside, my pent-up sobs released a cloudburst of tears. A feeling of wretched helplessness caused me to cry out, "Lord, what have I done to deserve this punishment?"

As if I were a young child who had stubbed a toe, Na'Cl'e gently clutched my head to her breast as she sat down beside me. With her gnarled and calloused hand, she caressed me with a tenderness I didn't know she possessed. Then she leaned her head against mine and burst into tears herself.

At that moment, we were no longer a white woman and a full-blood Cherokee. Neither were we a Christian and a heathen who came from different worlds. Nor were we different sorts of people because I was the wife and she the mother-in-law. Instead, we were as two peas from the same pod. Two lonely dejected women. We were foreigners, alone and unwelcome, in our own homeland.

For perhaps a quarter-hour we sat together sobbing away our sorrow not caring if the birds and animals heard us. Even after our tears had stopped, we remained on that log, sitting close together. We were equally reluctant to give up the warmth of our new found togetherness. It seemed that neither of us wanted to be the first to break the magic of that moment, nor did we have to. Dogs barking and cackling of guinea fowl broke the spell. The noise told us Werfford's friends were arriving for his warming of our home. It was too hard for me to look and I noticed that Na'Cl'e never turned for one last glance. "Do you feel better, Na'Cl'e?" I asked.

She grunted.

I didn't expect her to say more. Lifting our loads, we trudged east along the trail that led to the ford across the Coosawattee. Lost in our private thoughts, neither of us said a word for an hour or more. Long Hollow was just beyond the river crossing and up the mountain a bit. Little Flower would be watching for us.

MAMA'S REMEDY FOR DRINKIN'

"MAMA," the boys hollered from the yard, "Pa's coming"

"Can you see him plain?" she asked, not rising from her rocker on the porch.

"Light's too dim."

"Anyone with him?"

"Yeah. They's one."

"Who is it this time?"

"Can't make him out. Ain't enough sun."

"They walkin' straight up?" She asked.

"Nope. They's leanin'.

"Eliza, you and Pauline stir the fire," mama said. Because Pauline wasn't yet fifteen and I was past sixteen, mama always named me first when delegating a chore to both of us. "Ya'll know your pa. He'll soon be orderin' me to fix hot victuals for the two of them."

Pa had been staggering home tipsy for as long as I could remember. Like tonight, he usually brought a drunk friend home with him. My brothers, both younger than Pauline, were watching the two figures coming up the trail. "Mama," Matthew hollered. "We can see pa's friend now."

"Well. Who is it?"

"It's Charley Duck."

"Oohhh, my God," she groaned. "Not that no-count Duck boy. Why in the world would you pa take up with trash like Charley Duck?"

Mama had heard that Charley had forced himself on more than one of the young women who lived around Piney community. His shenanigans had brought shame to a number of unwed girls in the neighborhood. Mama didn't want Duck on our place sober. Now, he was coming up the trail drunk and Pa would soon be demanding that she fix supper for the two of them.

"Eliza," mama ordered. "You and Pauline stay out of the reach of that fellow while he's here. He's no good."

Then talking to herself as much as anyone else, she mumbled something that sounded like, "Husband, how come you a-bringin' that low-down varmint on our place? The last time we were grinding corn at the Dutchman's mill, I caught him leering at the girls. He's got eyes for our two, and he don't care which he lays first. You want him to force his attention on Eliza and Pauline like he did those other girls?"

Most of the time, mama carefully hid how she felt from family view. Tonight, however, the calm in our home was uneasy, much as it was sometimes just before a violent thunderstorm broke. Outwardly, mama usually gave no indication she was ever anything more than a person tired from a hard day's work. But tonight was different. Her quivering chin told me that she was boiling inside. I knew mama had a temper locked out of sight behind her apron, and I also knew first hand that it could escape. When it did she could scratch and claw as hard as any bobcat cornered by pa's dogs. All of us kids had felt the pain she could inflict, with a peach tree shoot for a switch, when she was really angry. Tonight, I thought mama was more than a little sore at pa. I believed her as mad as any hornet whose nest was being smoked. Always before, when he hollered for hot food, she took the easy road and fixed him something that would fill his mouth. Tonight, however, when he ordered hot food for him and Duck, mama didn't move. Instead she stood scowling, one hand on a hip and the other holding our biggest iron skillet. I had the feeling that she would rather hit pa with the skillet than fix something to eat for the two of them.

All of us kids loved our pa. When he was sober, he was a joy to be around. But we sided with mama on pa's drinking. The burden of an extra meal tonight was a good example of his uncaring shiftlessness. All of us, except him, had spent the daylight doing sweat work in the hot sun. It was time to plant corn and peas, our victuals for next winter, and we still had oak sprouts to grub and rocks to tote from a patch of new ground where we had girdled the trees last winter. Even though pa wasn't much of a farmer, we had resented him not being in the field wielding a grubbing hoe today. It just wasn't right that he would be gallivanting around, drinking the day away while we worked the farm like indentured farm hands.

I think mama tolerated pa's drinking because she thought it something he couldn't keep from doing. A lot of Cherokees were stigmatized with his affliction. We didn't doubt pa's good intentions. He left home every morning to go trading. Pa was a good trader, usually the gainer. But trading and friendly palavering were hand and glove. Around Piney idle talk wasn't regarded friendly unless it was accompanied by tippling from a demijohn. "Your pa is good at trading," mama said. "But," she quickly added "he was even better at drinking whiskey."

The truth of life around Piney was that trading and whiskey drinking were inseparable. Poor pa. His best skill and his worst weakness were harnessed to the same wagon. Pa rarely reached home with any of his gains. When he was drinking, he often mistook hangers-on, white and Indian alike, for long-time friends. They easily inveigled him into giving up his possessions. When he came in at night, he rarely had more to show for a day's trading than a snoot full of whiskey and an empty belly.

To tell the truth, mama, rather than pa, was the producer in our family. Folks around Piney said they didn't understand how mama worked the place like she did, seeing as how she was so little. Mama was on the smallish side, but us kids didn't dare say anything of that sort to her face. If ma was soaked in the well and weighed before she dripped, she might gross a hundred pounds. Although tiny in size, ma had a man's muscles and a mountain of grit. Mama and us kids worked the garden, tended the stock and fowl, farmed a few acres of potatoes, corn, peas, squash and pumpkin, smoked the fish, ham and bacon, and picked the pot herbs, and berries. For the cash to buy necessities we didn't grow, mama would sometimes hire all of us out to the neighbors as day labor. She didn't have any trouble finding work, 'cause everyone around Piney knew she'd see that we gave them an honest day's work.

Tonight, however, it was plain on her face. Mama was tired of having to work so hard around the place, tired of having to fix meals for a drunk husband who didn't produce as much as he ate, tired of having to put up with his drunk friends particular the ones that were like that sorry Charley Duck, and tired of working as day labor because he didn't get home with any of his trading gains. While she fixed his supper, she told pa how she felt. Even though her speech was almost loud enough to be hollering he was too drunk to pay her any mind.

If it hadn't been for Duck, mama would likely have cooled off before morning. But Duck was just as loud as pa, and much more repulsive. Besides, he smelled like he'd been sleeping in a pile of manure. All through supper, he kept after pa to let him get under the cover with his girls, meaning me and Pauline. Since both of us were being sparked by well-fixed neighbor boys, mama didn't want Pauline and me to even hear such talk. She made both of us go outside and sit on the porch. This was her way of getting us out of the reach of Duck's groping paws.

"Did you notice Mama?" Pauline asked, when we got outside. "She looked like she was close to pouring a skillet of hot grease on the Duck."

"I saw her. I wish she had done it. That buzzard patted me on my butt every time I went by him. And you're right, mama is about to bust. Something is going to happen for sure. Why, her jaw muscles are so tight she could crack hickory nuts with her teeth."

"Listen, Eliza."

"I don't hear anything."

That's it. Mama has stopped talking. That ain't like her at all."

"I bet she is in there hovering around pa like a bumblebee getting ready to set its stinger into pa's neck. Sis, I'm uneasy. Something's bad is liable to happen afore this night's over."

"I feel the same way," Pauline grunted . . .

"Do you remember that time I mistook Mama's tobacco sprouts for suckers, and hoed them away?"

"I remember," Pauline replied, smiling for her memory of my misfortune.

"She gave me a whipping with pa's strop that made my tail so sore, I didn't want to sit down for a nigh onto a week."

"That was some whipping, all right," Pauline said. "Every time you started to sit down, I just had to snicker. Shhhh. . .listen. Don't talk," Pauline said, putting a finger across her closed lips. "Mama has started talking again, but pa still ain't paying her no mind. The more he ignores ma, the madder she is going to get. We better stay close. You don't think she'd take a butcher knife to pa, do you?"

"I wouldn't put it past her," I said.

Soon as pa and Duck got their bellies full, they stretched out on the only beds we had. In a few minutes they were snoring loud. Then Mama called out, "Gather 'round me, children. I've got something to say that you'll want to hear."

Tingling with suspense, the four of us chimed in at the same time, "What'cha "gonna" do to pa?"

"You kids know I been putting up with a lot," mama said. "And I ain't never complained, leastwise not where you'uns could hear me."

"We know what you been putting up with, mama. I think we're all sorry for the way pa acts," I said.

"Your pa went too far tonight. He ain't got no right to bring drunk trash into our home, especially the kind that wants to get on top of you girls. My mind's made up. Unless he leaves off whiskey, I ain't gonna spend no more time with him."

"Mama" I said, tingling with suspense. "You ain't goin' to leave pa, are you? Where would we live?"

"We're staying right here," mama assured us. "Your pa might be leaving, but we ain't going nowhere. I'm goin' to try to beat the whiskey devil out of him. I'll either remedy his drinkin' or run him off. Now do what I tell you, and your pa may turn into something worth having around. If he stays, he's got to leave off whiskey. If he leaves for good, it'll finally free us from feeding drunks every night. Either way it goes, they ain't gonna be no more whiskey on this place. Not ever again!"

"Matthew," mama went on, as she parceled out the work. "Go

to the barn and fetch a spool of your pa's harness mending twine
and one of his big-eyed needles."

"Beaver," she said, looking towards my youngest brother.
"Fetch me your pa's quirt from the dog-run."

"Eliza, you and Pauline," mama said. "Dig out that new mus-
lin sheet we got and work it under your pa so's it covers him
from his neck to his knees."

When Matthew returned, he helped Pauline and me roll up
pa in the sheet. We really rolled him up tight. Then, me and
Pauline sewed it closed with pa's stout harness-mending twine.
The boys removed pa's boots and socks as mama told them to
do.

"You kids get back out of my way," mama said. "I don't want
to hit you with your pa's quirt."

Then she began striking the tender bottoms of pa's feet with
the handle of his quirt. Mama had muscles and she got pa's
attention with her first blow.

"Ooouucch!" pa screamed. "What in 'tarnation' you doin',
woman? You lost your damn mind? That hurts!"

"I meant it to hurt. You need to know a little pain, husband,"
mama retorted. "You've been a pain to me and the kids long
enough." Then, with all her might, mama rained blows with the
quirt on pa's belly, back or buttocks, whichever part of him was
handiest. With her lashing away at his body, pa wiggled off the
bed and headed outside, part hopping and part tiny-stepping.
"Matthew," Mama called out, "you and Beaver stay close beside
your pa. If he starts to fall help him steady himself."

"When I get free," pa threatened, "I'll wear your tail to a nub
with that quirt."

"Your words don't hurt none, husband. Your drinkin' hurts
plenty," mama retorted.

"Woman!" pa hollered, still threatening. "If you don't stop
whipping me right now, I'll kill you with my bare hands when I
get free."

Mama, busy with her "whomping," didn't say a word. Instead, she just kept right on thumping pa's backside with his
quirt.

"Please wife. I ain't no renegade horse. You got no call to
beat me like you're doin'," pa said. He was crying and pleading
now, as he moved closer to the front door.

On feet already tender from mama's beating, Pa tiny-stepped his way bare-footed across the front yard. His pain must have been more than doubled by the sticks and stones he stepped on. With ever step, his "ooucches and oooohhs" were loud enough to be heard all the way down to Dutch Mill, which was better than two miles away.

Mama coupled every blow with a complaint. What I heard that night would forever linger in my memory.

Swisshh. . .splat. "That's for bringing that foul-mouthed Charley Duck on the place!"

Swisshh. . .splat. "That's for not working our field when all the other men around here work their fields."

Swisshh. . .splat. "That's for making me cook a special meal for you every night."

Swisshh. . .splat. "That's for making me and the kids hire out to the neighbors, just to put food on the table."

Swisshh. . .splat. "That's for not listening to me when I talk to you."

Swisshh. . .splat. "That's to drive the whiskey demon out of you."

As pa staggered through the front gate, Mama landed a couple of strong swisshh. . .splats on his butt.

"Ooohh, woman, Why are you doing this to me?" pa moaned. No wonder he was groaning loud. Mama had put all of her hundred pounds behind every blow.

"Husband," mama called after pa. "When you're ready to stop drinkin' whiskey, you can come back through that gate. But don't you dare show your face on this place again smellin' of moonshine. They ain't goin' to be no more liquor in this home." After a pause to catch her breath, she added, "If'n you do come back, you got to work the place like you promised when we got married. Do you hear what I'm telling you, husband?"

"I hear you, woman! Lord have mercy on me. I hear you," he answered. "You've hurt me bad, wife. And you've shamed me. It'll be hard to forgive what you've done to me this night. Ain't you goin' to help me none?"

"When you're sober, come back. I'll help you then."

As she walked back from the gate, mama was saying something to herself. I couldn't make out her words, but they sounded like:

"Now, I'm gonna run that no-good Duck off'n the place."

The commotion with pa must have awakened Charley, because he'd staggered out on the porch just as mama stepped up on the porch from our yard. Catching ol' Duck by surprise, she started slashing at him with pa's quirt. After the first blow, he began dodging, only to lose his balance and fall off the porch right smack-dab into the middle of her climbing rose bush. That rose bush had been there as long as I could remember. Thick as a large man's thumb, the canes were covered with hooked, razor-sharp thorns. My guess Duck wasn't thinking of anything but to get out of reach of mama's whip, 'cause he chose to go through that old bush "front-ways" rather than back up into mama's flailing quirt. All the way across the yard, mama was right behind him swinging pa's quirt at Duck's backside.

Crossing the yard behind the Duck, she reminded me of a mockingbird pecking at the flying tail of a egg-sucking squirrel. As he went through the gate, Duck was bleeding from more'n a dozen cuts, some made by pa's quirt and some by the rose bush thorns. His shirt was in tatters. For a drunk, he was doing a good imitation of running, 'cept his running was more up and down than straight ahead. I can still hear the words that mama flung at the fleeing man.

"Charley Duck," mama screamed after him. Her voice was pitched much higher than normal; she was screeching. I supposed the high pitch was caused by her anger and frustration. Anyhow, she sounded just like a eagle plummeting out of the sky towards a prey. "If you ever show your ugly face on this place again, I won't whip you, I'll shoot you."

With her mouth froze in a thin line, she marched into the house, right past Pauline and me without saying a word.

"Let's leave her be," I said, as I restrained Pauline with a light hand. "She'll cool as she sleeps. Soon's the sun's up, I imagine she'll go down and tend to pa's wounds. It's best we don't interfere right now."

""You're right." Pauline agreed. "But you know something, Sis?"

"What?" I replied.

"I'll bet pa thinks twice before he ever takes another drink."

"I'd say you're probably right."

Glenn J. Twist (Cherokee/Muscogee) was born in July 1917. He graduated from Sallislaw High School, Sallislaw, Oklahoma in 1935 and the University of Tulsa at Tulsa in 1949.

In Glenn's words, "Fact is, when I started writing, my only purpose was to stay alive. I was a green hand, no experience, no training, and no teaching. But, I have learned a lot since I started writing, mainly because people have gone out of their way to help me improve. I have been grateful for every suggestion I've received, even those I didn't accept. I have been very fortunate.

"My life span started with the Bolshevik revolution, had me participating in World War II, watching Korea, and Viet Nam, as well as the 'fly swatter' wars in Greneda, Panama and Kuwait, not counting a number of other, so-called, police actions. Moreover, I experienced the Great Depression in the, so called, Dust Bowl, and witnessed the collapse of the Soviet Union, and lived 'trickled down economics' that has brought our nation to the brink of another depression. Histories tell of the great events, and how they affected nations. From a first hand viewpoint, I can tell how these events affected one person, and one family, and that too is history.

"Lt. Commander Richard E. Webb, United States Submarine Force who, while serving as the senior officer of a review board examining my fitness for the U.S. Naval Academy in 1936, showed me that much of American history, as it was taught in American schools, was in reality more propaganda than fact. What I write is my life, warts and all.

"I am a storyteller. I write from the oral tradition. My writing has to do with the culture of my people. I try to write history in a manner that will make people want to read what I write. My people were neither judges nor preachers, just plain old dirt farmers. I am the last generation in my family to be born in the Boston Mountains of Arkansas and Oklahoma, as well as on a Cherokee allotment. If I don't preserve the stories I've heard they will be lost forever."

Eddie Webb

GRAND MOTHER SUN

na da wa gi ni li si

> *This story came from my Keetoowah Cherokee Uncle Jim.*
> *wa do wa do, ga li e li ga to you for the many hardships you*
> *and your Keetoowah Cherokee People have suffered. May*
> *the differences of my Cherokee Nation and Your Great*
> *Keetoowah Cherokee Nation be resolved and my Peace and*
> *Harmony find a foot hold once more. With all respect, your*
> *nephew.*

A LONG TIME AGO the People walked about the Earth (E lo i) in darkness. They were always running into each other. They were always hurting each other because they could not see each other as they really were. One day one of the People said "I had a dream, and in the dream we had a great light. The light warmed us and we could see, we didn't run into each other and hurt ourselves."

Just then a warrior named Eagle (u wo ha li) stepped forward and said, "My People, I have something to say. Not long ago I was flying in the East (a hi da) and I saw a great light, it blinded me and I became afraid. I told no one because I am a warrior, but now I see I have hurt my People by not facing my fear. Because I have kept this place to myself my People walk in darkness."

All of the People came together and heard Eagle speak of his fear. Eagle again spoke, "I am a great warrior and I ask my People to let me go to this place and see if I can bring this light to our People." All of the People agreed to let Eagle go. So Eagle stepped back and with his mighty wings flew up into the darkness. As Eagle came to the place were the great light was burning high in the sky (ga lv lo i) his heart began to pump, and fear filled him. Eagle knew he must face his fear for his People so he flew high above the light. Once he was above the light he dove down and with his great wing grabbed a piece of the light and put it on top of his head. As he flew back to his People the light energy began to burn his head. By the time he reach his People all of the energy was gone and all of his feathers on his head burnt, and this is why the Eagle's feathers on his head are all white, and this is why he is called Bald Eagle. The People still had no light.

So Beaver (tse ya) stepped forward and spoke, "I am a great warrior and I ask my People to let me go to this place where there is light. The People there must be selfish or they would give us light, so we could see each other and stop running into each other." The People agreed and Beaver jumped into the river and began swimming into the East to find the light. Soon Beaver felt the water warming up and knew he was close to the light. He dove down deep into the river so no one could see him. He came to a place where light filled the bottom of the river and he made a great stroke with his tail and headed for the surface. Beaver shot out of the river and reached up and grabbed a piece of the light and placed it on his tail and began swimming back to his People. Soon the light energy began burning his tail. By the time he reached his People all of the light energy was gone and all of the fur on his tail had been burned off. This is why today the Beaver has no hair on his tail. The People were again in darkness, and could not see each other the way they really are.

One more time the People came together and Possum (Oo ni na) stepped forward. Possum spoke, "My brothers have failed and we have no light, I am a great warrior and I would like to go to this place. The People agreed and Possum began digging a hole into the ground towards the East. Soon Possum could feel the ground becoming warm so he knew he was under the light. Possum dug straight up and came out from the ground. He reached up and grabbed a piece of the light and placed it on his nose. He began to head back to the People. Soon the light energy began burning his eyes. When he reached the People his eyes were red and pushed back into his head so he could not see. This is why today the Possum can only come out at night because his eyes have been burned by the light. Again the warriors had failed and the People had no light.

The People came together and didn't know what to do. They were all talking when from underneath the blades of grass a small gentle voice said, "I will go." The People looked around and said, "Who speaks? We have sent all of our great warriors."

Again the voice said, "It is I, Grandmother Spider (a li si ka hna ne s gi), I have lived a good long life, I can go to this place and bring light to my People so we can see each other the way we really are, and so we will not run into each other and hurt ourselves. The People talked for a long time. Many of them said, "If our greatest warriors have failed, how can we send such an old Grandmother?"

The People talked some more and finally agreed to let her go. Grandmother Spider began spinning her web so she could find her way home. Finally she came to this place where the light lived. She could see the light so she reached up with her arm and grabbed a piece of the light. With her other arms she reached into the mud and made a clay pot. She put the light energy into the pot and made a lid to cover it. Grandmother Spider followed her web back to her People. When she reached home she took the lid off her clay pot and threw it high into the sky. All of the People began singing songs in honor of Grandmother Spider. This is when the People knew it is the Grandmothers who bring light into the land of the People so we can see each other the way we really are. It is her knowledge that keeps us from running into each other and hurting ourselves. The People sang songs to honor Grandmother Spider for her beautiful pottery (tsu tsu go tiv nv nv i), and this is why Grandmother Spider always spins her web towards the East before the Sun brings light into a new day.

JOHN REDEAGLE

"GOODBYE JOHN, I just wanted to call and thank you for helping me get sober and regain the desire to live, thanks and I love you. I promise I will live my life one day at a time, telling Indian people who they are and how to get sober."

That was the last telephone conversation I had with John Redeagle before I left Oklahoma for California. John was a tall tanskin Indian man who had hands the size of an old frying pan. He must have stood six foot two and wore thick square black frame glasses. John's rich Indian features demanded respect and dignity from those around him. I knew John was special and I wanted to be like him.

John was big, but at peace with himself not a trace of the macho, stay out of my way kind of attitude I had come to know in myself. John was sober and he had a certain kind of glow or serenity about him that was attracting. My grandfather displayed this kind of peace when I sat at the foot of his death bed watching him through his last hour of life. Anyway the best way to describe myself the first time I had met John, was I didn't want to live anymore, and John Redeagle gave me hope.

John may have been the first man I ever asked for help. I wanted to know how to live without drinking alcohol the way I did. I was an established athlete who at the age of twenty six was training in a gym where many world class athletes trained, but I couldn't seem to escape the drunkeness of dirty old bar rooms.

As I asked John for help, he stepped back putting his weight on his right foot then his left, allowing his body to rock slowly from one side and then the other. He stuck those big hands inside the front pockets of his off brand jeans and softly said, "Praise God, Ed. I will not help you learn how to stop drinking, but how not to start drinking." John gave my directions to his home and told me to be there at seven a.m. the following morning.

I stood knocking on John's front door at six fifty a.m. sharp. Slowly the door opened and there stood John wearing those black thick glasses that seemed to camouflage all he was thinking. John shifted his weight once again from one foot and then the other and asked me to have a seat on his sofa. I couldn't help but to be impressed by how clean and organized he was for a bachelor. John sat down and with that peace and serenity in his voice began telling me of "his story," he told me how he had once reached a place in his life that he didn't want to live anymore and how alcohol got the best of him. John then got up from the sofa slowly walked over by the front window turned to me and said, "Ed, I once had the same look in my eyes that you do today, but I know a way that you will never have to feel the way you do ever again if you don't want to." I remember looking up at him saying "How?"

John went into the other room, grabbed a suit case and told me we were going to the Osage reservation to meet his people. After about three hours on the highway we entered a large wooden gate, and John pointed to the large house on the right side of the road where his father, the assistant Chief of the Osage lived. We drove another four hundred yards to a giant tent that covered a big arena. We parked the truck and started walking toward the tent. John told me to wait over by the entrance.

I was trying my best to look inside the giant tent when an older Indian man walked up, put his hand in front of his chest and motioned it outward towards me and said, "O si yo, to hi tsu?" (hello, how are you?)

I replied, "to hi kwu, ni hi na hv?" (I am well and you?)

It was a pleasant surprise to be recognized as being Chero-kee (tsa-la-gi) and then addressed as such. His welcome worked and I felt like I was among family. Just then John returned and displayed the secrets of his suit case. He was dressed magnifi-cently. He was wearing a beautiful hand made shirt with blue and black ribbons hanging five inches long around his arms and down his back, there was a gourd belt hanging around his waist made of blue, red, and gold colors, a wonderful creation he told me his cousin had made for him. John also carried a hand made Eagle feather fan and a gourd stick that would serve him inside the tent at the dance.

Once inside there were many Indians standing around laugh-ing and joking with each other, there was so much love and joy in under that tent that you could cut it with a feather. John and I moved toward the center of the arena. I could see a big wooden drum placed in the middle of the floor.

We were standing forty feet from the drum, when the drum keeper and several Indian singers walked up to the drum. Boom! the first drum beat rang out sending vibrations through my body, boom! another beat of the drum and the singers joined in "Hao, Hao." All the dancers formed a circle around the drum and John told me to stand next to him in the circle and watch.

There I stood in the midst of traditions older than the white man's history books, traditions practiced on this land long be-fore Columbus ever set sail. Standing there a new awareness hit me. I whispered softly to myself "I haven't thought about drink-ing all day." Just then a spiritual man of the Osage tribe walked up to me with his wife and told me he knew I was coming, that he wanted me to have his gourd stick. I was slow at taking it because it was old, but his wife stepped around him and whis-pered in my ear, "Take it or you will offend my husband."

Boom! Boom! the drum's rhythmic vibrations began the day's dancing and all the Indian dancers tighten the circle. I looked down at John's feet to gain my rhythm, short little steps that slowly moved us towards the drum.

Boom!! Boom!! Looking back at John I realized my mind had wandered deep into thought. As though disappearing into the theater of my visual thoughts I see myself clearly, what I am, who I am, and what I need. The Hindus call this dharama, the Buddhas nirvana. Malcolm X experienced this in Mecca, Martin saw a dream, the apostle Paul was struck down on the way to Domascus and I simply had clarity of mind. Like a story being told to me I found myself hiding inside myself, I feel the shame of long ago, the guilt imposed on me through calculated oppression of my great People.

Boom!! Boom!! I shake my head trying to clear my thoughts Boom!! Boom!! again I disappear. I find my father existing in a farm labor camp in Firebaugh and then came me full of spirit, but no one to teach me my Indian traditions and who's to blame? Not my father. Boarding schools and shame left him unable, and like a sea without a river I slowly died, turning on myself. Subconsciously I had agreed with this generation shame. I was Indian and no good at that either.

Boom!! Boom!! The vibrations of the drum shake my flesh and cut through me to the marrow of my bones. "Hoa, Hoa" the singers' voices cut into my spirit, the way spiritual things should. Boom!! Boom!! Help me John, my eyes say to his. Boom, boom, the dancers slowly move toward the drum.

Slowly, slowly, my steps no longer feel out of balance with my body. It seems smooth and calm. I look at John as he begins to move away rocking from side to side, Boom!! Boom!! Boom!! I disappear once again, but this time my mind is quiet and my spirit feels as though it has awakened from a deep sleep. I begin to see my life in Los Angeles as a young teenager learning how to hate, learning how to be street wise.

On those streets I grew and excelled at sports. In high school and in college my coaches would call me "one tough mother." Yet little did they know my pain, little did they know the anger that drove me to beat those rich white kids, because from the radio announcer's booth it always looked like a great play.

Boom!! Boom!! The vibrations slow then stop. I look up to John and for the first time in my life I realize I don't have to talk, I don't have to win, I don't have to fight, I don't have to struggle to explain myself, and, as John always says, "Praise God I don't have to drink."

We end the song and walk around the drum, and I am a

different man. The circle has shown me power—not for being a circle, but for being from the creator GOD. I no longer have anything to prove. I know who I am.

Eddie Webb is an enrolled member of the Cherokee Nation in Tahlequah, Oklahoma. He has made his home in California and Oklahoma. "I see my writing as a way to live in the generations. The People believe in community, but they also believe we should express our own individual thought. This is why I listen to the stories, then I make them my own, in order to better understand the realities I and my children face."

Eddie has served on the National Indian Education Association's, Organization of North American Indian College Students, and Wordcraft's Board of Directors. Eddie is presently an Educator at Four Winds Indian Education, and a Team American Trainer for the Department of Education in California. He will enter graduate school at Arizona State University in the fall of 1995. Eddie is a Traditional dancer, Gourd dancer, and a Sun dancer. "My uncles died in Europe serving the 45th out of Oklahoma, I dance and sing for them. In return, I maintain my sobriety and try to carry on what they would have given to Our People."

Ron Welburn

THE GRANDFATHER CORN

EACH DAY of those later powwows she lifted the grandfather corn from her glass case and, breaking off a kernel, gave a piece of her ancestry to the open hands of a child. She knew she was completing a circle, and as often as she felt the weight of the blessing bestowed in giving, the blessing and its dominion overwhelmed her. The words *sacred* or *frightened* were spoken but that wasn't it. The kernels she twisted from the hull of dried pale sustenance she gave freely in honor of the stones whose bodies she adorned with beads and bone and shell and wire. Silver is a soft metal and corn is soft and each piece taken will give a child a night of rest in this world's restless tumult. Each piece given is a story of the samp eaten in Quogue and memories of Sugarloaf Mountain; each piece given is a story of walking back to Rome, Georgia all the way from Thalequah on a path marked by tears. With each kernel of this white corn she gave something of ancestry, the proud inevitable return.

THE MEETING PLACE

HARDENED BY XIT'S "cement prairie" we gathered in a storefront in central Brooklyn, or at whatever arena granting four hours space. Some big houses these! Not even seven sides. A language to speak and songs to be tried out for the first time – in *lieder*? Our meeting places shift around like shadow figures on the walls of a strange cave; and in our urban longhouse we take on clan identities, then all of us play skeptic with glass beads. Drum? Power? Identity? Our hearts have overlong searched for unity. And now where are all those Cherokees whose lip service traipsed through our neighborhoods? And how are we here, stumbling, standing, walking, and for a while, very alone?

Ron Welburn. "Though growing up in Philadelphia where I fell in love with jazz, I spent a lot of time in rural Berwyn where I started school. Both parents are of Cherokee ancestry; the Wests on Mom's side are listed in the 1851 Siler Roll. Other family branches come from the Delmarva and various parts of eastern Pennsylvania; and like many Natives here we are part African American. I've published other collections of poems but those in *Council Decisions* (American Native Press Archives, 1991) are my strongest. I teach a range of American literatures in the English department at the University of Massachusetts at Amherst, and my wife and I sell books for the Native American Authors Distribution Project at powwows throughout the Northeast. In the past few years my poems have appeared in *Gatherings*, *Pig Iron*, the *SAIL* poetry issue, and *Archeae*."